Department of Economic and Social Affairs

ST/ESA/363

World Economic and Social Survey 2016

Climate Change Resilience: an opportunity for reducing inequalities

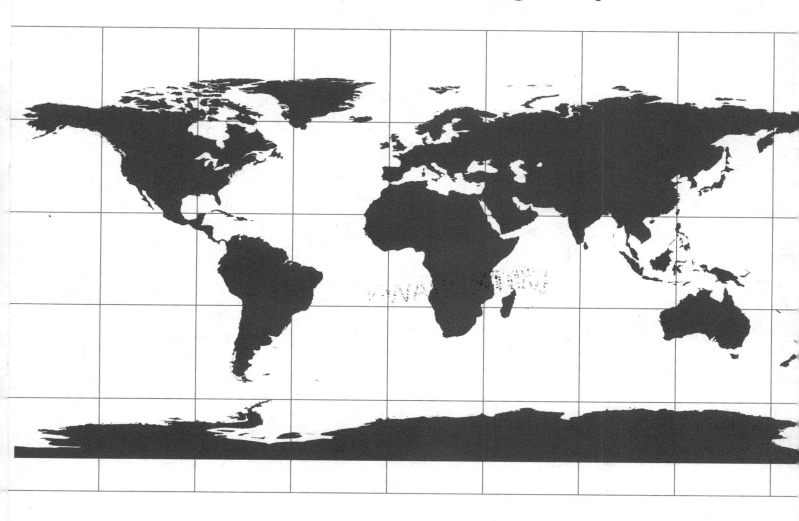

United Nations
New York, 2016

DESA

The Department of Economic and Social Affairs of the United Nations Secretariat is a vital interface between global policies in the economic, social and environmental spheres of sustainable development and national action. The Department works in three main interlinked areas: (i) it compiles, generates and analyses a wide range of economic, social and environmental data and information on which States Members of the United Nations draw to review common problems and to take stock of policy options; (ii) it facilitates the negotiations of Member States in many intergovernmental bodies on joint courses of action to address ongoing or emerging global challenges; and (iii) it advises interested Governments on the ways and means of translating policy frameworks developed in United Nations conferences and summits into programmes at the country level and, through technical assistance, helps build national capacities.

Note

Symbols of United Nations documents are composed of capital letters combined with figures.

E/2016/50/Rev.1
ST/ESA/363
ISBN: 978-92-1-109174-8
eISBN: 978-92-1-058231-5
Print ISSN: 1605-7910
Online ISSN: 2412-1509

United Nations publication
Sales No.: E.16.II.C.1
Copyright @ United Nations, 2016

Preface

At its seventieth session, in 2015, the General Assembly adopted the transformative 2030 Agenda for Sustainable Development as well as other landmark commitments on disaster risk reduction, financing for development, and climate change. These historic agreements embody our collective promise to build a life of dignity for all on a cleaner, greener planet.

The 2030 Agenda and the Sustainable Development Goals form the basis of a comprehensive, integrated and universal framework. As the world embarks upon implementation, countries must accelerate their efforts to keep the increase in temperature well below 2 degrees Celsius above pre-industrial levels.

We must also make greater efforts to adapt to the challenge posed by accumulation of greenhouse gases, which is driving higher temperatures, destroying homes, crops and livelihoods, and inflicting serious harm on millions of people.

The *World Economic and Social Survey 2016* advances our understanding of the many links between climate and development. Sadly, the people at greatest risk from climate hazards are the poor, the vulnerable and the marginalized who, in many cases, have been excluded from socioeconomic progress.

If we are to prevent climate change from exerting further devastating impacts, we must close the development gaps that leave people and communities at risk.

We have no time to waste—and a great deal to gain—when it comes to addressing the socioeconomic inequalities that deepen poverty and leave people behind. The powerful political consensus of 2015 presents us with the opportunity to act both collectively and decisively.

I commend the *World Economic and Social Survey 2016* to all Governments and development partners. The challenges are enormous, but the world possesses the know-how, tools and wealth needed to build a climate-resilient future—a future free from poverty, hunger, discrimination and injustice.

BAN KI-MOON
Secretary-General

Acknowledgements

The *World Economic and Social Survey* is the flagship publication on major development issues prepared by the Department of Economic and Social Affairs of the United Nations Secretariat (UN/DESA).

Under the overall guidance of Lenni Montiel, Assistant Secretary-General for Economic Development at UN/DESA, and the management of Pingfan Hong, Director of the Development Policy and Analysis Division at UN/DESA, the Survey 2016 was produced by a team led by Diana Alarcón. Core members of the team included Helena Afonso, Nicole Hunt, Kenneth Iversen, S. Nazrul Islam, Alex Julca, Hiroshi Kawamura, Marcelo LaFleur, Marco V. Sánchez, Sérgio Vieira and John Winkel. Ramona Kohrs, Israel Machado and Maricela Martinez facilitated access to reference documents. Administrative support was provided by Gerard F. Reyes.

Substantive contributions in the form of background papers and draft text for sections and boxes were made by Lykke Andersen, John Antle, Martin Cicowiez, Saleemul Huq, Sarah Jasmine Hyman, Luis Carlos Jemio, Robert Johnston, Israel Osorio Rodarte, Golam Rabbani, Julie Ann Silva and Roberto Valdivia.

Comments and inputs at various stages were provided by colleagues from other Divisions within UN/DESA and in other organizations, including Susana Adamo, Marion Barthelemy, Jorge Bravo, Matthias Bruckner, Madhushree Chatterjee, Pedro Conceição, Liu Daqui, Glen Dolcemascolo, Joanna Félix Arce, Oscar Garcia, Danan Gu, Maria Eugenia Ibarraran-Viniegra. Asha Kambon, Ran Kim, Arpine Koredian, Marianna Kovacs, Darryl McLeod, Maria Martinho, Lisa Morrison, Shantanu Mukherjee, John Mutter, David O'Connor, Eric Olson, Jonathan Perry, Rayen Quiroga, Anjali Rangaswami, Elida Reci, Valentina Resta, Christopher Ritcher, Marta Roig, Oliver Schwank, Reena Mahendra Shah, Claudia Sheinbaum-Pardo, Shamika N. Sirimanne, Friedrich Soltau, Patrick Spearing, Shari Spiegel, Sanjay Srivastava, Marcia Tavares and Barbara Tavora-Jainchill.

Editorial and design input at the various stages of the publication process were provided by Michael Brodsky, Leah Kennedy, Mary Lee Kortes, Nancy Settecasi and the Graphics Design Unit in the Department of Public Information.

Executive summary

The *World Economic and Social Survey 2016: Climate Change Resilience – An Opportunity for Reducing Inequalities* contributes to the debate on the implementation of the 2030 Agenda for Sustainable Development.[1] In addressing the specific challenge of building resilience to climate change, the *Survey* focuses on population groups and communities that are disproportionately affected by climate hazards, whose frequency and intensity are increasing with climate change. It argues that, in the absence of a continuum of policies designed to reduce the exposure and vulnerability of people to climate change, poverty and inequalities will only worsen.

Climate change and inequalities, as addressed in the 2030 Agenda for Sustainable Development

In 2015, world leaders took significant steps towards forging sustainable development pathways to fulfil the promise to eradicate poverty, reverse environmental degradation and achieve equitable and inclusive societies:

- In June 2015, the General Assembly endorsed the Sendai Framework for Disaster Risk Reduction 2015-2030,[2] recognizing the primary responsibility of Governments to reduce disaster risk and loss of lives, and preserve livelihoods.
- In July 2015, the Third International Conference on Financing for Development adopted the Addis Ababa Action Agenda,[3] including a global framework for mobilizing resources and facilitating policy implementation for sustainable development.
- In September 2015, Heads of State and Government, in the high-level plenary meeting of the General Assembly, made a commitment to reach the Sustainable Development Goals as part of the outcome document "Transforming our world: the 2030 Agenda for Sustainable Development".
- In December 2015, the Conference of the Parties to the United Nations Framework Convention on Climate Change, at its twenty-first session, adopted the Paris Agreement,[4] through which countries committed to reduce greenhouse gas emissions and to support adaptation efforts.

These historic agreements are all part of a global consensus on the need to address the inextricable linkages between the human development and environmental agendas as a necessary condition for sustainable development.

---

[1]   General Assembly resolution 70/1.

[2]   General Assembly resolution 69/283, annex II.

[3]   General Assembly resolution 69/313, annex.

[4]   See FCCC/CP/2015/10/Add.1, decision 1/CP.21.

The *World Economic and Social Survey 2016* identifies key challenges to implementing the 2030 Agenda for Sustainable Development, building upon the recognition that climate hazards have a differential impact on people and communities. It argues that, in the absence of far-reaching transformative policies, the goal of building climate resilience will remain elusive and poverty and inequalities will likely increase.

Climate change exerts uneven impacts across countries and population groups

According to the scientific evidence, climate change is likely to result in surface-water scarcity, increased frequency of storms and precipitation extremes, coastal flooding, landslides, wildfires, air pollution and droughts. This will cause loss of life, injury and negative health impacts, as well as damage to property, infrastructure, livelihoods, service provision and environmental resources.

In the period 1995-2015, there were 6,457 weather-related disasters registered, claiming the lives of more than 600,000 people and affecting an additional 4.2 billion people in other ways. Not all countries experienced the effects of climate hazards on their human and natural systems in the same way: low-income countries suffered the greatest losses, including economic losses estimated to have accounted for about 5 per cent of their gross domestic product (GDP).[5]

The global average annual cost of climatic disasters, including floods, storms, droughts and heat waves, is estimated to have risen substantially, from $64 billion during the period 1985-1994 to $154 billion in the period 2005-2014. A more complete estimate of global costs, taking into account the losses associated with slow-onset climate events (e.g., sea-level rise and desertification), is likely to be much larger. Climate scenarios predict unambiguously that tropical areas will be at higher risk of climate hazards, including countries in Africa and South and South-East Asia, small island developing States and the countries where livelihoods depend on climate-sensitive natural resources such as agriculture, fisheries and forestry. It is in these countries where there is a lesser capacity to prevent (or even cope with) most adverse impacts.

If left unaddressed, these manifestations of climate change are likely to make it more difficult to achieve many development goals as they disproportionally affect poor people and communities, causing an increase in poverty incidence and inequalities. They are likely to slow down economic growth and exacerbate food insecurity, health problems and heat stress of the most vulnerable populations. They may also induce significant displacements of people and involuntary migration.

Climate change and structural inequalities are locked in a vicious cycle

Evidence suggests that the impacts of climate change and structural inequalities are locked in a vicious cycle. Vulnerability and exposure to climate hazards are closely linked to existing underlying inequalities. Differences in access to physical and financial assets; unequal opportunities to access quality health services, education and employment; and

---

5   Centre for Research on the Epidemiology of Disasters and United Nations Office for Disaster Risk Reduction (2015).

inequality with respect to voice and political representation, as well as the perpetuation of discrimination under cultural and institutional norms, are the structural underpinnings of an aggravation of the exposure and vulnerability of large population groups to climate hazards.

The area of residence and the livelihood of people at disadvantage often expose them to mud slides, periods of abnormally hot weather, water contamination, flooding and other climate hazards. Groups whose livelihoods depend on climate-sensitive natural resources are exposed and vulnerable to land degradation, water scarcity, landscape damage, deteriorating ecosystems and other hazards. This is the case particularly if they do not possess the capacity to diversify into climate-resilient livelihoods.

When hit by climate hazards, people afflicted by poverty, marginalization and social exclusion suffer great losses in terms of lives and livelihoods. The disproportionate impact of climate hazards further aggravates existing socioeconomic inequalities and may actually undermine the capacity of people to cope and adapt.

Addressing the root causes of inequalities enables adaptation and the building of resilience to climate hazards. It requires a continuum of policies which include: i) immediate assistance in the wake of climate hazards and interventions for disaster risk reduction, for example, through early warning systems, creation of shelters and infrastructure improvements; ii) policies for adaptation to a changing climate entailing, for example, introduction of new crop varieties and water management techniques; iii) policies centred on ecosystem management and on income diversification; and iv) sound development policies focused on reducing inequalities to achieve poverty eradication and social inclusion. These specific measures will be most effective in reducing climate change vulnerability when they are part of longer-term transformative strategies which embrace coherent policies across the economic, social and environmental dimensions of sustainable development.

Bringing inequalities to the forefront of climate assessments

Environmental concerns, in general, and the impact of climate hazards on people's livelihoods, in particular, require policymakers to improve policy frameworks and analytical capacities, so that they can design and implement coherent policies. Integrated climate impact assessments assemble different modelling frameworks to help policymakers understand the challenges posed by climate hazards. Effective climate impact assessments assist policymakers in better understanding policy options aimed towards adaptation and climate change resilience with a sharper focus on inequalities.

However, this makes for a complex task. The construction of policy options with regard to achieving climate resilience for sustainable development requires good information systems for identifying people at risk in their (often very local) geographical contexts. The construction of policy options also requires sound integrated assessments to improve understanding of the interlinkages across the economic, social and environmental dimensions of development, including the impact of climate hazards on people and their livelihoods.

The present *Survey* shows how the improved use of integrated modelling frameworks will contribute to the assessment of the impacts of climate hazards and policies relating to:

- Climate-sensitive natural resources upon which livelihoods rely
- Distribution of income on the basis of ownership and employment of production factors such as land, capital and labour

- Human capital and access to basic public services and resources (education, health, sanitation and infrastructure)
- Vulnerabilities of disadvantaged groups based on their socioeconomic characteristics

Engaging different stakeholders (including policymakers, experts and communities) is essential to obtaining the detailed information and critical feedback required to improve the design of model-based scenarios and the interpretation of results. Meaningful participation of stakeholders assures the input of local political and expert judgment. The feedback of vulnerable population groups and communities is particularly important in facilitating an understanding of the factors that exacerbate people's vulnerability and exposure to climate hazards. It is also important when assessing adaptation options to ensure that adaptation policies are relevant to building climate resilience among people and communities.

Greater efforts to improve the production of the data and statistics necessary to document the socioeconomic impacts of a changing climate are urgently needed, along with the building of capacity to construct and use integrated assessments at the country level. Building scenarios illustrating possible impacts of climate hazards and assessing policy options for building resilience can yield sound scientific evidence for application to policy decisions. Institutionalizing the use of integrated analytical frameworks and of scenario results can both strengthen the policymaking processes by mobilizing technical expertise across sectoral ministries and contribute to improved policy coordination within the government, and in close collaboration with relevant stakeholders and researchers.

Coherent, participatory and adaptive policymaking for climate resilience

Better understanding of the impact of climate change on lives and livelihoods will lead to better-informed policymaking. Public policies have an important role to play in addressing people's vulnerability and building climate resilience. Disadvantaged groups typically possess few options for diversifying their income sources, gaining access to insurance and financial markets and improving their education and health status.

Breaking the vicious cycle in which inequalities and vulnerability to climate hazards are locked requires well-integrated and coherent policies designed to reduce current well-known vulnerabilities, including policies targeting poverty eradication, income diversification and improved access to basic social services such as education, health, and water and sanitation, among many others.

Reducing exposure and vulnerabilities as part of a process to strengthen people's capacity to cope with and adapt to climate hazards in the present and in the medium term requires a continuum of development policies strategically crafted to reduce the multiplicity of inequalities that make people vulnerable. A continuum of well-integrated economic, social and environmental policies for building climate resilience would also help harmonize present adaptation efforts within short-term political and funding cycles with longer-term development objectives. Policies designed to close the development gaps that leave people vulnerable to climate hazards are sound development policies and are essential to reducing the risk posed by climate change. Investing, for example, in prevention to halt the spread of malaria and other debilitating diseases, so as to improve the quality of life of the most disadvantaged population groups, is both a sound development policy and part and parcel of a sound adaptation policy, given that healthier and potentially wealthier people will be more resilient to future climate hazards.

In the continuum of policies, addressing the root causes of inequalities requires transformative policies that generate change in the fundamental attributes of systems, particularly the existing governance systems and norms that perpetuate inequalities. Transformative policies should aim, for example, towards generating shifts in behaviours to encourage sustainable consumption and production practices, in line with the goals set out in the 2030 Agenda for Sustainable Development.

This *Survey* argues that policy processes based on the principles of coherence and integration, participation and flexibility should help address underlying inequalities by identifying vulnerable populations, particular intersecting inequalities, and concrete actions for strengthening resilience.

Policy coherence is important for achieving climate resilience, particularly because of the need to integrate, or mainstream, adaptation objectives into longer-term development processes across the different dimensions of sustainable development.

Direct consultation with and participation of multiple stakeholders in policy decision-making improve understanding of specific risks and vulnerabilities at the local level. Further, a better understanding of risks and priorities achieved through the engagement of local communities and stakeholders improves policy design, policy implementation and policy outcomes.

Within the context of a changing climate and greater weather variability, uncertainty must be fully embedded in policy decision-making processes. This requires a flexible policy process, capable of incorporating lessons derived at each step of the process, with a view to improving knowledge and outcomes. Within the context of uncertainty, no-regret and low-regret policies constitute a good starting point for adaptation, as they can address immediate vulnerabilities and structural inequalities, without compromising the foundations of future resilience.

Enhanced cooperation for climate-resilient development

Delivering on the commitments set out in the 2030 Agenda for Sustainable Development will be critical to strengthening resilience to climate change among the most vulnerable countries and population groups. Improving access to stable and adequate sources of finance for adaptation and contributing to the building of the information systems needed to guide policymaking for climate resilience are two concrete undertakings for which greater international cooperation is required.

A strengthened Global Partnership for Sustainable Development has an important role to play in supporting countries' efforts in building climate resilience. The historical agreements adopted by the international community in 2015, including the 2030 Agenda for Sustainable Development and the Addis Ababa Action Agenda of the Third International Conference on Financing for Development, provide a unique opportunity to solidify effective global cooperation and coordination in support of global, regional and national efforts towards achieving sustainable development in general and climate-resilient development more specifically.

The imperative of limiting global warming together with the task of effectively reducing the impact of climate hazards on vulnerable populations requires a profound transformation of international cooperation. Much of the previous focus of climate action has been on mitigating the effects of anthropogenic activity so as to limit the rise in global temperature. In addition to this effort, unprecedented levels of cooperation in a number of critical development areas are needed for the specific purpose of achieving climate change adaptation.

Two types of international support are discussed in the *Survey*: (a) support for the provision of stable, predictable and sufficient sources of financing for climate-resilient development; and (b) support for improving capacities needed to produce and utilize large and complex sources of data and information so as to facilitate identification of population groups particularly vulnerable to climate hazards.

In December 2015, the Conference of the Parties to the United Nations Framework Convention on Climate Change committed to mobilizing at least US$ 100 billion per year for climate change mitigation and adaptation activities in developing countries.[6] While there is no central accounting mechanism for climate finance flows, adaptation activities are clearly underfunded: the Climate Policy Initiative estimates that funding for mitigation efforts is 16 times greater than that for adaptation projects. This gap in financing for adaptation — the "adaptation gap" — is a cause for concern, particularly given that climate hazards have a disproportionate impact on the poorest countries and on vulnerable population groups within countries.

According to the IPCC Fifth Assessment Report (2014), adaptation costs will range from $70 billion to $100 billion per year by 2050 in the developing countries alone. An updated review conducted by the United Nations Environment Programme indicates that these figures are likely to be an underestimate. Yet, the $100 billion climate finance pledge is for both mitigation and adaptation. Put simply, climate finance streams need to far exceed the target under the Paris Agreement if climate change-related needs are to be met.

Given that many adaptation efforts, such as the creation of levies and the installation of weather monitoring systems, support the public good, there is a strong case to be made for support from the public sector. Increased funds from public domestic and international efforts are required to fill the gap in areas where the private sector is unlikely to invest adequately, in particular in projects aimed at the most marginalized areas and population groups. Adaptation efforts are successful only when they integrate the needs of the disenfranchised and are responsive to the inequalities that underpin exposure and vulnerability. While in some cases (such as that of philanthropy) the private sector will aim for redistributive outcomes, in most, an adaptation agenda will require public funding.

Mobilization of resources and actions to build resilience and adaptive capacity will also entail meeting the challenge of identifying those vulnerable to climate hazards, understanding the risk they incur and monitoring the effect of interventions in reducing that vulnerability. Production of statistics on the impact of climate hazards requires the development of consistent concepts and classifications as a component of official national and international programmes. Understanding the interlinkages between vulnerability and climate hazards requires intensive collaboration, harmonization and integration across a range of disciplines and among a wide range of data programmes, including official statistics of population, its main characteristics and its distribution in different ecological areas.

Understanding the socioeconomic attributes of vulnerable groups and further assessing the potential impacts of climate hazards and policies on their livelihoods require sound statistics at the lowest possible geographical resolutions. This is critical for enabling

---

6   See FCCC/CP/2015/10/Add.1, decision 1/CP.21, para. 53.

policymakers and population groups and communities to be better informed and to acquire an understanding of the true nature of the problems to be confronted, as well as the expected impact of policy alternatives. When such disaggregated data and information are missing, rigorous climate impact assessments and the capacity of policy systems to respond are seriously challenged.

In building the information systems needed for climate resilience, a wide range of official data developers beyond the national statistical offices and across sectors (including agriculture, water, sanitation, energy, mining and environment) will need to engage in intensive collaboration and adequate coordination. At this point in time, the institutional experience, capacity and responsibility needed to generate statistics for analysing climate change and its impact on exposed populations are diffused across Governments and international organizations, with little communication among the different specialties.

These challenges have been recognized in the 2030 Agenda for Sustainable Development and are being taken up by international organizations led by the Statistical Commission. Efforts in this direction will require unprecedented levels of cooperation at the global and national levels. Strengthened international cooperation is needed for a new form of data development and to support the building of capacity to use data effectively, including within the context of integrated climate impact assessments.

Contents

Boxes

Figures

Tables

Explanatory Notes

The following symbols have been used in the tables throughout the report:

..	**Two dots** indicate that data are not available or are not separately reported.
–	**A dash** indicates that the amount is nil or negligible.
-	**A hyphen** indicates that the item is not applicable.
—	**A minus sign** indicates deficit or decrease, except as indicated.
.	**A full stop** is used to indicate decimals.
/	**A slash** between years indicates a crop year or financial year, for example, 2011/12.
-	**Use of a hyphen** between years, for example, 2012-2012, signifies the full period involved, including the beginning and end years.

Reference to "dollars" ($) indicates United States dollars, unless otherwise stated.

Reference to "billions" indicates one thousand million.

Reference to "tons" indicates metric tons, unless otherwise stated.

Annual rates of growth or change, unless otherwise stated, refer to annual compound rates.

Details and percentages in tables do not necessarily add to totals, because of rounding.

The following abbreviations have been used:

AgMIP	Agricultural Model Intercomparison and Improvement Project
CGE	computable general equilibrium
CLEWS	Climate, Land, Energy and Water Systems
CRED	Centre for Research on the Epidemiology of Disasters (Louvain, Belgium)
ECLAC	Economic Commission for Latin America and the Caribbean
EM-DAT	CRED International Disaster Database
FAO	Food and Agriculture Organization of the United Nations
GCM	global circulation model
GDP	gross domestic product
IFPRI	International Food Policy Research Institute
ILO	International Labour Organization
IMF	International Monetary Fund
INDCs	intended nationally determined contributions
IPCC	Intergovernmental Panel on Climate Change
NAMA	nationally appropriate mitigation actions
NAPA	national adaptation programme of action

ODA	official development assistance
OECD	Organization for Economic Cooperation and Development
PE	partial equilibrium
RAP	representative agricultural pathway
REDD+	reducing emissions from deforestation and forest degradation and fostering conservation, sustainable management of forests, and enhancement of forest carbon stocks
RIA	regional integrated assessment
SDMX	Statistical Data and Metadata eXchange
SSPs	shared socioeconomic pathway
SWITCH	Sustainable Water Management Improves Tomorrow's Cities' Health
UN/DESA	Department of Economic and Social Affairs of the United Nations Secretariat
UNDP	United Nations Development Programme
UNEP	United Nations Environment Programme
UNFCCC	United Nations Framework Convention on Climate Change
UNICEF	United Nations Children's Fund
WHO	World Health Organization

The designations employed and the presentation of the material in this publication do not imply the expression of any opinion whatsoever on the part of the United Nations Secretariat concerning the legal status of any country, territory, city or area or of its authorities, or concerning the delimitation of its frontiers or boundaries.

The term "country" as used in the text of this report also refers, as appropriate, to territories or areas.

For analytical purposes, unless otherwise specified, the following country groupings and subgroupings have been used:

Developed economies (developed market economies):

Australia, Canada, European Union, Iceland, Japan, New Zealand, Norway, Switzerland, United States of America.

Group of Eight (G8):

Canada, France, Germany, Italy, Japan, Russian Federation, United Kingdom of Great Britain and Northern Ireland, United States of America.

Group of Twenty (G20):

Argentina, Australia, Brazil, Canada, China, France, Germany, India, Indonesia, Italy, Japan, Mexico, Republic of Korea, Russian Federation, Saudi Arabia, South Africa, Turkey, United Kingdom of Great Britain and Northern Ireland, United States of America, European Union.

European Union (EU):

Austria, Belgium, Bulgaria, Croatia, Cyprus, Czech Republic, Denmark, Estonia, Finland, France, Germany, Greece, Hungary, Ireland, Italy, Latvia, Lithuania, Luxembourg, Malta, Netherlands, Poland, Portugal, Romania, Slovakia, Slovenia, Spain, Sweden, United Kingdom of Great Britain and Northern Ireland.

EU-15:

Austria, Belgium, Denmark, Finland, France, Germany, Greece, Ireland, Italy, Luxembourg, Netherlands, Portugal, Spain, Sweden, United Kingdom of Great Britain and Northern Ireland.

New EU member States:

Bulgaria, Croatia, Cyprus, Czech Republic, Estonia, Hungary, Latvia, Lithuania, Malta, Poland, Romania, Slovakia, Slovenia.

Economies in transition:

South-Eastern Europe:

Albania, Bosnia and Herzegovina, Croatia, Montenegro, Serbia, the former Yugoslav Republic of Macedonia.

Commonwealth of Independent States (CIS):

Armenia, Azerbaijan, Belarus, Georgia,[a] Kazakhstan, Kyrgyzstan, Republic of Moldova, Russian Federation, Tajikistan, Turkmenistan, Ukraine, Uzbekistan.

Developing economies:

Africa, Asia and the Pacific (excluding Australia, Japan, New Zealand and the member States of CIS in Asia), Latin America and the Caribbean.

Subgroupings of Africa:

Northern Africa:

Algeria, Egypt, Libya, Morocco, Tunisia.

Sub-Saharan Africa:

All other African countries, except Nigeria and South Africa, where indicated.

Subgroupings of Asia and the Pacific:

Western Asia:

Bahrain, Iraq, Israel, Jordan, Kuwait, Lebanon, Occupied Palestinian Territory, Oman, Qatar, Saudi Arabia, Syrian Arab Republic, Turkey, United Arab Emirates, Yemen.

South Asia:

Bangladesh, Bhutan, India, Iran (Islamic Republic of), Maldives, Nepal, Pakistan, Sri Lanka.

East Asia:

All other developing economies in Asia and the Pacific.

Subgroupings of Latin America and the Caribbean:

South America:

Argentina, Bolivia (Plurinational State of), Brazil, Chile, Colombia, Ecuador, Paraguay, Peru, Uruguay, Venezuela (Bolivarian Republic of).

Mexico and Central America:

Costa Rica, El Salvador, Guatemala, Honduras, Mexico, Nicaragua, Panama.

Caribbean:

Barbados, Cuba, Dominican Republic, Guyana, Haiti, Jamaica, Trinidad and Tobago.

---

[a] As of 19 August 2009, Georgia officially left the Commonwealth of Independent States. However, its performance is discussed in the context of this group of countries for reasons of geographical proximity and similarities in economic structure.

Least developed countries:

Afghanistan, Angola, Bangladesh, Benin, Bhutan, Burkina Faso, Burundi, Cambodia, Central African Republic, Chad, Comoros, Democratic Republic of the Congo, Djibouti, Equatorial Guinea, Eritrea, Ethiopia, Gambia, Guinea, Guinea-Bissau, Haiti, Kiribati, Lao People's Democratic Republic, Lesotho, Liberia, Madagascar, Malawi, Mali, Mauritania, Mozambique, Myanmar, Nepal, Niger, Rwanda, Sao Tome and Principe, Senegal, Sierra Leone, Solomon Islands, Somalia, South Sudan, Sudan, Timor-Leste, Togo, Tuvalu, Uganda, United Republic of Tanzania, Vanuatu, Yemen, Zambia.

Small island developing States and areas:

American Samoa, Anguilla, Antigua and Barbuda, Aruba, Bahamas, Barbados, Belize, British Virgin Islands, Cape Verde, Commonwealth of the Northern Mariana Islands, Comoros, Cook Islands, Cuba, Dominica, Dominican Republic, Fiji, French Polynesia, Grenada, Guam, Guinea-Bissau, Guyana, Haiti, Jamaica, Kiribati, Maldives, Marshall Islands, Mauritius, Micronesia (Federated States of), Montserrat, Nauru, Netherlands Antilles, New Caledonia, Niue, Palau, Papua New Guinea, Puerto Rico, Saint Kitts and Nevis, Saint Lucia, Saint Vincent and the Grenadines, Samoa, Sao Tome and Principe, Seychelles, Singapore, Solomon Islands, Suriname, Timor-Leste, Tonga, Trinidad and Tobago, Tuvalu, United States Virgin Islands, Vanuatu.

Parties to the United Nations Framework Convention on Climate Change:

Annex I parties:

Australia, Austria, Belarus, Belgium, Bulgaria, Canada, Croatia, Czech Republic, Denmark, Estonia, European Union, Finland, France, Germany, Greece, Hungary, Iceland, Ireland, Italy, Japan, Latvia, Liechtenstein, Lithuania, Luxembourg, Monaco, Netherlands, New Zealand, Norway, Poland, Portugal, Romania, Russian Federation, Slovakia, Slovenia, Spain, Sweden, Switzerland, Turkey, Ukraine, United Kingdom of Great Britain and Northern Ireland, United States of America.

Annex II parties:

Annex II parties are the parties included in Annex I that are members of the Organization for Economic Cooperation and Development but not the parties included in Annex I that are economies in transition.

Non-Annex I parties:

Non-Annex I parties are mainly developing countries. Certain groups of developing countries are recognized by the Convention as being especially vulnerable to the adverse impacts of climate change, including countries with low-lying coastal areas and those prone to desertification and drought. Others (such as countries that rely heavily on income from fossil fuel production and commerce) experience greater vulnerability to the potential economic impacts of climate change response measures. The Convention emphasizes activities that promise to respond to the special needs and concerns of those vulnerable countries, such as investment, insurance and technology transfer.

The 48 parties classified as least developed countries by the United Nations are given special consideration under the Convention on account of their limited capacity to respond to climate change and adapt to its adverse effects. Parties are urged to take full account of the special situation of least developed countries when considering funding and technology transfer activities.

Chapter I
Climate change resilience for sustainable development

Key messages

- Climate change is increasing the frequency and intensity of the extreme weather and climate events that are affecting all countries. However, because of their geographical location, reliance on climate-sensitive natural resources and development gaps in general, developing countries, and low-income countries in particular, are at the greatest risk of climate hazards. Left unattended, climate hazards are likely to increase poverty, worsen inequalities, exacerbate food insecurity and cause health problems, among other hardships, which may reverse years of development progress in some countries.

- Climate hazards also have differential impacts on people and communities within countries. These impacts are largely determined by deep-rooted socioeconomic inequalities. As a result, they tend to be particularly detrimental to the most disadvantaged groups of society, which are hence disproportionately exposed and vulnerable to climate hazards.

- The universal consensus attested by the adoption of the 2030 Agenda for Sustainable Development provides a unique opportunity to build climate change resilience for sustainable development by addressing the structural inequalities that perpetuate poverty, marginalization and social exclusion and thus increase vulnerability to climate hazards.

- To be successful, disaster risk reduction and disaster management, social protection and adaptation strategies must all be part of a broader development framework which incrementally leads the way to the empowerment of today's disadvantaged groups, by improving their asset positions and access to input and product markets; by extending their access to quality basic services; and by changing the norms that foster their social and political exclusion.

The international consensus on sustainable development

In 2015, world leaders took significant steps towards forging sustainable development pathways holding out the promise of eradicating poverty, reversing environmental degradation and achieving equitable and inclusive societies. From 25 to 27 September 2015, Heads of State and Government and High Representatives gathered at United Nations Headquarters in New York to adopt the 2030 Agenda for Sustainable Development,[1] which

In 2015, States Members of the United Nations took significant steps towards building sustainable development pathways

---

1   General Assembly resolution 70/1, entitled "Transforming our world: the 2030 Agenda for Sustainable Development".

will drive global efforts towards achieving sustainable development until 2030. Previous efforts gave impetus to the adoption of this Agenda.

On 16 July 2015, the Third International Conference on Financing for Development, held in Addis Ababa from 13 to 16 July 2015, adopted the Addis Ababa Action Agenda of the Conference,[2] which puts forward a global framework for mobilizing resources and facilitating policy implementation for sustainable development. On 3 June 2015, the General Assembly endorsed the Sendai Framework for Disaster Risk Reduction, 2015-2030,[3] which had been adopted by the Third World Conference on Disaster Risk Reduction, held in Sendai City, Japan, from 14 to 18 March 2015. The Sendai Framework recognizes that it is the primary responsibility of Governments to reduce disaster risk and loss of lives, and preserve livelihoods, which will be critical to averting development reversals in the future.

The 2030 Agenda for Sustainable Development recognized that climate change, whose adverse impacts undermine the ability of all countries to achieve sustainable development, constitutes one of the greatest challenges of our time and, in that regard, acknowledged the sessions of the Conference of the Parties to the United Nations Framework Convention on Climate Change as the primary forum for negotiating the global response to that challenge. On 12 December 2015, the Conference of the Parties to the Convention at its twenty-first session adopted the Paris Agreement in which the parties to the Agreement announced quantitative commitments to reducing their greenhouse gas emissions, the major driver of climate change, and to supporting adaptation efforts.[4]

There is global consensus on the need to address the inextricable links between the human development and environmental agendas

These historic agreements are part of a global consensus on the need to address the inextricable links between the human development and environmental agendas. They signal acknowledgement, on the part of developed and developing countries, of the universal need for an integrated and coherent approach to tackling global development challenges, including consistent adaptation to climate change. Recognition of the urgency of moving towards sustainable development pathways comes at times when "warming of the climate is unequivocal" (Intergovernmental Panel on Climate Change, 2014e, p. 2, SPM 1.1) and is "increasing the likelihood of severe, pervasive and irreversible impacts for people and ecosystems" (ibid., p. 8, SPM 2).

Building climate resilience presents a unique opportunity to reduce inequalities through far-reaching transformative policies supported by effective global partnerships

World Economic and Social Survey 2016: Climate Change Resilience - An Opportunity for Reducing Inequalities contributes to the identification of some of the challenges of implementation of the 2030 Agenda for Sustainable Development. The evidence points to the great economic, human and environmental losses brought about by climate hazards which, if left unattended, are likely to continue. The *Survey* addresses the challenges of strengthening the capacity of countries and people to avoid development reversals from those hazards. Recent data suggest that the world has already warmed 0.85° Celsius from pre-industrial levels and will continue to experience warming even if greenhouse gas emissions were immediately brought to a complete halt (Intergovernmental Panel on Climate Change, 2013). The consequences of the warming of the planet will continue to challenge the capacity of countries to prevent devastating impacts on people and ecosystems.

This *Survey* argues that building climate resilience presents a unique opportunity to reduce inequalities. The persisting inequalities in multiple dimensions have led to recognition that climate hazards have a differential impact on people and communities. It

---

2   General Assembly resolution 69/313, annex.

3   General Assembly resolution 69/283, annex II.

4   See FCCC/CP/2015/10/Add.1, decision 1/CP.21.

has also been recognized that the association between climate hazards and inequalities has not been sufficiently researched.[5] In response, the *Survey* has chosen to tackle the issue of climate change resilience, with a focus on the population groups and communities that are disproportionately vulnerable. It argues that, in the absence of well-assessed, far-reaching transformative policies at the national level, supported by effective global partnerships, building climate resilience will remain elusive and poverty and inequalities will likely be exacerbated. This would pose a fundamental challenge to the implementation of the 2030 Agenda for Sustainable Development.

Moving climate resilience forward in implementing the 2030 Agenda for Sustainable Development

The 17 Sustainable Development Goals and 169 targets set out in the 2030 Agenda explicitly elaborate on the interlinkages across the economic, social and environmental dimensions of development and the opportunities to build positive synergies among them. Some of these interlinkages and synergies are fundamental to facets of building climate change resilience and reducing inequalities.

Sustainable Development Goal 13 affirms the urgency of taking action to combat climate change and its impacts by calling for actions to strengthen resilience and adaptive capacity with respect to climate hazards; to integrate climate change measures into national policies; and to improve education, awareness-raising and human and institutional capacity on climate change mitigation, adaptation, impact reduction and early warning. The interlinkages between climate change and other dimensions of development are also well reflected in other Goals. If the frequency and intensity of climate hazards increase, it will be harder for countries to end poverty and hunger, achieve food security, improve nutrition, promote sustainable agriculture and ensure healthy lives (Goals 1-3). Furthermore, the sustainability of water and energy systems (Goals 6 and 7) and the safety and resilience of infrastructure, cities and human settlements (Goals 9 and 11) will be challenged by climate hazards. Similarly, if climate hazards continue to undermine the ability of countries to achieve sustained growth and development, full employment and decent work will be harder to achieve (Goal 8).

Sustainable Development Goal 10, which explicitly addresses the goal of reducing inequality within and among countries, includes targets focused on improving the income of the bottom 40 per cent of the population; promoting the social, economic and political inclusion of all, irrespective of age, sex, disability, race, ethnicity, origin, religion or economic or other status; eliminating discriminatory laws, policies and practices; and achieving fiscal, wage and social protection policies for greater equality. With their references to universality, many other targets within the framework of the Goals provide the basis for reducing inequality in its multiple dimensions, encompassing access to key basic services such as health, education, water and sanitation, and energy (Goals 3, 4, 6 and 7), gender (Goal 5) and inclusive economic growth (Goal 8).

---

5   The Intergovernmental Panel on Climate Change (IPCC) has already recognized that climate-resilient development pathways will have only marginal effects on poverty reduction unless structural inequalities are addressed. At the same time, the Panel has underlined that the importance of structural inequalities and their association with climate change remain insufficiently researched (Olsson and others, 2014, pp. 797 and 819).

The SDGs provide the framework for tackling the structural inequalities that increase vulnerability to climate hazards

Together, these Goals provide a framework for the implementation of policies that address the underlying causes of poverty, vulnerability and the risk of climate change. Yet, it is important to deepen the understanding of the interlinkages across these Goals and their policy implications in order to tackle the structural inequalities that perpetuate poverty, marginalization and social exclusion, the factors that increase the risk of climate hazards. Critical aspects of this understanding encompass integration of the various facets of the environment into development policy; the interaction of climate change with mega-trends which may magnify its impacts; and a continuum of policies that, while addressing immediate vulnerabilities, make it possible to incrementally achieve adaptation and transformative change for sustainable development.

Ensuring consistency across the economic, social and environmental dimensions of development policy is a core challenge in achieving sustainable development

Nowadays, the relationship between the economic and social dimensions of development is better understood owing to an extensive body of research and the experience of countries over the last decades. The trickle-down paradigm which prevailed in the 1980s was seriously challenged when new research and country experiences demonstrated that economic growth did not necessarily translate into human development. This understanding led to a major revision of development policies aimed at improving the consistency between economic growth and human development objectives. Developing countries made major efforts to increase investments in education, health, water and sanitation. They introduced comprehensive social protection programmes and experimented with new regulations and incentives designed to redirect private investments towards job creation and larger development objectives. However, those efforts were disconnected, more often than not, from efforts to meet environmental goals (United Nations, 2016).

Hence, there is much less experience and policy guidance on the integration of the various aspects of the environment into development policy. Building consistency across the economic, social and environmental dimensions of development policy will be a core challenge in building climate resilience and achieving sustainable development. It will demand greater technical capacities among policymakers and all stakeholders for building on the interlinkages across the multiple dimensions of development in the event of climate impacts and for policy responses. It will also be necessary to strengthen the capacities to negotiate commonly agreed objectives through building upon single-group interests. More broadly, policy systems as a whole will require systemic changes to enable the more coherent and more flexible design of integrated policies for climate resilience, with participation from all relevant stakeholders. For many developing countries, these changes will not be possible without global partnerships.

Important mega-trends that interact with climate change will shape development prospects and policy

The complexity inherent in addressing the links between the human development and environmental agendas is compounded by the uncertainty surrounding important mega-trends which will shape development prospects and policy in both the near and the distant future. Despite overall convergence in average per capita income across countries, within-country inequalities are on the rise. This important trend along with others, such as globalization and technological change, demographic dynamics, rapid urbanization and climate change itself, will exert additional pressures leading towards increasing inequalities both among and within countries. Moreover, if investment in green technologies is inadequate, if population growth continues to be high, if investment in human capital is low and if current socioeconomic inequalities remain, then income poverty and inequality are likely to increase in the future under scenarios where current unmitigated emissions are high. (See appendix I.1 for a full description of alternative development pathways.) This clearly points to the importance of understanding the options for building climate resilience with full consideration given to climate change and socioeconomic mega-trends.

Based on the evidence, there exists no doubt that moderating or avoiding the risks associated with climate change and reducing poverty and inequality, involve both mitigation (preventing future warming) and adaptation (finding better or safer ways to live on a warming planet). Unquestionably, the only way to prevent the adverse consequences of climate change for human and natural systems is through mitigation. However, effective policies focused on adaptation are urgently needed as well to enable the building of resilience; those policies may also assist both in preventing the negative impacts arising from climate hazards and in slowing the process of climate change. For a number of reasons, however, adaptation has received less attention than mitigation in the discussions centred around climate change and it is only recently that efforts directed towards adaptation are being incorporated in the global policy agenda. First, as adaptation is a public good, private provision will typically remain below socially desirable levels unless the public sector intervenes. Second, adaptation, is difficult to address as it requires actions along the economic, social and environmental dimensions of development, which depend on the specific context of each country. Finally, there are no clear metrics for assessing adaptation impacts; that is, unlike mitigation, for which there is a clearly defined metric (namely, tons of greenhouse gas emissions), assessing adaptation efforts requires a larger number of indicators closely related to wider development efforts.

> For many reasons, adaptation has received less attention than mitigation and it is only recently that adaptation has become a focus of global attention

This *Survey* focuses more on adaptation than on mitigation. In doing so, it situates adaptation along a continuum of broader development policies for transformation—critical components of which are efforts to address immediate needs (for example, poverty alleviation and disaster risk reduction and management) while reducing structural inequalities. The capacity for integrating these policies will be at the centre of the challenge of implementing the 2030 Agenda. However, it is important to understand that while these policies will contribute to sustainable development in general, they will at the same time help build the climate resilience of the particular countries and population groups that are most at risk.

> Successful adaptation requires broad development policies aimed at reducing the structural inequalities that leave people vulnerable to climate hazards

Climate change and variability, and the uneven impacts of climate hazards

Understanding the association between climate change and inequality requires proper identification of (a) the climate-induced events that people experience most and (b) the countries and the population groups within countries that are most vulnerable to those events.

The United Nations Framework Convention on Climate Change[6] (article 1) defines climate change as a change in the climate attributed directly or indirectly to human activity that alters the composition of the global atmosphere and which is, in addition to natural climate variability, observed over comparable time periods.[7] Climate change takes place

---

6   United Nations, *Treaty Series, vol. 1771*, No. 30822.

7   Climate change, as defined by IPCC, refers to a change in the state of the climate that can be identified (e.g., through use of statistical tests) by changes in the mean and/or the variability of its properties, and that persists for an extended period, typically decades or longer. It may be caused by natural internal processes or external forcings such as modulations of the solar cycles, volcanic eruptions and persistent anthropogenic changes in the composition of the atmosphere or in land use. The United Nations Framework Convention on Climate Change makes a distinction between climate change attributable to human activities altering the composition of the atmosphere and climate variability attributable to natural causes. For more details, see the glossary of terms in IPCC (2014b, annex II). For the purpose of this *Survey*, the focus of attention is on climate hazards as the manifestation of potentially damaging impacts from climate-induced events, regardless of their origin.

over a period of decades or centuries; what people experience in their daily life is climate variability and climate extremes.[8]

There is consensus in the scientific community that climate change is increasing the frequency, intensity, spatial extent, duration and timing of extreme weather and climate events, which results in an unprecedented level of climate hazards (IPCC, 2012, p. 7). Climate hazards are understood as being the potential occurrence of a climate-induced physical event that may cause loss of life, injury or other health impacts, as well as damage to and loss of property, infrastructure, livelihoods, service provision and environmental resources.[9] The destruction generated by climate hazards when they hit countries and people with greater frequency may derail years of development efforts.

For the twenty-first century, scenarios unambiguously predict continuing slow-onset changes such as higher surface and ocean temperature, ocean acidification and global rise of sea level. They also predict increased or more intensified extreme weather-related events, such as heat waves and precipitation extremes. In particular, those scenarios predict the most severe effects in tropical areas, where most developing countries are located.

If left unaddressed, these manifestations of climate change are likely to cause an increase in poverty incidence and inequalities by slowing down economic growth and exacerbating food insecurity, health problems and heat stress; and to result in surface-water scarcity and increased exposure to storms and precipitation extremes, coastal flooding, landslides, air pollution and droughts. They may also induce displacement of people and involuntary migration, among other hardships.

Weather-related disasters are becoming more frequent in all corners of the world, with a total of 6,457 events in 1995-2015, which represents an average of 323 disasters per year. Those disasters claimed more than 600,000 lives and affected about 4.2 billion people during the same period (table I.1). Floods constitute the major cause of deaths and had the greatest effect on people's lives. The number of people exposed to water-related hazards, together with storms, lies in the billions. Land-related disasters, such as droughts, landslides and wildfires, are other major factors affecting people's lives and their livelihoods. Importantly, the impacts of these climate hazards are not distributed evenly across countries, or across and within population groups in countries. This is a critical fact underlying the association between climate change and inequality.

---

8   Climate variability refers to variations in the mean state of the climate and may result from the same factors that explain climate change, as noted above. A climate extreme (i.e., an extreme weather or climate event) occurs when the value of a weather or climate variable is above (or below) a threshold value near the upper (or lower) end of the range of observed values of the variable. For simplicity, both extreme weather events and extreme climate events tend to be referred to collectively as "climate extremes" (IPCC, 2014b, annex II).

9   The City Climate Hazard Taxonomy developed by C40, a network of the world's megacities committed to addressing climate change, classifies climate hazards within five groups of events: (a) meteorological: short-term or small-scale weather conditions; (b) climatological: long-term or large-scale atmospheric processes; (c) hydrological: mass movement of water or a change in the chemical composition of water bodies; (d) geophysical: originating from mass movement of solid earth; and (e) biological: a change in the way living organisms grow and thrive, which may lead to contamination and/or disease (see http://www.c40.org/).

Table I.1

Number of people killed or affected by disasters, by type, 1995–2015[a]

Thousands		
Disaster type	Number killed	Number affected[b]
Floods	157	2 300 000
Drought	22	1 100 000
Storms	242	660 000
Extreme temperature	164	94 000
Landslides and wildfires	20	8 000
Total	**605**	**4 162 000**

Source: Centre for Research on the Epidemiology of Disasters (CRED) (2015).

a Up to August 2015.

b Those injured, left homeless or in need of emergency assistance, not including those killed.

Uneven impacts across countries

Not all countries experience the effects of climate hazards on their human and natural systems in the same way or proportion. Scenarios unambiguously predict that tropical areas are at higher risk of climate hazards. According to the Notre Dame Global Adaptation Index (ND-GAIN) (Chen and others, 2015),[10] for example, countries at the highest risk of climate change are concentrated in Africa and South and South-East Asia, where the capacity to prevent (or even cope with) most negative impacts is poor (figure I.1). While some high-income countries (Italy, Japan and the United States of America) exhibit relatively high risk levels owing to their high exposure to climate hazards, they possess greater capacity (resources) to manage those risks.

In absolute terms, total economic losses owing to climate hazards are most significant for high-income countries. In CRED (2015), total economic losses are defined as the estimated cost of damage to property (housing and infrastructure), crops and livestock. However, because of the distribution of risks and level of development, the greater economic losses relative to national income are observed in countries at lower levels of income. Low-income countries lost an estimated 5 per cent of gross domestic product (GDP) during the period 1995-2015 (figure I.2).[11]

The effects of climate hazards on the human and natural systems are uneven across countries and among population groups

10 This Index ranks countries' risk of climate change. Risk is constructed by summing rankings for vulnerability and exposure to climate change and the number of weather-related events. Vulnerability is assessed by considering six "life-supporting sectors": food, water, health, ecosystem services, human habitat and infrastructure. Each sector in turn represents three cross-cutting components: the exposure to climate-related hazards, the sensitivity to those impacts and the adaptive capacity to cope or adapt. Exposure is measured by projected changes in (not levels of) the following components, some of which are due to projected climate change: cereal yields, population, water run-off, groundwater recharge, deaths from climate change induced diseases, length of transmission season of vector-borne diseases, biome distribution, marine biodiversity, warm period, flood hazard, hydropower generation capacity and sea-level rise impacts. For the technical treatments of the index, see Chen and others (2015).

11 See, in this regard, the definition of "estimated damage" found in the glossary for the Emergency Events Database EM-DAT. Available at http://www.emdat.be/Glossary.

Figure I.1
Risk of climate change of all countries, by quintile, 1995–2014

Source: UN/DESA, based on University of Notre Dame Global Adaptation Index (available at http://index.gain.org) and Centre for Research on the Epidemiology of Disasters (CRED) (2015).

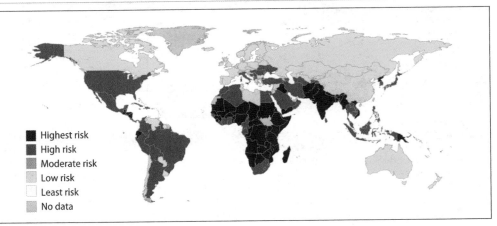

Figure I.2
Economic losses of countries from climate hazards, by income group, 1995–2015

Source: Centre for Research on the Epidemiology of Disasters (2015).

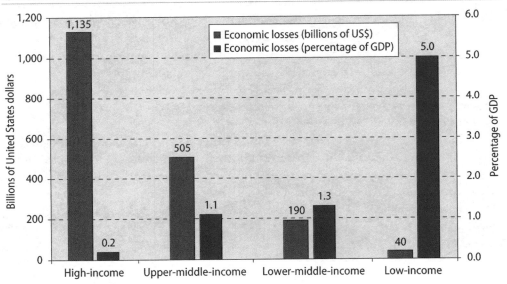

Least developed countries, countries in Africa and small island developing States are the most vulnerable to climate change

Countries with a high reliance on agriculture, the majority being least developed countries, are particularly vulnerable. Current agricultural practices are a major contributor to environmental degradation through greenhouse gas emissions and poor management of land and water resources. At the same time, agriculture is highly sensitive to climate change. As temperature rises, crop productivity is predicted to decrease at lower latitudes — although it is also expected to increase at mid-high latitudes. Warming, together with changes in water precipitation and unpredicted climate variability, affects the timing and length of growing seasons and yields, with strong impacts on farmers' livelihoods and on food security more generally (United Nations, 2011b, pp. 74-76). There is evidence for the period 1981-2003 that land productivity decreased in sub-Saharan Africa, in South-East Asia and southern China, in north-central Australia, in the pampas and in the swathes of boreal forest in Siberia and Northern America (ibid.).

According to IPCC projections, countries in Africa are particularly vulnerable to climate change impacts. By 2020, between 75 million and 250 million people in Africa are projected to be exposed to increased water stress owing to climate change and as a consequence, yields in some countries could be reduced by up to 50 per cent. Agricultural production, including access to food, in many African countries is projected to be severely compromised. By 2080, in Africa, an increase from 5 to 8 per cent in arid and semi-arid land is projected under a range of climate scenarios. Further, the projected cost of adaptation could amount to 5-10 per cent of GDP.[12]

In the worst cases, climate change and the associated sea-level rise threaten the very existence of some small island developing States (such as Kiribati and Tuvalu) because of the latent risk that their territories may become submerged under water.[13] Other island States are facing severe drought and water shortages.

Uneven impacts across population groups

Not only are the impacts of climate hazards uneven across countries, they are also felt differently across population groups within countries. While identifying particularly vulnerable groups globally and at country level remains challenging, it is particularly important for policymaking directed towards building climate resilience.

Unfortunately, current information systems are not adequate to the challenge of following trends at the intersection between climate-related events and socioeconomic vulnerabilities. People living in low-lying coastal areas, drylands, and mountainous and remote areas and population groups whose livelihoods rely on forest products are particularly at risk. Yet, basic information on population size, socioeconomic characteristics and risk factors which could help identify those groups remains in the form of very rough approximations. Some of those groups are difficult to reach owing to their geographical location, but the lack of basic information is also associated with an insufficiency in the resources for producing statistics at the level of disaggregation required to identify specific population groups.

In spite of limited information, existing data and studies have enabled important inferences to be made with regard to the uneven distribution of climate-induced vulnerabilities and impacts across population groups. For example, despite the increased frequency of water-related risks such as sea-level rise and coastal erosions, more and more people in both developing and developed countries have settled in low-lying coastal areas, thereby

People in low-lying coastal areas, drylands, and mountainous and remote areas are particularly vulnerable

---

12 See fact sheet entitled "Climate change in Africa: what is at stake?", comprising excerpts from IPCC reports, the United Nations Framework Convention on Climate Change and the Bali Action Plan, as compiled by the African Ministerial Conference on the Environment secretariat. Available at http://www.unep.org/roa/amcen/docs/AMCEN_Events/climate-change/2ndExtra_15Dec/FACT_SHEET_CC_Africa.pdf. Information given above derived from IPCC (2007), "Summary for Policymakers".

13 The Government of Kiribati, for example, acknowledges that the relocation of its people may be inevitable, owing to climate change, which would threaten the survival of the country. The Government has stated that "it would be irresponsible to acknowledge this reality and not do anything to prepare our community for eventual migration". See Republic of Kiribati, Office of the President, "Relocation", Kiribati Climate Change. Available at http://www.climate.gov.ki/category/action/relocation/ (accessed 25 January 2016).

exposing themselves to greater risks (see figure I.3). A study issued by the US Census Bureau shows that since 1960, there has been a steady increase in the population living in coastal areas of the United States and concludes that the trend, driven by social, economic and environmental factors, can be expected to continue (Wilson and Fischetti, 2010).

Figure I.3
Population living in coastal cities with 300,000 inhabitants or more on 1 July 2014, 1950–2015[a]

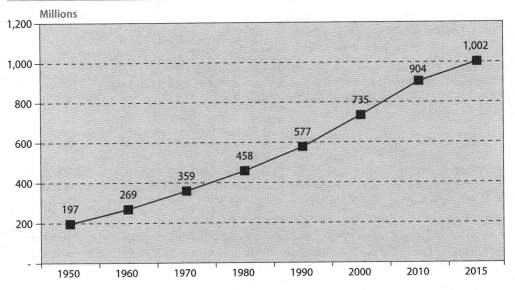

Source: United Nations (2015b);
Gu and others (2015).
a Preliminary estimates for
2015 only.

The problem is particularly acute for developing regions where, according to Johnston (2016), just over 10 per cent of the population (518 million out of 4,912 million) were living in low-elevation coastal zones (that is, zones less than 10 metres above sea level) in 2000 (table I.2) and 3 per cent (148 million) were living in a 100-year floodplain (that is, a plain that has a 1 per cent probability of being hit by a flood event in any given year). The same study predicts that in 2030, 767 million people (about 11 per cent of the population of developing regions) will be living in a low-elevation coastal zone and 224 million in a 100-year floodplain. These estimates suggest greater exposure to climate hazards and thus larger climate-related human costs in the future for particular population groups if effective climate adaptation and mitigation policies are not in place.

The rapid rise in the number of people living near the coast is doubtless to a large extent a manifestation of two mega-trends: one towards rapid population growth and the other towards urbanization. However, socioeconomic factors play a role as well: in the absence of more diversified economies that provide job opportunities in less-exposed areas, people are settling in low-lying coastal areas in search of a livelihood.

For example, the fishing population was estimated to have reached 43.5 million by 2006, with much of the "absolute growth in numbers largely explained by the wide expansion of the aquaculture sector" (Food and Agriculture Organization of the United Nations, Fisheries and Aquaculture Department, n.d.). Moreover, "(f)ishers, aquaculturists

Table I.2

Populations living in low-elevation coastal zones and 100-year floodplains in developing regions, 2000 and 2030

Millions						
	Population		Population living in low-elevation coastal zones		Population living in 100-year floodplains	
	2000	2030	2000	2030	2000	2030
Africa*	811.0	1 562.0	54.0	109.0	13.0	24.0
Asia[a]	3 697.0	4 845.0	461.0	649.0	137.0	201.0
Latin America and the Caribbean	521.0	702.0	32.0	40.0	6.0	8.0
Pacific islands	7.0	12.0	1.0	2.0	0.3	0.4
Developing regions, total	4 912.0	7 002.0	518.0	767.0	148.0	224.0
Least developed countries	662.0	1 257.0	93.0	136.0	13.0	21.0
World	6 101.0	8 298.0	625.0	893.0	189.0	271.0

Source: Johnston (2016).

a Including Japan.

and those supplying services and goods to them assure the livelihoods and well-being of a total of about 520 million people, 7.9 per cent of the world's population" (ibid.). However, exploitation and climate change are threatening the collapse of livelihoods derived from fishing (Jackson and others, 2001). This situation is problematic because the fishing industry has historically played a major role in providing food security and income and more recently, aquaculture has played a rapidly growing role. Fishing is, to a large extent, a low-wage or subsistence-based activity and its decline due to climate change would be expected to affect large population groups.

Large vulnerable population groups are also found in drylands and mountainous and remote areas. Populations in these areas largely comprise nomadic, semi-nomadic and sedentary agricultural inhabitants. Large areas of populated drylands with growing subsistence populations, in particular, pose challenges to agricultural development and food security in Africa and large parts of central and South Asia. It is estimated that nearly 2 billion inhabitants in the developing regions were vulnerable to desertification and drought in 1995, the latest year for which data are available, and the number is considered to be increasing owing, as in the case of coastal zones, to population growth and migration. According to Millennium Development Goals reports for Ghana and Kenya, while the proportion of the population in extreme poverty declined in many regions of those countries, their poorest and most remote parts witnessed rising poverty rates (Johnston, 2016).

The problem of deforestation is also raising concerns for important population groups (United Nations, Economic and Social Council, United Nations Forum on Forests, 2009a; 2009b). According to the Food and Agriculture Organization (FAO) (2016a), forests are estimated to contribute to the livelihoods of at least 1.6 billion people in the world, with some 60 million people, mainly in indigenous communities, living within forests and another 350 million being highly dependent on forests. The forest industry, both formal and informal, is estimated to employ roughly

50 million of the world's people.[14] Deforestation is fundamentally challenging the existence of those livelihoods. As FAO also estimates, deforestation accounted for a loss of forest cover of approximately 13 million hectares per year between 2000 and 2005 — a loss that could not be compensated by the 5.7 million hectares recovered during the same period from the natural expansion of forests and forest plantations.

Indigenous people, in particular, are under siege, as their livelihoods are seriously affected owing to the alteration of forests. Local human activities that are being undertaken in and near forests—mostly unsustainable logging, conversion of forests to agricultural land, conversion of coastal mangrove forests for aquaculture, mining, infrastructure creation and the expansion of human settlements—as well as forest fires, further accelerate deforestation and degradation.

Deforestation also increases a community's risk of experiencing disasters. Forest degradation lowers the capacity of forests to provide the community with the livelihood resources needed to withstand and recover from disasters. Deforestation is known to cause severe floods, river-basin flooding, flash floods, mudslides and landslides (Hammill, Brown and Crawford, 2005) and leads to an increased number of disasters and extensive damage.

Indigenous people are a particularly vulnerable group. Their vulnerability is linked not only to deforestation but also to other manifestations of climate change. Their close relationship with their natural environment makes them particularly sensitive to the effects of climate change (Baird, 2008). In the worst cases, their way of life, and even their existence, is being threatened by climate change. For example, in the Arctic, where rises in temperature are most noticeable, there are some 400,000 indigenous peoples, which include the Sami of northern Norway, Finland, Sweden and the Russian Federation, for whom herding reindeer is a way of life. The Sami people had observed signs of climate change as early as the mid-1980s, when winter rainfall increased. Higher temperatures and increased rainfall began to make it difficult for reindeer to reach the lichen that they consume. When temperatures drop, and lichen is covered with ice, many reindeer are likely to starve. In addition, the thinning of the Arctic ice has made tracking reindeer herds more dangerous, as the inherited local knowledge regarding safe tracking is then no longer useful.

Uneven impacts within population groups

The evidence demonstrates that some people and some communities are particularly vulnerable compared with the rest of the population. This is clear when considering the case of Nepal, a least developed country, where rising temperatures, erratic rain- and snowfall, and the unpredictability of the beginning of the monsoon season have resulted in slow growth and decreased crop production. In principle, all people and communities whose livelihood is associated with crop production should be negatively affected by these hazards. However, Gentle and others (2014) have shown that the impacts are not uniform among people and communities. Their study shows that the severity of climate-related impacts depends on geographical location and the vulnerability of households, which is in turn determined by a number of socioeconomic characteristics such as household size, quality

---

14   These numbers are all rough estimates lacking a basis in clearly defined concepts and sources. While the Global Forest Resources Assessment 2015 gives detailed country data on forest employment, it does not provide an estimate for the total.

of farmland, social status within the community, education of the head of household, and access to financial resources.

These socioeconomic factors shape the structural inequalities that perpetuate poverty, marginalization and social exclusion in the face of climate hazards. In fact, the interviews conducted by the authors of the study revealed that the number of climate hazards experienced by Nepalese households was largely concentrated among the poor. On average, poor households experienced 2.63 climate hazards over the six-year period of the study; better-off households experienced 1.76 hazards on average. The proportion of the members of poor households who were injured or killed was 6.3 per cent, while 81.3 per cent experienced damage to their house, land or livelihood. The corresponding proportions for well-off households were 2.6 and 55.3 per cent, respectively.

In the Sahel region of Africa, where the livelihood of considerable portions of the population derives from farming and raising livestock, all farmers and pastoralists are witnessing the same reductions in the level of rainfall and rising desertification. It is poor farmers and pastoralists, however, who have been shown to be most vulnerable, given their limited ability to mobilize the resources necessary for adapting to these climate changes, which include water and land, and their lack of political power in society (Cotula, 2006; Silva, 2016).

A framework for understanding risk and policy

All of the above evidence attests to what is to be the core focus of the present *Survey*. Climate change is increasing the frequency and intensity of the extreme weather and climate events that are affecting all countries. However, it is developing countries, in particular small island developing States, and countries where livelihoods depend on climate-sensitive natural resources, that are the most exposed to climate hazards; additionally, they have fewer resources and less capacity to adapt. In those countries, there is a clear-cut association between inequality and vulnerability to climate change. Certain population groups are particularly at risk owing to their socioeconomic characteristics which leave them disproportionately exposed and more vulnerable to climate hazards. In most countries, the disproportionately high risks experienced by particular population groups are determined by structural inequalities which reproduce poverty, marginalization and social exclusion. Deepening the analysis of this problem with a view to identifying policies that can act upon the structural drivers of vulnerability requires a consistent analytical framework.

Structural inequalities that reproduce poverty, marginalization and social exclusion leave some population groups at higher risk of climate-related hazards

Exposure, vulnerability and structural inequalities

The IPCC Fifth Assessment Report considers people to be at risk when they are faced with the potentially adverse consequences of an uncertain outcome and where something of value is at stake in the human and natural systems, such as human lives; livelihoods; health; ecosystems and species; and economic, social and cultural assets and service flows arising out of them (see IPCC, 2014c, annex II: Glossary). In this framework, the intersection between the occurrence of climate hazards and the exposure and vulnerability of people and natural systems to them is the central source of risk (figure I.4). Exposure refers to the presence of people (including their livelihoods), ecosystems and species, or economic, social, or cultural assets in places that could be adversely affected by climate hazards. Vulnerability is defined as the propensity or predisposition to be adversely affected, which encompasses

The degrees of exposure and vulnerability of people determine climate risk

Figure I.4
Human interface with the climate

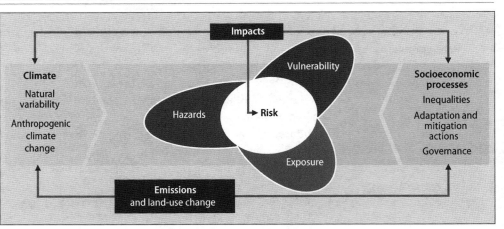

Source: UN/DESA, based on
IPCC (2014d), p. 3.

two elements: (a) sensitivity or susceptibility to harm and (b) lack of capacity to cope and adapt. Exposure and vulnerability are thus determined implicitly by the conditions of poverty, marginalization and social exclusion as they affect specific population groups.

Exposure and vulnerability are determined by the socioeconomic processes leading to persisting inequalities

Except for a few countries at very low levels of development, where poor living conditions are widespread, poverty, marginalization and social exclusion are, in most cases, the result of deeply entrenched inequalities regarding access to physical and financial assets; and access to quality health services, education and employment; and as regards the unevenness of the opportunities of people and communities to voice their concerns and participate in political decision-making. As discussed in the *Report on the World Social Situation 2016: Leaving No One Behind – The Imperative of Inclusive Development* (United Nations, forthcoming), the term social exclusion refers to both the inability of individuals to participate fully in the economic, social, political and cultural life of the community to which they belong and the processes leading to their exclusion. The structural inequalities that result in social exclusion are reproduced by the economic rules, institutions and social norms that govern societies. Cultural, institutional and political regimes that determine the differential rights of people according to the difference in their status, as based on gender, tribal, ethnic or racial markers, have reproduced those inequalities over time.[15]

Structural inequalities matter when examining the impacts of climate hazards on people and communities. People and communities are relatively more exposed and vulnerable to climate hazards when their livelihoods depend on natural resources and they have few options for diversifying their income sources; when they are without appropriate access to insurance and financial markets; and when they have low levels of education and inadequate access to health services or inadequate access to appropriate facilities for persons with disabilities and older persons.

Policies whose goal is climate change resilience must address the underlying structural inequalities that leave people at high risk

To be effective, the building of climate change resilience must entail addressing the processes underlying such structural inequalities. This *Survey* will strive to delineate the structural inequalities that most increase vulnerability and exposure to climate hazards.

15   See chap. I of the *Report on the World Social Situation 2016* (United Nations, forthcoming) for an extensive discussion on the concept of social inclusion/exclusion.

The policy implications of such an analysis are most important. If effective actions for climate resilience are not put in place, climate hazards are likely to exacerbate inequalities, leading to increasing poverty, marginalization and social exclusion.

Transformative policies for climate resilience

Sound development policies are the kind of policies, above all, needed to build climate resilience through building people's resilience to socioeconomic and climate-related shocks. Addressing the root causes of vulnerability requires a continuum of policy interventions leading to the structural transformations that strengthen people's opportunities and agency.

Today's policies must lead the way towards achieving the kind of transformations required to build inclusive and climate-resilient societies. Disaster risk reduction and disaster management are obviously playing an important role in strengthening the preparedness and early warning capacities needed to confront climate hazards. Social protection policies are necessary to protect lower-income groups against the threats of climate hazards. Adaptation policies, such as those entailing the adoption of new crops or improved irrigation systems in agriculture, are critical to preventing a deterioration of livelihoods as a result of climate hazards. To be successful, however, these highly specific policy responses must be part of a broader development framework which leads the way incrementally to the empowerment of today's disadvantaged groups by improving their asset positions and access to input and product markets, by extending their access to quality basic services such as health, education and sanitation, and by changing the norms fostering their social and political exclusion.

> A continuum of policy interventions is required to address immediate needs and enable the structural transformations needed to build climate-resilient and sustainable societies

The adoption of the 2030 Agenda for Sustainable Development, with its vision of "transforming our world", provides a unique opportunity to strengthen policymaking systems in such a way as to enable them to effectively take the lead in the transformation process required for sustainable development, including the building of climate resilience. While broad international consensus has supported this view,[16] the challenge going forward is nevertheless centred around the adoption of national policies which will, within each country's context and constraints, drive efforts towards poverty eradication, human development and climate resilience.

There is an extensive literature devoted to the past experiences of countries on alternative interventions in response to extreme climate hazards. However, there is less experience with and less recognition of the challenges posed by both slow setting events and the accumulation of weather-related hazards, which can have devastating consequences on livelihoods. In the absence of government support, even small changes in temperature or rain and wind patterns can push people into poverty traps (Olsson and others, 2014). Those who are the most exposed and vulnerable are also the ones who are already economically and socially disadvantaged and the least likely to have access to support systems.

Public policy will have to play a critical role in providing public goods for adaptation and ensuring that social processes and institutions are flexible enough to learn and adapt and assess policy options. Climate change presents a public goods-related problem, one that

> Climate change adaptation presents a public-goods related problem requiring public policies to address it

16   In fact, in the 2030 Agenda, as adopted by the General Assembly (resolution 70/1), the Heads of State and Government and High Representatives declared that "(o)n behalf of the peoples we serve, we have adopted a historic decision on a comprehensive, far-reaching and people-centred set of universal and transformative Goals and targets", that "we are setting out a supremely ambitious and transformational vision" and that "(w)e envisage a world free of poverty, hunger, disease and want, where all life can thrive".

produces socially undesirable results. Information and accurate climate forecasts, public infrastructure, flood control systems, early warning systems, knowledge and technology are public goods, all of which are essential for adaptation. But it is precisely because they are public goods that they cannot be provided adequately by the private sector.[17] It is thus public policies that play the critical role in their provision.

In the presence of large development gaps and incomplete markets,[18] public policies also have an important role to play in creating the incentives and regulations capable of increasing provision by the private sector of the goods and services (including their accessibility) that facilitate climate change adaptation among vulnerable groups. Inadequate access to credit and insurance markets constrain people's options with regard to investing and protecting their assets under the effects of shocks. Creating the incentives needed to expand access to credit and insurance markets is an example of government activity that would contribute to reducing the structural inequalities constraining the capacity of people to diversify their livelihoods and adapt to climate change.

At the same time, social processes and institutions need to be flexible enough for learning adaptation and assessment with regard to development options. Climate change resilience will demand that social, economic and ecological systems become capable of reorganizing so as to maintain their essential functions, identity and structure, while also maintaining their capacity for adaptation, learning and transformation.[19] This will pave the way towards sustainable development—as long as the structural inequalities that drive poverty, social exclusion and vulnerability are addressed.

Building resilience requires improved technical and political capacity to implement integrated policies with participation from all stakeholders

This *Survey* has been structured to elucidate the distinct ways in which national efforts in the most vulnerable countries can confront these challenges. At the same time, it identifies concrete areas where national efforts will need to be supplemented through enhanced international cooperation.

Organization of the chapters of this *Survey*

Chapter II reviews the literature on the impact of climate change on human systems and stresses the need to advance understanding of the link between climate change and inequalities, both conceptually and empirically. The chapter builds upon the idea that climate hazards and inequalities are locked in a vicious cycle, whereby those hazards affect people experiencing socioeconomic vulnerability disproportionately. If resources are not adequate

---

17 A public good is both non-excludable (i.e., individuals cannot be prevented from using it) and non-rivalrous (i.e., the use of the good by one individual does not reduce its availability or utility to others). Common examples include fresh air, national security and street lighting. Providers cannot discriminate among users or exclude non-payers from the good and therefore have no incentive for providing the good.

18 Incomplete markets are those where the conditions for market formation are not fully met. In these circumstances, service provision by private firms satisfies only a small part of potential demand, which is typically the case for credit and insurance markets within the rural environments of developing countries.

19 As defined by Shaw (2012, p. 309), climate resilience is a dynamic process of "bouncing forward" (as opposed to "bouncing back to what it was"), which requires reacting to crises by moving up to a new state that is more sustainable in the current environment. So described, the resilience-building process is often called evolutionary resilience, as it entails the ability of complex human and natural systems to change, adapt and crucially transform in response to climate hazards rather than return to normality (Davoudi, 2012).

to the challenge of recovery from climate hazards, inequality in its multiple dimensions will deepen. Using evidence from the existing literature, chapter II explores the economic, social and political channels that shape the structural inequalities through which climate hazards both increase the level of exposure and susceptibility to damage of disadvantaged groups and weaken their capacity to cope and to recover. The evidence reviewed points to the need for a well-integrated continuum of policies, planning and practices for addressing the root causes of inequalities which impose disproportionate impacts on people when they are hit by climate hazards. The transformations leading to adaptation and climate resilience need to be well sustained by assessments and fully supported by a sound policymaking system.

Chapter III introduces the methodologies used in "integrated climate impact assessments" which combine different types of modelling tools to uncover the interlinkages across the environmental, economic and social dimensions of development. To the extent that the occurrence and impacts of climate hazards are associated with a high degree of uncertainty, integrated assessments have to provide robust estimates of plausible climate outcomes and policy responses. The chapter argues for the need to sharpen the focus of these assessments in several ways, targeting the importance of bringing inequalities to the fore. It is also argued that engaging stakeholders (policymakers, experts and researchers, vulnerable groups and local communities) in the design of policy scenarios and in the discussion of policy options is critical to strengthening the political process through which policy decisions are made. Bringing forth the evidence provided by integrated climate impact assessments with full transparency regarding both the use of data and the assumptions built into the modelling tools that facilitate those assessments will critically improve the knowledge base, policy options and political processes in countries seeking to build climate change resilience as an integral part of sustainable development policies. In addition, chapter III focuses on areas where capacities need to be strengthened so that developing countries can expand the construction and use of assessments.

Improving assessments is only one of the many possible means of strengthening policymaking. Chapter IV introduces the subject of the complexity of policy decision-making processes that is introduced when multiple objectives are being pursued within the continuum of policies required for resilience and sustainability. A central claim of the chapter is that, given the presence of three factors—the underlying uncertainty of climate change, the locality where it exhibits its effects, and the interconnected nature of the various sectors in which its impacts are felt—a policymaking system is required that meets three core criteria: it has to be coherent, participatory and flexible.

International cooperation will have a critical, supportive role to play in ensuring that the most vulnerable countries possess the means to strengthen their capacity to forge climate-resilient development pathways as part of their strategies for sustainable development. While the 2030 Agenda for Sustainable Development respects the mechanisms by which countries make their own policy choices, it also recognizes the importance of development cooperation, especially within the context of countries with special needs. Chapter V explores two important areas of international cooperation: international financing for climate change adaptation and the development of improved systems of information and data sharing.

Appendix I.1

Uncertainty of the prospects for the global distribution of income in 2050 based on alternative development pathways

Development trends are hedged in by large uncertainties arising from the uncertainty associated with the estimation of future climate change. Those uncertainties are compounded by the interaction of climate change with mega-trends related to demographic dynamics, urbanization, globalization and technological progress. In order to in some way address these conditions of uncertainty, the international research community has adopted a set of narratives which consider possible pathways for development. The estimation of plausible scenarios in the future are produced by different combinations of those mega-trends.

These narratives, known as shared socioeconomic pathways (SSPs), were proposed initially by Kriegler and others (2012). They have gone on to serve in the creation of a correspondence, which has featured prominently in climate change assessments, between shared socioeconomic pathways and greenhouse gas concentration trajectories under different mitigation scenarios (or representative concentration pathways (RCPs)).

Each shared socioeconomic pathway is associated with different mitigation and adaptation challenges depending on the distinct evolution of mega-trends, as illustrated in table A.I.1.

Alternative shapes of the global distribution of per capita income in the year 2050 have been determined for each of the SSPs from the Global Income Distribution Dynamics database of the World Bank (Osorio Rodarte, 2016; and van der Mensbrugghe, 2015). An important finding of this exercise has been that, as shown in figure A.I.1, the overall level of welfare, inequality and poverty varies significantly, depending on the path taken. Poverty incidence is highest in those cases where adaptation efforts are weak (SSP3 and SSP4).

Figure A.I.1
Global distribution of income in 2050 based on different shared socioeconomic pathways

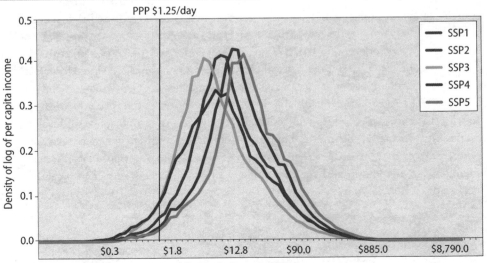

Source: Osorio Rodarte (2016).

Table A.I.1

Mitigation and adaptation challenges associated with different shared socioeconomic pathways

SSP	Challenges	Illustrative starting points for narratives
SSP1 (Sustainability)	Low for mitigation and adaptation	Sustainable development proceeds at a reasonably fast pace, inequalities are lessened, and technological change is rapid and directed towards environmentally friendly processes, including lower-carbon energy sources and high productivity of land
SSP2 (Middle of the road)	Moderate	A case intermediate between SSP1 and SSP3, viewable perhaps as business-as-usual
SSP3 (Fragmentation)	High for mitigation and adaptation	Unmitigated emissions are high owing to moderate economic growth, a rapidly growing population and slow technological change in the energy sector, making mitigation difficult. Investments in human capital are low, inequality is high, a regionalized world leads to reduced trade flows and institutional development is unfavourable, leaving large numbers of people vulnerable to climate change and many parts of the world with low adaptive capacity
SSP4 (Inequality)	High for adaptation, low for mitigation	A mixed world, with relatively rapid technological development in low-carbon energy sources in key emitting regions, leading to relatively large mitigation capacity in places where it matters most for global emissions. However, in other regions, development proceeds slowly, inequality remains high and economies are relatively isolated, leaving those regions highly vulnerable to climate change, with limited adaptive capacity
SSP5 (Conventional development)	High for mitigation, low for adaptation	In the absence of climate policies, energy demand is high and most of this demand is met by carbon-based fuels. Investments in alternative energy technologies are low, and readily available options for mitigation are few. Nonetheless, economic development is relatively rapid and is itself driven by high investments in human capital. Improved human capital also produces a more equitable distribution of resources, stronger institutions and slower population growth, leading to a less vulnerable world which is better able to adapt to climate impacts

Source: UN/DESA, based on van der Mensbrugghe (2015), table 2.

Chapter II
Climate change and inequality nexus

Key messages

- Climate change and inequality are locked in a vicious cycle. Initial socioeconomic inequalities determine the disproportionate adverse effects of climate hazards on people at disadvantage. The impact of climate hazards in turn results in greater inequality.

- Climate hazards affect the poor and vulnerable groups disproportionately by (a) increasing their exposure to those hazards, (b) increasing their susceptibility to damage and (c) decreasing their ability to cope with and recover from that damage.

- Existing exposure and vulnerability have been shaped by the economic and political factors, social norms and individual characteristics that put vulnerable groups at a disadvantage. Because of the lack of capacity to cope and recover, vulnerable groups frequently experience a disproportionate loss of life, human capital, assets and income.

- Addressing the root causes of inequalities to enable adaptation and the building of resilience to climate hazards will require a continuum of development policies, planning and practices which result in transformative change and sustainable development.

Introduction

The interlinkages between climate change and inequality need to be understood and addressed here and now. This is a critical aspect This is a critical aspect in the process of strengthening the capacity of countries and people to avoid development reversals from climate hazards. Owing to structural inequalities, loss of life, injury and other health impacts, as well as the damage to and loss of property, infrastructure, livelihoods, service provision and environmental resources caused by climate hazards, are not felt evenly by all people.

The nexus between climate change and inequality is complex: there is not only the threat of multiple climate hazards (see chapter I), but also because not all inequalities and their root causes are the same. In fact, inequalities are multi-dimensional and they need to be understood and addressed as such to build resilience to climate hazards and avoid development reversals.

The nexus between climate change and inequalities is complex

There is need for a better understanding on why climate hazards affect people unevenly owing to structural inequalities. This requires shifting from a narrow focus on identifying only the physical impacts of climate change, towards a broader analysis which also incorporates the socioeconomic impacts of climate hazards.

Initially, the discussion on climate change focused mostly on the physical impacts (i.e., nature). With time, however, the social consequences of climate change received more attention, and evidence regarding the relationship between climate change and poverty began to emerge. Even so, the interlinkages between climate change (and hazards) and multidimensional inequalities have yet to be fully explored. The role of the underlying structural causes of inequalities is also poorly understood. The objective of the present chapter is therefore to bridge these gaps, which will in turn provide the foundation for a discussion centred on the policy challenges related to building resilience to climate hazards.

Climate hazards intersect with multi-dimensional inequalities to generate uneven impacts on people and their livelihoods

The chapter examines the links between climate change and inequalities. More specifically, it shows that they are locked in a vicious cycle, whereby initial socioeconomic inequalities determine the disproportionate adverse effects arising from climate hazards, which in turn results in greater inequality. This discussion is followed by a thorough review of the evidence demonstrating that the multiple dimensions of inequality (as they relate, inter alia, to income, assets, political power, gender, age, race and ethnicity) underlie a situation where disadvantaged groups are more exposed and susceptible to climate hazards and possess less capacity to cope and recover when those hazards have materialized. Further, it is shown that as a result, inequality is exacerbated. The review of the evidence covers different types of hazards in different geographical areas, although it pays particular attention to the experiences associated with Hurricane Katrina in the United States of America, flooding in Bangladesh, and severe water loss and desertification in the Sahel region of Africa. The chapter concludes with a discussion of the policy implications of addressing the root causes of inequalities for adaptation and building resilience to climate hazards.

The social impact of climate change

The initial discussion of climate change was focused on its physical impact

As noted above, the discussion on climate change originally focused on its physical impact. Relatively less attention was paid to the implications of that physical impact for the lives, livelihoods of the people who are most vulnerable and most affected. To quote Skoufias, ed. (2012, p. 2):

> While the eyes of the world have been riveted on polar bears, Antarctic penguins, and other endangered inhabitants of the Earth's shrinking ice caps, relatively few researchers have turned serious attention — until recent years — to quantifying the prospective long-term effects of climate change on human welfare.

Part of the problem is that it took time for researchers across different disciplines to develop and then test the methodologies that allowed for a broadening of the focus to include socioeconomic impacts and the need to address them.

Poverty and livelihoods

Over time, the broader social impacts of climate change and their feedback effects garnered more attention. New studies emerged, particularly as biophysical and socioeconomic impacts began to be examined in an integrated manner through the use of specialized modelling techniques (see chap. III).

One early study in this regard (World Bank, 2003), which was launched at the eighth session of the Conference of the Parties to the United Nations Framework Convention on

Climate Change, noted that climate change was making achievement of the Millennium Development Goals difficult by reducing access to drinking water, threatening food security and bringing about adverse health effects.

Other studies on the issue followed. The Stern report (Stern, 2006) noted that climate change was expected to increase poverty owing to its effects on agriculture, flooding, malnutrition, water resources and health. The 2007/2008 Human Development Report (United Nations Development Programme, 2008) devoted an entire chapter (2) to a discussion of the vulnerability and risk arising from climate change in an unequal world. The interaction between climate change and human development has also been analysed in Carvajal-Velez (2007), United Nations Economic Commission for Africa (2010) and Hughes and others (2012). Previous reports of the Intergovernmental Panel on Climate Change (IPCC) drew upon this discussion as well.[1]

Similarly, the *Global Monitoring Report 2008: MDGs and the Environment – Agenda for Inclusive and Sustainable Development* (World Bank, 2008) pointed to the potential impacts of climate change on poverty and development. Brainard, Jones and Purvis, eds. (2009) explored a wide range of impacts of climate change on poverty and some recent studies have examined the issue using cross-country data. Skoufias, Rabassa and Olivieri (2011) reviewed several such studies, taking note of the different methodologies used, the units of analysis adopted and the various policy suggestions put forth.

Some studies considered the impact of climate change on poverty and livelihoods in particular countries. For example, Paavola (2008) focused on the Morogoro region of the United Republic of Tanzania; Somanathan and Somanathan (2009) on India; and Gentle and Maraseni (2012) on mountain communities in Nepal. Many studies focused on poverty impacts in specific sectors, such as agriculture (see, for example, Ahmed, Diffenbaugh and Hertel (2009); Hertel, Burke and Lobell (2010); Hertel and Rosch (2010); and Müller and others (2011), or in particular settings, such as urban areas (see, for example, Satterthwaite and others (2007); Douglas and others (2008); and Hardoy and Pandiella (2009)). These studies cover a broad range of climate change issues, including crop and structural damage, reduced agricultural output and higher food prices, reduced food security, increased unemployment, general uncertainty, involuntary migration, potential maladaptation, the need for responsive adaptation, rising social inequality, and differences in exposure and susceptibility to climate hazards.

From gathering the broad evidence of the effects of climate change on poverty and livelihoods, research gradually shifted to investigating the mechanisms through which those effects operate. Shared socioeconomic pathways (SSPs), introduced in chapter I, were devised to consider the human development-related aspects of climate change under such different narratives. Using SSPs in an integrated fashion with other methodological tools, Hallegatte and others (2014) identified prices, assets, productivity and opportunities as four key channels through which households may move in and out of poverty, and further examined the effect of climate change on each of them.

Many studies examined the social impact of climate change at the global level...

...while others focused on the impact of climate change on poverty and livelihoods in particular countries

---

[1] Considerable research was devoted to studying the potential health impacts of climate change, with a World Health Organization Task Group addressing the issue as early as 1989 (World Health Organization, 1990). The report of the Task Group was later expanded into the volume entitled *Climate Change and Human Health* (McMichael and others, 1996). In 2010, the Interagency Working Group on Climate Change and Health published a report highlighting 11 different pathways through which climate change could be expected to exacerbate detrimental health outcomes (Portier and others 2010).

The IPCC made an
important contribution
to the discussion on
effects of climate on
poverty and livelihoods

Further, in its contribution to the periodic IPCC Assessment Reports, Working Group II gradually increased its focus on the human dimensions of climate change impacts. In its contribution to the Fifth Assessment Report, particularly to chapter 13 of part A (see Olsson and others, 2014), Working Group II provided an extensive review of the evidence from all parts of the world, both statistical and anecdotal, regarding the dynamic interaction between climate change and livelihoods and poverty. Leichenko and Silva (2014) provided a synthesis in which they noted that the connections between climate change and poverty are "complex, multifaceted, and context-specific". Hallegatte and others (2016) provides comprehensive guidance on joint solutions through which poverty reduction policies and climate change mitigation and adaptation policies can reinforce each other.

Because of the complexity underlying the physical and socioeconomic impacts of climate change, time was required to develop the integrated climate impact assessment methodologies that have supported the studies described above (see chap. III). However, the nexus between climate change and structural inequalities still requires further research, as the focus has been mainly on poverty-related implications, rather than on the multiple inequalities that may have exacerbated poverty and vulnerability.

From poverty and inequality to structural inequalities

The discussion on the impact of climate change on poverty has more recently been expanded to include consideration of the impact of climate change on inequalities. As noted in Olsson and others (2014, p. 796), the Fourth Assessment Report had already pointed out "that socially and economically disadvantaged and marginalized people are disproportionately affected by climate change". Similarly, in Skoufias, ed. (2012, p. 6) it was observed that "climate change impacts tend to be regressive, falling more heavily on the poor than the rich"; the study also noted (within the context of the effects of climate change on Brazil) that "there is significant geographical variation, with already-poor regions being more affected than prosperous regions" (p. 5).

However, despite the progress highlighted above, the discussion of the interlinkages between climate change and inequalities suffers from three important deficiencies.

Most studies treat
inequality as a secondary
issue: the focus of
concern continues to be
poverty

First, most studies treat inequality as a secondary issue: the focus of concern continues to be poverty. Moreover, few studies incorporate equity considerations; and the methodologies are generally not suited to tracing the impacts on specific groups that are particularly vulnerable (see table III.1 in chap. III for more details). Poverty and inequality are indeed clearly interwoven: At a given level of income, a more unequal distribution is likely to raise poverty; and similarly, an increase in poverty, at a given level of income, is likely to be associated with worsening inequality. Furthermore, while studies focused on poverty do take note of income and assets, inequality is in fact multidimensional and is determined by myriad factors which both intersect and are structurally entrenched, including discrimination based on gender, age, ethnicity, race, religion and culture; unequal access to basic services (such as health and education); and unequal opportunities for political participation and exercising a voice in policy decision-making, among others. The structural inequalities resulting from the interaction among these different factors impose a differential impact of climate hazards across population groups.

As emphasized in chapter I, it is important to advance beyond a narrow monetary concept of inequality towards a broad understanding of multiple inequalities and their structural causes. Even in countries with low income poverty, as is the case for many developed countries, climate hazards have a disproportionate impact on individuals and communities facing other forms of discrimination based on race, ethnicity and other characteristics. In countries where poverty is widespread, the people living in poverty suffer disproportionately from climate hazards not only because they are poor but because of their unequal standing in society.

References to inequalities are more frequent in the contribution of Working Group II to the Fifth Assessment Report than in its contribution to previous reports. In the Fifth Assessment Report, Working Group II notes that socially and geographically disadvantaged people, including those facing discrimination based on gender, age, race, class, caste, ethnicity and disability, are particularly affected by climate hazards (Olsson and others, 2014, p. 796). Exacerbation of inequalities which place such people at a disadvantage can occur through disproportionate erosion of physical, human and social assets;[2] Working Group II offers evidence in this regard with respect to those types of assets. Even climate change adaptation expenditures are often found to be driven more by wealth than by need, with the result that those expenditures end up aggravating income and wealth inequality both within and between countries (Georgeson and others, 2016). In addition, some adaptation measures shift risks onto populations already facing greater exposure and susceptibility to climate hazards (Lebel and Sinh, 2009).

Second, the evidence on the relationship between climate change and inequalities provided so far is often indirect. In many cases, the discussion remains limited to general statements, or the reference to inequality is only contextual. Often, the evidence provided is location- and impact-specific and extrapolations are made on this basis. Relatively few studies have attempted to examine the effect of climate change on inequalities *directly*.

Third and most important, there is a lack of the unifying analytical framework necessary for a discussion of the relationship between climate change and inequalities. As a result, the evidence presented is characteristically scattershot. The Fifth Assessment Report itself recognizes this deficiency, noting that "(d)espite the recognition of these complex interactions [between climate change and inequality], the literature shows *no single conceptual framework* that captures them concurrently" (Olsson and others, 2014, p. 803; italics added). That such a problem exists is to a large extent explained by the fact that inequalities have not featured prominently in the most comprehensive climate impact assessments which have shaped the discussion on climate change (see chap. III for further consideration of this issue).

The following sections provide a systematic analysis of the links between different dimensions of inequality and climate change and in this regard offer empirical evidence concerning the main interconnections. This exercise is a critical first step towards bridging the gulf separating climate change policy and development policies.

Evidence provided on the relationship between climate change and inequalities is often indirect

There is a lack of a unifying analytical framework

---

2   In the contribution of Working Group II to the Fifth Assessment Report, the term *asset* refers to "natural, human, physical, financial, social, and cultural capital". Livelihoods are understood to be the "ensemble or opportunity set of capabilities, assets, and activities that are required to make a living" (Olsson and others, 2014, p. 798). The present chapter will continue its exploration with this concept in mind.

Links between climate hazards and inequalities

Climate change and structural inequalities are locked in a vicious cycle

Existing evidence suggests that climate change and structural inequalities are locked in a vicious cycle. To begin with, climate hazards aggravate the pre-existing socioeconomic inequalities that determine poverty, marginalization and social exclusion. Structural inequalities increase the exposure and vulnerability of certain groups of people and communities to climate hazards and through this greater exposure and vulnerability, disadvantaged people and communities experience disproportionate losses in terms of their lives and livelihoods. If left unaddressed, the stress induced by climate hazards will worsen inequalities (in respect of physical, financial, human, social and cultural assets), thus perpetuating the above-mentioned vicious cycle between climate change and inequalities (figure II.1).

Figure II.1
The vicious cycle between climate hazards and inequalities

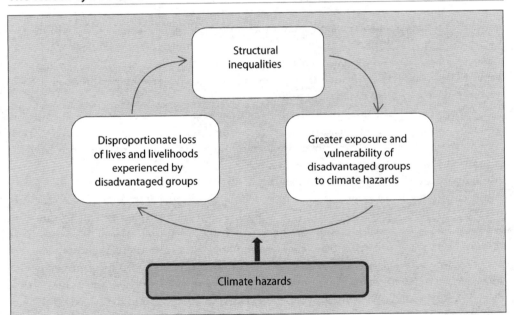

Source: UN/DESA.

The main focus of the present chapter is on elucidating how inequalities increase the risk of climate hazards among particular groups and providing evidence in this regard, as well as on examining the multiple generators of those inequalities.

Inequalities increase the risk of climate hazards

Structural inequalities increase exposure and susceptibility and decrease people's ability to cope with and recover from the effects of climate change

IPCC situates climate change risk at the intersection of exposure and vulnerability (see chap. I, figure I.4). Exposure refers to the presence of people, livelihoods, infrastructure, or economic, social or cultural assets in places and settings that could be adversely affected. Vulnerability has two facets which need to be distinguished. One is the propensity or predisposition to be adversely affected by climate hazards, which is referred to in this chapter as susceptibility to the damage inflicted by climate hazards. The other is the inability to cope with and recover from that damage. Evidence and analysis show that structural inequalities increase both the exposure and susceptibility[3] of certain groups of people to climate hazards; structural inequalities also decrease their ability to cope with and recover from damage.

Exposure, susceptibility and the inability to cope and recover are interrelated. However, while exposure and susceptibility apply to situations and processes that are ex ante in nature, the ability to cope and recover apply to situations and processes ex post, that is to say, those in which climate hazards have already materialized.

Structural inequalities increase the exposure of some groups of people to climate hazards, such as flooding, erosion, cyclones and hurricanes, when they live in areas that are more prone to such hazards. The various reasons that make this so are usually associated with the cost of housing, which in some contexts is combined with political and administrative restrictions arising from discriminatory policies. Greater exposure to climate hazards often leads to greater susceptibility as is the case, for example, for people living in areas of flooding whose houses have been built with flimsy materials and often contain a poor drainage infrastructure. Under these conditions, they are not only exposed but also susceptible to climate hazards. Finally, inequalities decrease the ability of disadvantaged groups to cope with and recover from hazards if they lack insurance, if they cannot diversify their income sources and if the provision of public services is insufficient to assist them in their recovery.

Multidimensional channels of inequality

People's greater exposure and vulnerability to climate hazards is largely influenced by economic, political and social factors which intersect and create inequalities. In unequal societies, there are large differences in the capacity of people to avoid the devastating impacts of climate hazards.

Economic, political and social inequalities increase exposure and vulnerability to climate hazards

There are people who can protect themselves from climate hazards through their control of capital which enables them to make choices in respect of investment (Stiglitz, 2012; Dabla-Norris and others, 2015), accumulate wealth (Piketty, 2014), withstand the effects of fluctuations in aggregate demand (Carvalho and Rezai, 2014), influence politics and policies (Page, Bartels and Seawright, 2013; Gilens and Page, 2014) and exert greater control over their participation in the labour force (which is particularly significant in the case of women) (Gonzales and others, 2015) and over employment decisions (Dabla-Norris and others, 2015). By contrast, people with limited economic resources, especially those living in poverty, have less capacity to exercise control over their participation in the labour market and to protect themselves in general (*Report on the World Social Situation 2016*, chap. II), let alone in the face of climate hazards.

Inequalities are also reinforced through the political channel. In this regard, disadvantaged groups have less access to public resources (such as health, education, infrastructure and the judicial system) and fewer opportunities to participate in and influence policy decisions (United Nations, forthcoming, chap. III). They also receive relatively fewer of the public resources needed to respond to climate hazards (Silva, 2016). The existence of entrenched inequalities in the domain of access to power and political representation leads to the adoption of public policies that leave people vulnerable and more exposed to climate hazards.

---

3   As illustrated in figure I.5, susceptibility and the lack of the ability to cope are the factors that define vulnerability.

The social channel interacts with the economic and political channels to limit the provision of both private and public resources to those most in need of them. In particular, marginalization and social exclusion lead to a reduction of social capital and access to community resources.[4] The social channel works in a number of ways, including through the establishment of social norms which determine that women and minorities are to engage in certain occupations, and through the effects of discrimination and exclusion. Certain groups are able to exercise control over common property based on their social position vis-à-vis other marginalized groups. As noted above, these norms and distinctions also interact with the mechanisms of other channels to determine who is to be deemed capable of participating in economic and political activities. This curtailing of access thereby limits the opportunities of marginalized individuals and groups to build up their own supply of resources and to access public resources.

The following sections review the empirical evidence, as contained in the literature, on the relationship between pre-existent socioeconomic inequalities and their impact on the exposure, susceptibility and ability to cope and recover of people and communities at disadvantage. The evidence often concentrates on extreme weather events whose timing has sharp cut-off points, which makes those events suitable for "before and after" impact studies. While slow-onset hazards also have devastating consequences for livelihoods, their impact is more difficult to capture, as it is often blurred by other sources of socioeconomic vulnerability. Slow-onset hazards pose a major challenge to the policymakers and correct identification of their impact on people's livelihoods is critical for the design of actions appropriate to building resilience. Notwithstanding, the uneven effects of slow-onset hazards do find empirical support in the existing literature.

Inequalities and exposure to climate hazards

Exposure to climate hazards often depends on the location of dwelling and location of work

Exposure to the adverse effects of climate change is generally determined by the location of one's dwelling and the location of one's work to secure a livelihood. Intersecting economic, political and social factors play a role in determining those locations. The ways in which these factors operate demonstrate that degrees of resilience to climate hazards are not equal. Asset positions and livelihoods determine whether people can afford to move away from areas of risk in the face of climate hazards. The problem of exposure is particularly acute in densely populated and land-scarce countries (e.g., Bangladesh, India and the Philippines, among many others) and affects both rural and urban areas. As households with higher incomes bid up the price of real estate, those with lower incomes are forced into living spaces and geographical areas that are more exposed.

The confluence of economic and political factors

Vulnerable population groups frequently live in marginal areas and...

Often, economic and political factors interact and influence the location decision and exposure outcome. Low-income groups and those subject to other forms of discrimination are frequently forced to live in marginal areas as a result of restrictions on available land and housing units. This may occur through official or unofficial restrictions or other socially devised constructions.

---

4   For a full discussion of the concept of social exclusion, see *Report on the World Social Situation 2016* (United Nations, forthcoming), chap. I.

Inequality also gives shape to the administrative regulations that influence where some people will reside and whether they will experience exposure in climate hazard-prone areas (United Nations Human Settlements Programme (UN-Habitat), 2003). For example, it was not only economic but also administrative restrictions that had led to the concentration of large numbers of disadvantaged people in Irrawaddy Delta, the lowest-lying expanse of land in Burma, which was hard hit by Cyclone Nargis in 2008 (Mutter, 2015).

In the case of slums, there are interaction effects: social exclusion may drive the members of some groups into slums, with slum dwelling then becoming the basis for further social exclusion (Arimah, 2011).

As a result of combined economic and racial inequalities, African Americans living in poverty constituted the majority of the residents of vulnerable low-lying sections of the city of New Orleans. By contrast, the wealthier residents were more likely to live — literally — on higher ground. Both economic and politically mediated influences of inequality, including discriminatory practices, joined in producing this particular spatial distribution of the population. In consequence, the impact of Hurricane Katrina was felt disproportionately by populations that were African American (Brookings Institution, 2005; Logan, 2006). Indeed, people in areas damaged by the hurricane were twice as likely to be African American as not (Brookings Institution, 2005).

The phenomenon of Katrina also attests to the role of inequality as shaped through the political channel. For example, the districts inhabited primarily by wealthy households had better protective infrastructure, even if their elevation was also low; by contrast, in areas where residents were poor, less attention was paid to protection. In fact, it can be argued that the Industrial Canal, which bounds the Lower Ninth Ward to the west, was constructed in that particular area because of the limited political power of its residents. While it is true that other components of the critical infrastructure failed during the hurricane, it was parts of the Industrial Canal that were among the first to do so (Mutter, 2015).

The experience of floods in Bangladesh provides another illustration of how the effects of climate change are aggravated by inequalities. Given that Bangladesh is a delta, the overflowing of its rivers onto the floodplains is a natural and expected phenomenon; climate change, however, is aggravating inland flooding in several ways.[5] Approximately 20.3 per cent of the population, amounting to almost 30.5 million people, is expected to be affected by river floods in a given year, with a significant portion of gross domestic product (GDP) to be decreased by inland flooding. Different scenarios demonstrate that the population exposed to this phenomenon will increase, with climate change being one of the drivers of this trend (Luo and others, 2015; World Bank, 2013; Dasgupta and others, 2010).

In general, low-income and other disadvantaged groups in Bangladesh face greater exposure to flooding as a result of their having settled in areas that are more flood-prone. Twenty-five per cent of poor households, for example, were exposed to the effects of Cyclone Aila in 2009, versus 14 per cent of non-poor households (Akter and Mallick, 2013). Further, 75 per cent of people living in poverty were exposed to the 1998 floods, compared with 71 per cent of the non-poor (del Ninno and others, 2001).

...when hit by a climate hazard, they are disproportionately affected

Given the ethnic homogeneity of the population of Bangladesh, discrimination of a political and administrative nature plays a less important role in forcing people to live in areas — either inland riverine or coastal — that are prone to flooding. The compelling motive is therefore for the most part an economic one. In Bangladesh, the most densely

---

5   For more details on the ways in which climate change is aggravating flooding in Bangladesh, see, for example, Islam and others (2014) and Rana and others (2011).

populated country in the world, land is scarce. As a result, people with low incomes flock to the areas that are the most risk-prone and hence less in demand among the more advantaged sections of the population.

Similarly, economic factors force people to live in flood-prone sections of urban areas. In examining the factors motivating people to migrate from rural areas to the slums of Dhaka city, Ullah (2004) found that the search for employment, lack of land, easier access to the informal sector and overall extreme poverty were the most relevant. Similarly, the United Nations Children's Fund (2009) noted that the lack of comprehensive land planning coupled with the pressures of economic migration has led to a considerable expansion of the slum populations in Bangladesh. In most cases, the slums are located in relatively low-lying areas that are exposed to flooding.

Demographic trends

Many of the disadvantaged population in developing regions live in low-elevation coastal and flood-prone zones, and...

A significant proportion of the population in developing regions live in low-elevation coastal zones and 100-year floodplains, and their number is increasing both in absolute terms and as a share of the population (Neumann and others, 2015; see also chap. I). A large proportion of the populations of low-elevation coastal zones is rural: 84 per cent in Africa, 80 per cent in Asia, 71 per cent in Latin America and the Caribbean and 93 per cent in the least developed countries. Rural areas are in general poorer, more remote and the inhabitants tend to be marginalized, particularly with respect to access to services and infrastructure. In general, the ecosystems of coastal and near-shore habitats are expected to have greater exposure to the effects of climate change and climate variability (Barbier, 2015). It is also instructive to note that more people now live in deltas, which are frequently subject to both coastal flooding due to sea-level rise and river flooding due to higher precipitation (see chap. I, table I.2). Researchers find that a greater proportion of the people living in the precarious parts of deltas belong to disadvantaged groups (Luo and others, 2015; Brouwer and others, 2007). Generally, it is the people living in poverty and other disadvantaged groups that find themselves compelled to live in those areas, despite their awareness of the inherent risks associated with such exposed locations.

...they are affected as well by increased salinity intrusion

In addition to experiencing flooding and erosion, the people living in coastal areas and deltas must confront salinity intrusion, a process that is exacerbated by climate change (Dasgupta and others, 2014; Rabbani, Rahman and Mainuddin, 2013). Salinization can cause a considerable decrease in agricultural productivity; increased aridity leading to a greater need for irrigation can bring about secondary salinization, thereby aggravating the impact of this problem (Pitman and Läuchli, 2002). Shameem, Momtaz and Rauscher (2014) estimate that 70 per cent of the farmers in some coastal areas gave up farming partially or fully owing to high levels of salinity. Due to their concentration in coastal areas and deltas, disadvantaged groups are thus more exposed to the salinity intrusion caused by climate change.

Greater exposure of disadvantaged groups to climate hazards is not limited to rural areas. A similar phenomenon can be observed in urban areas. For example, Braun and Aßheuer (2011) have found that slum dwellers in Dhaka are more likely to live in areas prone to natural hazards and similar findings are presented in Morin, Ahmad and Warnitchai (2016) for Manila. In general, many slums are located in low-lying land at high risk of flooding. As reported by Petley (2010), Painter (2007) and Sepúlveda and Petley (2015), it has been found that in many countries, including those in South and East Asia and Latin America and the Caribbean, disadvantaged groups build their dwellings at the bottom of hill slopes, thereby exposing them to mud slides, which are becoming more frequent owing to climate change.

About 40 per cent of the Earth's land surface comprises, and 29 per cent of the world's population lives in, arid, semi-arid and dry sub-humid zones, which are facing additional challenges owing to climate change. There is a larger concentration of the poor and other disadvantaged groups of people (such as pastoralists and ethnic minorities) in these areas.

Two thirds of the global population are estimated to live under conditions where water scarcity is severe for at least one month per year (Mekonnen and Hoekstra, 2016). Water scarcity is expected to increase as the climate changes. For example, under scenarios where emissions growth rates are not reduced, the number of people exposed to droughts could rise by 9-17 per cent by 2030 (Winsemius and others, 2015). Exposure to drought is higher in rural compared with urban areas (43 per cent versus 32 per cent). This implies a greater exposure to drought of disadvantaged groups, which make up a larger portion of the rural population. Climate change is also expected to increase the frequency and intensity of heat waves, with particular effects on the elderly, who are more susceptible, as further explained below (Kovats and Hajat, 2008; Luber and McGeehin, 2008; Olsson and others, 2014).

Cross-country data also point to the greater exposure of disadvantaged people to water scarcity. According to Christenson and others (2014), exposure to water scarcity is much greater in countries with a lower human development index (HDI) value than in those with a high HDI value: 50 per cent of countries with a low HDI value are exposed compared with 14 per cent of countries with a very high HDI value. Given the higher rates of households engaged in agricultural production in rural areas and low-income countries, a further increase in the exposure of these households to droughts can be expected.

Cross-country data show the greater exposure of disadvantaged people to water scarcity

Gender and livelihood patterns

Inequalities that are rooted in gender differences play a role in determining the degree of exposure to climate hazards. The inequalities associated with the norms, social role and socioeconomic status imposed on women together with other forms of inequality account for the particular exposure and vulnerability of women to climate hazards (Neumayer and Plümper, 2007). Gendered differentials in access to resources, power and processes of decision-making, including on the allocation of resources and responsibilities within the household, make women particularly vulnerable to climate hazards. In other words, it is the intersection of various dimensions of inequalities, including those associated with gender, that produce the differential outcome, as noted by Perez and others (2015).

Women often face the issue of lower asset positions. This is particularly the case in rural areas, where access to land tenure, formal rental land markets and credit tends to be more restricted for women. Particularly in Africa, women are employed overwhelmingly in agricultural activities that are most at risk from the deleterious effects of climate change. As a result of drought and deforestation, women are spending more time sourcing food, fuel and water for the household, which is traditionally the responsibility of women in rural areas. Some evidence also indicates that it is women and children who are most affected by natural disasters. For example, the majority of victims of Hurricane Katrina were African

Gender-based inequalities play an important role in determining exposure to climate hazards

American women and their children, a group whose members are more likely to be poor, to lack health care and to earn low wages (Gault and others, 2005; Williams and others, 2006).

More broadly, in many countries, a large proportion of female working-age spouses are not economically active or are working without remuneration. Within the context of the Plurinational State of Bolivia, for example, this is the single most important factor associated with high vulnerability to shocks, not least of all those that are climate-related (see chap. III, box III.3).

Certain occupations increase people's exposure to climate hazards

Along similar lines, certain occupations increase people's exposure to climate hazards. For example, members of fishing communities living near rivers or the coast are more exposed to flooding, erosion, cyclones and other such climate hazards; and they are particularly vulnerable to those hazards in the absence of effective adaptation. There is also evidence that the culturally defined farming responsibilities of women in Nepal limit their ability to adapt to climate change through adjustments in their livelihoods, which thereby increases the risk of their exposure to future climate hazards (Silva, 2016).

There are many regions of the world at risk of experiencing climate hazards where the livelihoods of disadvantaged groups depend on agriculture. This is the case for the Sahel region of Africa, which suffered a dramatic change in climate in the period between the early 1970s and the late 1990s, with a decline in average rainfall of more than 20 per cent (Hulme and others, 2001).[6] Desertification is estimated to be spreading at the southern edge of the Sahel by 6-10 kilometres per year, as water stress increases as a result of climate change (Silva, 2016). The region is also notable for having considerable climate variability, with relatively extreme shifts between wetter and drier periods (Ben Mohamed, 2011). Much of the region also has a high frequency of droughts, over longer timescales.[7]

Pastoralist populations of the Sahel region are facing greater exposure to climate change impacts

The problem is that much of the agricultural activity in the Sahel region is rain-fed, particularly for asset- and income-poor farmers. According to the evidence, the greater exposure of poorer households to droughts in the region varies by country, with Ethiopia, Nigeria and Senegal showing significant increases, and Burkina Faso and the Niger showing minor and moderate non-poor biases, respectively (Winsemius and others, 2015). The overall proportions of people exposed to drought are expected to rise considerably across much of West Africa under high-emissions scenarios (ibid.). At the same time, some parts of the Sahel are expected to see increases in rainfall, which will likely result in the expansion of agriculture and the further displacement of pastoralists (Brooks, 2006). In other areas, such as in Mali, changes in rainfall patterns are anticipated to increase the exposure of significant portions of the population as certain areas become more arid, with significant effects on livelihoods and undernutrition (Jankowska, Nagengast and Perea, 2012). Pastoralist populations—the Tuareg, for example, in the Niger—are also subject to high levels of location-based exposure to climate change impacts (Silva, 2016). Poor access to labour markets by these populations, coupled with the rural locations of livelihoods, limits the ability of some of them to relocate to less-exposed locations (ibid.).

---

6   While initially the change in climate was attributed to overgrazing and other direct human effects leading to land degradation and desertification, more recently it has been established that the change in rainfall patterns was largely due to broader changes in global surface temperatures (Brooks, 2006).

7   Despite these trends, there is still considerable debate regarding the prospective effects of climate change, with some areas expected to see increased desertification, other areas expected to see increased rainfall, and some others presenting a picture of uncertainty (Met Office Hadley Centre, 2010).

Inequalities and susceptibility to climate hazards

Even if they experienced the same level of exposure as the rest of the population, which runs counter to reality, disadvantaged groups would in general be more susceptible to damage from the adverse effects of climate hazards. Of the people living in the same floodplain, those residing in houses constructed with flimsy materials are more susceptible to damage from floods than those in houses put together sturdily. Similarly, poor farmers and pastoralists are more susceptible to changing rain patterns because they lack the resources to adapt.

At a similar level of exposure, the disadvantaged groups are more susceptible to the damage caused by climate hazards

Income, assets and livelihoods

Susceptibility increases when there is lack of income and asset diversification in absolute and relative terms. Wodon and others, eds. (2014) report that households in the lowest income bracket in five countries of the Middle East and North Africa—Algeria, Egypt, Morocco, the Syrian Arab Republic and Yemen—experienced higher losses of income, crops, livestock and fish caught as a result of adverse effects of climate change than did rich households. Lost income reported for the lowest-income households was more than double the proportion for the richest (46 per cent versus 21 per cent). Similarly, Gentle and others (2014) found that poor households in the Middle Hills region of Nepal are more susceptible to damage from climate hazards than wealthy ones. Hill and Mejia-Mantilla (2015) have shown that, because of limited options for changing crop patterns, limited ability to apply water saving technology and limited access to agricultural extension services and water storage sources, the farmers belonging to the lowest income bracket in Uganda lost greater shares of income from limited rainfall than did average farmers.

Lack of income and of asset diversification make people more susceptible

Patankar (2015) has shown that families in Mumbai within low-income brackets repeatedly require repairs to their homes in order to secure them against flood damage, with the cumulative cost as a proportion of income often proving to be much greater than the corresponding proportion for the rich. It is noteworthy that despite their lower levels of exposure to Hurricane Mitch, a considerably higher proportion of households in Honduras belonging to the lowest income bracket reported asset loss (31 per cent) compared with the corresponding proportion of those belonging to the higher income brackets (only 11 per cent) (Carter and others, 2007).

In Bangladesh, 42 per cent of people living in poverty reported loss of household income as a result of flooding versus 17 per cent of the non-poor (Brouwer and others, 2007); and people living in poverty also reported a greater number of houses with structural damage in the wake of Cyclone Aila. Furthermore, people living in poverty also reported higher levels of damage in dollar terms. This paradoxical outcome was the result of the fact that the houses of people living in poverty were constructed using very flimsy materials; as a result, those houses suffered considerably greater damage than did the houses of richer households, which had been built with sturdier materials (Hallegatte and others, 2016).

Flooding can be damaging in a multiplicity of ways. For example, flooding may wash away crops and livestock, in addition to destroying houses, and disadvantaged groups suffer disproportionately from these effects as well. In addition, they suffer to a greater extent from indirect market-based effects. For instance, many of the disadvantaged groups living in flood-prone areas in Bangladesh belong to fishing communities. Evidence suggests that they take an additional hit to their incomes when prices fall, as a result of the increased availability of fish made possible by the flood waters (Rahman, 2009).

People with fewer assets, worse health and less education are more susceptible to the effects of climate hazards

In the Sahel region of Africa, the livelihood of considerable portions of the population comes from farming or raising livestock. Given the predominantly rain-fed nature of these activities, farmers and pastoralists are particularly susceptible to the impact of climate hazards (Heinrigs, 2010). Lower-income households, and those whose members have fewer assets, poorer health and less education, along with those headed by women, have all been shown to be more susceptible to the effects of climate hazards in that region, particularly the effects of desertification (Adepetu and Berthe, 2007). Poor farmers and pastoralists tend to be more susceptible in general, given their limited ability to mobilize the resources necessary to adapt to lower levels of rainfall. That existing unequal arrangements already prioritize the access to water of large landholders over that of family farmers means that reductions in available water due to climate change will only exacerbate this inequality (Cotula, 2006). In addition, imbalances in political power, which have resulted in unstable land tenure as well as institutional and market failures, reinforce the marginalization of some groups (Silva, 2016). Further, desertification, the increased number of droughts and land degradation have been implicated in greater income inequality as well as decreased food security (Abdi, Glover and Luukkanen, 2013).

Lack of access to formal financial markets makes disadvantaged people more susceptible to climate-related damage

Susceptibility of lower-income households is also compounded by other limitations. Lack of access to formal financial markets, for example, makes people particularly vulnerable to shocks, including those from climate-related events, as is particularly the case for people who cannot build diversified asset portfolios and have restricted access to savings and insurance instruments. As a result, they are forced to channel the bulk of their savings into single assets. For example, the savings of low-income urban dwellers tend to take the form of housing stock, which is vulnerable to floods (Moser, 2007). Similarly, low-income persons in rural areas often keep their savings in the form of livestock, which are susceptible to droughts (Nkedianye and others, 2011), in contrast with the members of wealthier households, who are able to diversify their assets, both spatially and financially, and are therefore less susceptible to the damage arising from the adverse effects of climate change. Owners of financial assets may in fact face drought exposure similar to that experienced by the low-income rural poor whose assets take the form of livestock. However, since financial assets are far less likely than livestock to be affected by lack of water, the owners of financial assets are less susceptible to the damage caused by the decline in water availability. The greater levels of damage as well as the more limited diversification of savings and assets feed into a greater inequality of assets as a result of climate hazards. The greater susceptibility of disadvantaged groups can therefore usher in a future of widening of inequality, as children of families living in poverty are left with diminished assets and fewer opportunities and thus a reduced future capacity to improve their livelihoods.

Comparing the impact of flood hazards on street children, residents of low-income urban settlements and residents of wealthy neighbourhoods in Manila, Zoleta-Nantes (2002) found that the susceptibility of lower-income households was compounded by limited access to government and community resources, including water, sanitation and health services.

In parts of Punjab, Pakistan, neglect of some of the areas that are vulnerable to flooding has become institutionalized, the justification being that those areas should not be prioritized for development because of the risk from flooding. In the absence of policies aimed at relocating them or building their resilience to climate change, the members of these communities are being further exposed and will be susceptible to future impacts of flooding (Sindhu, Ensor and Berger, 2009).

Gender and age

Gender is a driver of susceptibility, particularly when it intersects with other socioeconomic factors, and in that context highlights important inequalities. A study of Turkana pastoralists found that gender, marital status, length of residency in a region, level of education and (lack of) access to extension services and early warning information were dominant factors in determining susceptibility, particularly given that the population lives predominantly below the poverty line. As a result of the impact of these factors, members of households headed by women, along with those characterized by a low educational level, a shorter time of residency and less access to extension services and early warning systems, were disproportionately susceptible to adverse effects of climate change (Silva, 2016).

Macchi, Gurung and Hoermann (2015) have noted that lower-caste families, women and other marginalized groups in Himalayan villages in north-west India and Nepal are more susceptible to effects of climate change and are also less able to adapt. Using household surveys and village focus-group studies conducted across nine countries in Africa, Perez and others (2015) found that a number of issues affecting women—including limited control of land (in terms of both quantity and quality), less secure tenure, less access to common property resources, less cash with which to obtain goods and services, and less access to formally registered public and private external organizations that foster agriculture and livestock production—make them more susceptible than men to impacts from climate hazards. Those issues arise from feedback effects between social norms that limit women's participation in some economic and social activities and the generally lower socioeconomic status of women that results from those limitations. Their lower socioeconomic status then limits the ability of women to access other services or to accumulate resources that would be beneficial in counteracting those social norms. Those women therefore get caught in a "disadvantage trap". Sherwood (2013) found that prolonged drought created just such traps for women in Gituamba, Kenya. In some locations, women's marital status, apart from the issues mentioned above, can be a driver of unequal access to resources. For example, Silva (2016) has found that widows and divorced women in many parts of the rural United Republic of Tanzania had less access to water resources. Similarly, Olsson and others (2014, p. 796) note that climate hazards increase and heighten existing gender inequalities because in many cases, women have to perform tasks, such as fetching water from afar or gathering fuelwood from forests, that entail a greater exposure to climate effects (Egeru, Kateregga and Majaliwa, 2014).

Within the context of flood-prone areas in Bangladesh, women are the most susceptible group owing to the fact that some of their socially determined livelihood activities, such as cleaning, washing and caring for children and the elderly, make them disproportionately susceptible to the effect of contaminated water (Rabbani, Rahman and Mainuddin, 2009). Issues of land tenure and elite capture of resources are other important factors associated with susceptibility in the flood-prone areas of Bangladesh (ibid.).

Apart from gender, age is another important determinant of susceptibility to climate hazards. For example, IPCC reports that flood-related mortality in Nepal among girls (13.3 per 1,000) was twice as high as that for women; similarly, the mortality was also higher for boys than for men (Olsson and others, 2014, pp. 807-808). These differential impacts apply across a variety of disadvantaged groups. For example, it was found that in Viet Nam, the elderly, widows and people with disabilities, in addition to single mothers

Lower-caste families, women and other marginalized groups are more susceptible to the impact of climate change

and women-headed households with small children, were most vulnerable to floods, storms and slow-onset events such as recurrent droughts (ibid., pp. 808-809). One of the main reasons for differential susceptibility across age groups is the difference in the ability to withstand disease and other adverse health effects of climate change.

The experience of Hurricane Katrina in New Orleans also brought to the fore this susceptibility differential across age groups. Overall, the elderly were the most impacted by the hurricane, as they were less able to relocate and were more susceptible to health-related impacts. More elderly white residents died, but when demographic differences are taken into account,[8] it was elderly African Americans who were the most affected (Mutter, 2015).

Ethnicity and race

The degree of susceptibility often depends on ethnicity and race

The degree of susceptibility often depends on ethnicity and race. Matin and others (2014) provide evidence showing that dominant ethnic groups are able to control resource management and resource use at the expense of other ethnic groups, thereby exacerbating the susceptibility of the latter. In Myanmar, poor and minority farmers who make up the bulk of the population in the Irrawaddy Delta, an area that had significantly greater exposure to Cyclone Nargis in 2008, were more susceptible to damage owing to a lack of effective warning systems and infrastructure. It is no wonder that they suffered most in terms of loss of lives, incomes and assets as a result of the cyclone. In this case, the lack of effective warning systems was, in part, the result of the discrimination faced by those ethnic groups in respect of resource allocation (Mutter, 2015).

Afro-Latinos and indigenous groups in Latin America have a higher degree of susceptibility to climate effects

IPCC has noted the important role of the social positions of different groups in determining susceptibility to the impact of climate change. For example, in many areas of Latin America, Afro-Latinos and indigenous groups were found to experience a higher degree of susceptibility to climate effects (Olsson and others, 2014, p. 810). Moreover, differential susceptibility to the effects of climate change among different races is found in both developing and developed countries, although in both country groups, low-income status is often intertwined with race and ethnicity status.

African Americans living in poverty and other disadvantaged groups were, relatively, the most susceptible to the damage inflicted by Hurricane Katrina. The housing stock in New Orleans at the time was considerably older than average, with 41 per cent of houses in 2003 having been built before 1949, partly as a result of historic preservation-related laws (Shrinath, Mack and Plyer, 2014). As the houses of African Americans living in poverty and of other disadvantaged groups were not only old but also fragile, they were totally damaged by inundation. In addition, a considerable portion of the population of the city were living in renter-occupied housing units—and the rate was higher among low-income and African American households—which were more susceptible to damage (Masozera, Bailey and Kerchner, 2006; Logan, 2006).

---

8   While the proportion of elderly white residents was greater than that of elderly African American residents in the city at the time, the fact remains that fewer African Americans, based on their differential health outcomes overall, reach ages at which they can be classified as elderly. When this factor along with the city's proportion of African Americans versus that of white residents is taken into account, it becomes clear that elderly African Americans were the most affected compared to their share of total population.

Susceptibility to health damage

One of the important ways in which inequality increases the susceptibility of disadvantaged groups is through the health-related effects of climate hazards. Hallegatte and others (2016) have found that for several reasons, people living in poverty are more susceptible to the diseases that many climate hazards help to spread, including malaria and the water-borne diseases that cause diarrhoea. For one thing, they live closer to malaria-breeding grounds. Further, they have more limited access to piped water sources, which forces them, during floods, to drink water containing pathogens. For example, residents of low-income slums in Mumbai have indicated greater levels of flooding during the monsoon season, resulting in an increase in the number of reports of disease outbreaks (ibid.). In the wake of the 1998 floods in Bangladesh, there were higher reported rates of diarrhoea among groups with lower income, lower levels of education and lower-quality housing without access to tap water (Hashizume and others, 2008).

People living in poverty are more susceptible to the diseases that some climate hazards help spread

Children and the elderly are particularly affected by the adverse health effects of climate hazards. This is not surprising, given their relative fragility. Hallegatte and others (2016) have reported a greater incidence of ailments among children following floods in Ho Chi Minh City. Kovats and Akhtar (2008) noted outbreaks of leptospirosis among children following flooding in Mumbai. Lloyd, Kovats and Chalabi (2011) estimated that the effects of climate change on crop yields will lead to an increase in undernutrition, resulting in turn in higher rates of child stunting, particularly in sub-Saharan Africa and South Asia. The majority of the victims of Cyclone Aila in Bangladesh were children and the elderly, groups that have difficulty achieving rapid mobility (Rabbani and Huq, 2016).

Children and the elderly are particularly susceptible to adverse health effects

Similarly, disadvantaged people suffer more adverse health effects from heat waves and high temperatures, because they cannot afford heat alleviating amenities, including proper housing ventilation and air conditioning. Heat waves have significant effects on the elderly, particularly as they are already more likely to suffer from chronic illnesses, such as coronary heart disease and respiratory diseases, which can be exacerbated by heat (Hutton, 2008).

Elderly people are also more susceptible to a greater magnitude of health effects from floods and, in addition, are less able to relocate in the event of disasters (ibid.). For example, as elderly residents of Limpopo, South Africa, lacked access to the labour necessary to construct their houses to enable them to withstand flooding, their dwellings suffered greater damage (Khandlhela and May, 2006).

As noted above, it was the elderly in New Orleans who were the most impacted by the hurricane, as they were less able to relocate and were more susceptible to health-related impacts. In general, poorer and minority populations were less able to relocate in response to the pre-storm warnings and were therefore more likely to suffer injuries and death. The lack of ownership of, or access to, a means of transportation was a significant factor affecting the probability of evacuation and relocation (Colton, 2006; Masozera, Bailey and Kerchner, 2006). Another significant factor was the lack of the financial and social resources needed to secure a dwelling to relocate to. As a result of all of these factors, low-income and African American inhabitants suffered greater levels of loss and damage than the wealthier and white households.

Effects on health were noted as a particular concern with regard to the impacts of climate change on indigenous populations, already located in marginal areas, in Latin America. Those effects were exerted through changes that allowed diseases to spread in areas where they could not have thrived previously. As a result, rates of respiratory and diarrhoeal diseases increased. Climate change also adversely affected the nutritional status of those populations, thereby worsening their health status (Kronik and Verner, 2010). The time devoted to household labour by women also increases as a result of climate hazards and this has a direct effect on child nutrition (Silva, 2016).

The greater susceptibility to health effects frequently undermines the income and asset position of disadvantaged groups not only in the short term but also in the long run. In the short term, they may suffer from loss of productivity, employment and income. An example for the Plurinational State of Bolivia shows that income poverty increases when climate-related productivity shocks strike, as labour wages (upon which disadvantaged groups most rely) are hit adversely in absolute terms and also in relation to the rents of other factors of production (see chap, III, box III.2). In the long run, disadvantaged groups suffer from loss of human capital (through lost school days and the development of chronic conditions such as stunting) and a lower rate of income growth (Somanathan and others, 2014; Li and others, 2016; Zivin and Neidell, 2014).

Inequalities and the ability to cope and recover

Fewer resources are available to disadvantaged groups for coping and recovery

Ability to cope and recover is the third channel through which inequalities aggravate the impact of climate hazards on disadvantaged groups. The situations and processes to which exposure and susceptibility apply are ex ante, while those to which coping and recovery refer are ex post. The persistence of multiple inequalities implies that disadvantaged groups will have access to fewer of the resources required to take coping and recovery measures. Those resources generally take any of four forms: (a) households' own resources, (b) community resources, (c) resources provided by non-governmental organizations, private companies or citizens and (d) public resources provided by the government. Disadvantaged groups are likely to lack some—if not all—of the resources that are necessary for coping and recovery. As a result, their situation worsens after a climate hazard has materialized.

Recovery trajectories

Differences in the recovery trajectories of advantaged and disadvantaged groups lead to greater inequalities

In this analysis, the recovery trajectories of different groups matter. In the wake of a climate hazard, the rate of recovery is not the same across the population owing to existing inequalities and can ultimately become an important factor in terms of a further worsening of inequalities. If, hypothetically, both rich and poor households recover at the same rate, the welfare gap may remain constant (see figure II.2, panel A). On the other hand, if rich households are able to recover faster and increase their income further (panel B) or if poorer households see their welfare growth decline (panel C), then the welfare gap will increase. This will likely worsen existing inequalities.

How matters proceed in the real world is better represented by a situation where (a) owing to existing inequalities, either the rich have a faster rate of recovery or the poor have a lower rate of recovery, or both, and (b) as a consequence, inequality generally increases in all cases. There is considerable evidence that people affected by multiple inequalities undergo slower recoveries from more pronounced impacts (Verner, ed., 2010; Carter and others, 2007; Kraay and McKenzie, 2014; Jalan and Ravallion, 2001). These differential recovery rates contribute to an increase in the welfare gap. Lack of resources forces people living in poverty and other disadvantaged groups to cope with climate hazards in ways so detrimental as to put their future adaptive capacity at risk (Barbier, 2010; Barrett, Travis and Dasgupta, 2011; McDowell and Hess, 2012).

Figure II.2
Differential rates of recovery from climate hazards of wealthy and poor households

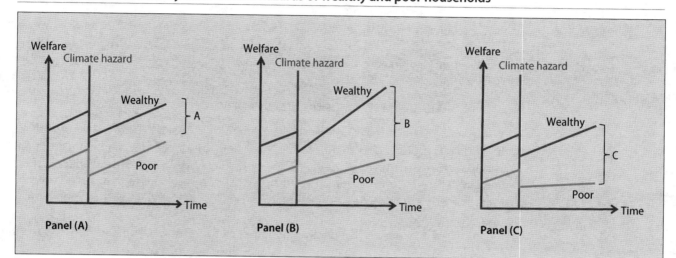

Source: Based on Mutter (2015) technical appendix 1.
Note: The slopes of the recovery curves for the wealthy and poor illustrate how inequality changes over time. Inequality remains constant (panel A) or increases based on the effect of the shock on the recovery path of the wealthy (panel B) or on that of the poor (panel C).

Coping capacity using own resources

Differences in an individual's or a household's own resources are obviously an important factor with respect to the ability to cope and recover from climate hazards. Thus, the ability to accumulate assets can play an important role in this regard. For example, in northern Burkina Faso, the ability among farmers to accumulate land and livestock played an important role in facilitating their ability to diversify income sources and improve adaptive capacity to climate hazards. The fact that increasing land prices and growing land scarcity limited younger farmers' ability to accumulate resources added to intergenerational poverty (Silva, 2016). In the Nkayi region of Zimbabwe, farms without cattle, which are poorer than farms with cattle, may eventually end up worse off with respect to climate change if they do not adapt so as to ensure resilient farming (see chap. III).

Importance of insurance

An important issue related to coping and recovery is that of insurance. Availability of insurance plays an important role in determining how different groups of the population fare when climate hazards actually materialize. Regrettably, not all groups have the same access to insurance. Lack of own resources often prevent people living in poverty and disadvantaged groups from buying necessary insurance. For example, Verner (2010) has reported that in Latin America, the asset losses of households with higher income levels are much more likely to be insured than those of low-income households.

Microinsurance offers the possibility of extending insurance coverage to those at the lower end of asset and income distributions (Mosley, 2015). This insurance modality is generally targeted towards disadvantaged groups and tends to focus on particular risks, most frequently those related to health. More recently, it has been extended to crops, although provision is based not on actual crop damage (estimates of which can be subjective, thereby

The fact that disadvantaged groups have less access to insurance makes recovery difficult

causing moral hazard-related problems) but on objective information generally related to rainfall, on which crop production crucially depends. Beneficial impacts of these schemes have been reported; for example, the BASIX rainfall insurance scheme operating in India has been shown to increase both investments by clients and stability of income. However, unlike microcredit, microinsurance schemes still face formidable challenges and have yet to achieve wide coverage.

The choice between human and physical capital

In coping with climate hazards, people facing multiple inequalities often have to make the difficult choice between protecting their human capital (health and education) and preserving their physical capital. In view of the absence of health insurance, these households face large expenses when hit by diseases in the wake of climate hazards. To meet these expenses, they often sell their physical assets, which frequently undermines their future efforts to reap income earnings (Clarke and Dercon, 2015).

It has been reported that while poor households in Ethiopia were forced to sell assets during periods when their finances were stressed by drought, this was not the case for the more well-off households (Little and others, 2006). After the famines in Ethiopia during the period 1984-1985, a decade was required for asset-poor households to bring livestock-holding back to pre-famine levels (Dercon, 2004). On the other hand, poor households sometimes reduce their consumption in order to avoid asset sales and preserve productive assets (Carter and others, 2007). This reduction in consumption, however, can have deleterious health and education outcomes, particularly for children. It also results in the perpetuation of inequality for future generations (Baez, de la Fuente and Santos, 2010; Maccini and Yang, 2009).

In the wake of the 1998 floods in Bangladesh, poorer households, as compared with wealthier households, were forced to borrow greater fractions of their income and at higher rates in order to survive and rebuild (del Ninno and others, 2001). This resulted in greater debt burdens, thus limiting poorer households' efforts to build assets and human capital. In view of their limited ability to cope and recover, disadvantaged groups in flood-prone areas of Bangladesh often face the choice between selling assets or reducing consumption. Poor households that were exposed to the 1998 floods reduced their caloric intake by 11 per cent. As a result, 48 per cent of poor households were reported to be food-insecure, in contrast with 16 per cent of all households (ibid.). People at disadvantage lose their physical or their human capital in the face of such hazards. Rabbani, Rahman and Mainuddin (2009) found that during periods of flooding, women prioritize the consumption of men and children by consuming less food and water themselves.

Along similar lines, there could be long-term effects on the education of children if they are taken out of school as a means of coping with climate hazards, even if this is only as the result of a temporary shock. It was found that in Mexico, children experiencing such a situation were 30 per cent less likely to complete primary school than those children that stayed in school (de Janvry and others, 2006). In sub-Saharan Africa, asset-poor households are more likely to provide their children with lower-quality nutrition and are less likely to take sick children for a medical consultation following weather shocks, which can have long-term impacts on those children and their prospects for development (Hallegatte and others, 2016). In addition, it has been found that lower-income households that were exposed to weather-related risks become more risk-averse, which can impact their future income and asset accumulation. These households are more likely to choose low-risk, low-return activities where income is more predictable, as opposed to investing in higher-income activities that entail a higher risk (ibid.). All of these patterns are linked to worse outcomes for disadvantaged households which as a result may translate into increased inequalities.

Diversification capacity and adaptive strategies

The ability to diversify income sources improves people's capacity to adapt to climate hazards, improving their capacity to cope and recover as illustrated in various examples from the Sahel region in Africa. Households deriving their livelihoods from agriculture and a sizeable pastoralist population coexist in this region, as already noted. Interestingly, some perceive the rise of pastoralism in the region as an adaptive mechanism designed to "respond to a rapidly changing, and increasingly unpredictable environment" (Marshall and Hildebrand, 2002) and past movements appear to have been driven by "arid crises" (di Lernia, 2006). However, pastoralists in some countries have been marginalized within the context of efforts to achieve economic development (Holthuijzen and Maximillian, 2011).

Often, capacity to cope and recover depends on the ability to diversify income sources

There is also conspicuous horizontal inequality. In Mali, for example, this exists between minority pastoralist populations (such as the Tuareg, Fula and other Arab-Berber groups) and majority agricultural ethnic groups (sub-Saharan tribes such as the Mande) (Straus, 2011). Tuareg communities in the Niger have experienced long-standing marginalization, amplified by French colonial policies which privileged agricultural communities' access to land. Furthermore, the traditional strategies for coping with extreme weather conditions in these communities have become less effective with the onset of climate change, thereby increasing the precariousness of their situation (Silva, 2016). In addition, population growth and urbanization have increased pressure on food supplies, which has led to projections of food insecurity for more than 40 per cent of the population (Verhagen and others, 2003).

In general, in the Sahel of West Africa, "[w]ealthier and larger farm households are more likely to be in a position to implement adaptive strategies, such as storage of food, technical measures to increase and stabilize food production, either by expansion of the land resources or by intensification, or outside agriculture through marketing of non-agricultural products, or selling services and/or labour to reduce or avoid future likelihood of stress and food shortages" (Dietz and Verhagen, eds., 2004).

Wealthier households in some regions have been better able to diversify and adapt

In food producing regions in Burkina Faso, adverse rainfall conditions have contributed to household participation in non-farm activities (D'haen, Nielsen and Lambin, 2014). This is an adaptive response, but the change in livelihoods can potentially have spillover effects. Wealthier households in Burkina Faso take advantage of these circumstances through the gaining of access to cheaper farm labour supplied by poorer households that are experiencing hardship (Silva, 2016). Climate change is also anticipated to have effects on the location and viability of particular livelihoods. For example, changing rainfall patterns in Mali are expected to lead to a changed perception of which crops are viable and which households are vulnerable (Jankowska, Nagengast and Perea, 2012). It can be expected that, with wealthier households being better able to diversify their crop mixture and with their increased access to water sources, there will be an exacerbation of inequality (Mertz and others, 2011). At the same time, despite other agricultural adaptation measures, 39 per cent of the Burkinabè population remains susceptible to considerable impacts from rainfall variation, forcing the adoption of migration as another adaptation strategy (Barbier and others, 2009). There are also instances of conflicting interests in coping and adaptation strategies. In the Niger, for example, water resources have been prioritized for agricultural populations to the detriment of pastoralists (Snorek, Renaud and Kloos, 2014). Thus, in the Sahel region, climate change is aggravating horizontal inequalities in addition to increasing inequality in terms of income and assets.

Common property, ecosystems and social resources

For many low-income people, access to common property resources is vital for coping with and recovering from climate hazards

Access to common property resources shared by the community can play an important role in coping and recovery strategies. People living in poverty may treat access to ecosystems as a de facto asset to the extent that they may use goods derived from local ecosystems, such as crops, timber and fish, either for self-consumption or for the purpose of smoothing income shocks (Barbier, 2010). For example, coastal populations in Bangladesh with closer proximity to mangrove reserves were better able to cope in the wake of Cyclone Aila (Akter and Mallick, 2013). Women's more limited access to common property resources has been noted as a factor that aggravates the difficulty of their situation in the wake of climate hazards (Perez and others, 2015).

A survey of the literature on climate change and ecosystem services shows that resource stocks such as fish and timber that are growing continuously are less sensitive to weather fluctuations than annual crops (Howe and others, 2013). The use of these types of ecosystem resources can therefore act as coping mechanisms during periods of reduced income. Effects of climate change on these ecosystems will therefore affect the livelihood and coping capacity of the low-income people who rely on them to generate income, thus exacerbating inequality. It has been reported that households within tropical and subtropical smallholder systems derive a considerable fraction of their income from ecosystems, ranging from about 55 per cent in South Asia to 75 per cent in sub-Saharan Africa. In these communities in Latin America and South and East Asia, those in the top quintile rely on those services to a lesser degree than those in all other quintiles, meaning that the highest-income residents are least exposed to the impact of climate hazards on such ecosystems (Noack and others, 2015). At the same time, overextraction of fish and timber can lead to resource exhaustion and ecosystem damage (Hallegatte and others, 2016).

Through the availability of and access to social capital, households that have limited access to other resources can be provided with the means to cope with climate hazards. For example, Braun and Aßheuer (2011) found that social capital plays an important role with respect to the ability to cope with floods in Dhaka. There is also evidence that pre-existing power imbalances within villages may result in adaptation responses that exacerbate inequalities. In Malawi, members of households with less land often adapt to climate hazards by working for wealthier families as farm labourers, often under exploitative conditions, which thereby increases local-level inequality and reinforces subsequent susceptibility of the labouring households to the impact of erratic rainfall, droughts and flooding (Silva, 2016).

The role of public resources

Public resources are critical for coping and recovery but they must be available to those who need them most

While the use of public resources can be critical for coping and recovering, its characteristics are frequently a function of the political dynamics of the society. Women farmers in many countries, for example, do not have equal access to climate adaptation funds when compared with male and larger-scale farmers (Silva, 2016).

Similar phenomena were observed in New Orleans in the wake of Hurricane Katrina. Lakeview is one of the neighbourhoods with the lowest elevation in Orleans Parish, and yet it was able to recover faster than other areas, partly owing to its relative wealth (Mutter, 2015). Households with low income and low credit ratings (factors that apply to a greater degree to African Americans in New Orleans) were more likely to have their application for a home loan for disaster recovery rejected (Masozera, Bailey and Kerchner, 2006). In the absence of dedicated efforts to support the reconstruction efforts of the most vulnerable in New Orleans, pre-existing inequalities were aggravated. This also resulted in considerable demographic shifts. Those able to return were better positioned in the labour market compared with non-returnees (Groen and Polivka, 2008).[9] There is evidence that income inequality in New Orleans, measured by the ratio of the income of the top 5 per cent to that of the bottom 20 per cent, increased between 2000 and 2013 (Shrinath, Mack and Plyer, 2014).[10]

The evidence shows that adaptation efforts are often driven by wealth rather than by need. Wealthier cities spend relatively more on adaptation despite the fact that poorer cities are more vulnerable. In addition, the outcomes of adaptation may reinforce existing social inequalities. For example, local chiefs in Mozambique were able to maintain disproportionate access to prime land, capital and social power in post-flood resettlement locations (Silva 2016). Furthermore, resources for adaptation, such as research on crop varieties, are often dominated by politically connected and wealthier groups. For example, the focus of research in the area of saline-tolerant rice crops in Sri Lanka has been directed towards large-scale rice growers, with less attention paid to marginalized groups such as the farmers of Hambantota (Weragoda, Ensor and Berger, 2009).

Policy implications

The comprehensive empirical evidence derived from the literature reviewed above, albeit not fully complete, points to the fact that the combination of economic and political restrictions, social norms and individual characteristics put large groups of people at a disadvantage in regard to their area of residence and their livelihood, thus exposing them to mud slides, periods of abnormally hot weather, water contamination, flooding and other climate hazards (see figure II.3). Groups whose livelihoods specifically depend on climate-sensitive natural resources and who do not possess the capacity to diversify into climate-resilient livelihoods are exposed and vulnerable to land degradation, water scarcity and landscape damage, among other hazards. Because of a lack of capacity to cope and recover, these disadvantaged groups frequently experience loss of human lives and human capital, assets and income. In the face of deteriorating ecosystems, people who rely on them for a living are at risk of falling into poverty traps.

Structural inequalities push people towards greater exposure and susceptibility while lowering their ability to cope with and recover from climate hazards

---

[9]   Almost 100,000 African American residents had not returned to Orleans Parish (i.e., to the city of New Orleans not the New Orleans metropolitan area) by 2013, versus about 11,500 white residents. This changed the racial composition of the city. The proportion of African Americans in the city's population declined from 66.7 per cent in 2000 to 59.1 per cent in 2013 (Shrinath, Mack and Plyer, 2014).

[10]   While some have argued that those who did not return were better off in their new locations, in terms of employment, education and health-care opportunities (Deryugina and others, 2014; Imberman, Kugler and Sacerdote, 2012), such an analysis is beyond the scope of this *Survey*.

Figure II.3
Drivers of exposure and vulnerability to climate hazards through the lens of the empirical evidence

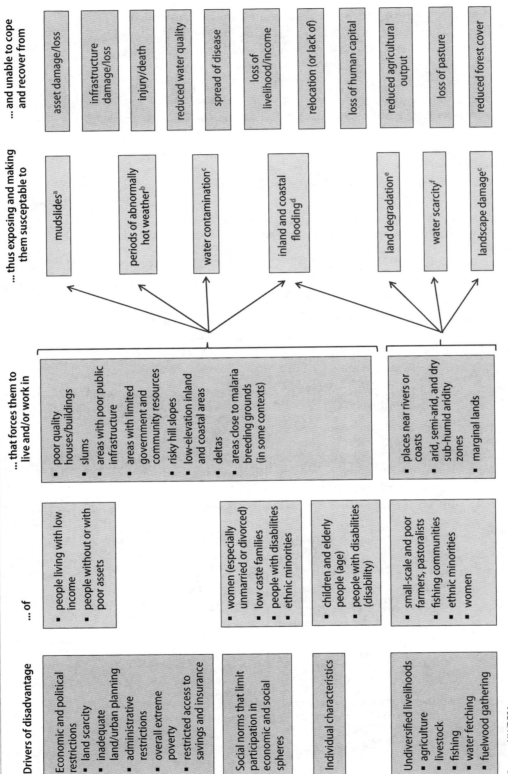

Source: UN/DESA.

a Caused by heavy rainfall.
b Caused by heatwaves.
c Caused by flooding from excessive rainfall.
d Caused by excessive rainfall and sea-level rise, respectively.
e Caused by increased salinity (in coastal areas), erosion, desertification, drought and long-term water scarcity.
f Caused by drought.

The implications of the present analysis are twofold. On the one hand, structural inequalities lie at the core of an understanding of vulnerability to climate hazards. On the other hand, addressing the root causes of inequalities to enable adaptation and the building of resilience to climate hazards will require a continuum of policies, planning and practices which include immediate assistance in the wake of climate hazards, disaster risk reduction measures and policies for adaptation to a changing climate, as well as good development policies focused on reducing inequalities. These specific measures will be effective in reducing climate change vulnerability only if they are part of longer-term transformative strategies for sustainable development.

Policies designed to build climate resilience should be pursued simultaneously and aimed at reducing immediate vulnerability, at the same time that they enable incremental transformative changes for achievement of longer-term objectives. Such policies are "low regret" in nature and the underlying logic is compatible with approaches for managing the risks of climate change through adaptation, as proposed by IPCC (see appendix II.1, table A.II.1).

Policies designed to reduce immediate vulnerability include interventions for poverty alleviation and income diversification; disaster risk reduction (through, e.g., early warning systems, shelters and infrastructure improvements); and adaptation strategies (e.g., introduction of new crop varieties, water management techniques and ecosystem management).

Policies will be low-regret if, irrespective of the (uncertain) evolution of climate change, through their incremental nature they help build resilience to climate hazards and meet development objectives. In some instances, in fact, incremental policies may actually be a precondition for change. For example, a policy that targets expanded access to resilient crops in previously fertile lands that became desert can improve the livelihoods of small-scale and poor farmers. A policy expanding the access to health care and cooling technology, making them more affordable for all, can reduce the pernicious effects of heat waves, particularly on the elderly. Not only will these policies together help facilitate adaptation but they will also contribute to addressing the root causes of inequality and poverty. Improving infrastructure, health care and sanitation will not only minimize exposure and vulnerability to climate hazards, such as those presented in figure II.3, but also enable sustainable development.

A focus on building climate change resilience by decreasing the vulnerability of those who are most exposed also provides a unique opportunity to tackle institutional deficits particularly the existing governance systems and cultural conditions, that perpetuate inequalities. Transformative policies can aim for shifts in production and consumption behaviours to encourage sustainable practices. Policies can also target reforms in political, social, cultural and ecological decision-making in order to open up space for the participation of population groups usually excluded.

In facing the challenges posed by this continuum of development policies, policymakers and all stakeholders potentially affected will have to build an iterative and flexible policy decision-making process. Integrated assessments that challenge the expertise of traditional development thinking and policy will be necessary as a means of informing the process (see chap. III). At the same time, policies will have to be coherent and well integrated, with the involvement of relevant stakeholders in identifying the risks and helping to implement the solutions (see chap. IV).

Addressing the root cause of inequalities that aggravate exposure and vulnerability will require a continuum of policies...

...as part of a transformative agenda for long-term adaptation and mitigation

Policies should aim at strengthening institutions to ensure a greater role for disadvantaged groups

Appendix II.1

Table A.II.1
Approaches to managing the risks of climate change through adaptation

Overlapping approaches	Category	Examples
Vulnerability and exposure reduction (throughout development, planning and practices) / Adaptation (including incremental and transformational adjustments)	Human development	Improved access to education, nutrition, health facilities, energy, safe housing and settlement structures, and social support structures; reduced gender inequality and marginalization in other forms
	Poverty alleviation	Improved access to and control of local resources; land tenure; disaster risk reduction; social safety nets and social protection; insurance schemes
	Livelihood security	Income, asset and livelihood diversification; improved infrastructure; access to technology; increased decision-making power; changed cropping, livestock and aquaculture practices; reliance on social networks
	Disaster risk management	Early warning systems; hazard and vulnerability mapping; diversifying water resources; improved drainage; flood and cyclone shelters; building codes; storm and wastewater management; transport and road infrastructure improvements
	Ecosystem management	Maintaining wetlands and urban green spaces; coastal afforestation; watershed and reservoir management; reduction of other stressors on ecosystems and of habitat fragmentation; maintenance of genetic diversity; manipulation of disturbance regimes; community-based natural resource management
	Spatial or land-use planning	Provisioning of adequate housing, infrastructure and services; managing development in flood-prone and other high-risk areas; urban planning and upgrading programmes; land zoning laws; easements; protected areas
	Structural/physical	Engineered- and built-environment options: sea walls and coastal protection; flood levees; water storage; improved drainage; flood and cyclone shelters; building codes; storm and wastewater management; transport and road infrastructure improvements; floating houses; power plant and electricity grid adjustments
		Technological options: new crop and animal varieties; indigenous, traditional and local knowledge, technologies and methods; efficient irrigation; water-saving technologies; desalinisation; conservation agriculture; food storage and preservation facilities; hazard and vulnerability mapping and monitoring; early warning systems; building insulation; mechanical and passive cooling; technology development, transfer and diffusion
		Ecosystem-based options: ecological restoration; soil conservation; afforestation and reforestation; mangrove conservation and replanting; green infrastructure (e.g., shade trees, green roofs); controlling overfishing; fisheries co-management; assisted species migration and dispersal; ecological corridors; seed banks, gene banks and other ex situ conservation; community-based natural resource management
		Services: social safety nets and social protection; food banks and distribution of food; municipal services, water and sanitation; vaccination programmes; public-health services; enhanced emergency medical services
	Institutional	Economic options: financial incentives; insurance; catastrophe bonds; payments for ecosystem services; pricing water to encourage universal provision and careful use; microfinance; disaster contingency funds; cash transfers; public-private partnerships
		Laws and regulations: land zoning laws; building standards and practices; easements; water regulations and agreements; laws to support disaster risk reduction; laws to encourage insurance purchasing; defined property rights and land tenure security; protected areas; fishing quotas; patent pools and technology transfer
		National and government policies and programmes: national and regional adaptation plans including mainstreaming; sub-national and local adaptation plans; economic diversification; urban upgrading programmes; municipal water management programmes; disaster planning and preparedness; integrated water resource management; integrated coastal zone management; ecosystem-based management; community-based adaptation
	Social	Educational options: awareness raising and integrating into education; gender equity in education; extension services; sharing indigenous, traditional and local knowledge; participatory action research and social learning; knowledge-sharing and learning platforms
		Informational options: hazard and vulnerability mapping; early warning and response systems; systematic monitoring and remote sensing; climate services; use of indigenous climate observations; participatory scenario development; integrated assessments
		Behavioural options: preparation and evacuation planning; migration; soil and water conservation; storm drain clearance; livelihood diversification; changed cropping, livestock and aquaculture practices
Transformation	Spheres of change	Practical: social and technical innovations, behavioural shifts or institutional and managerial changes that produce substantial shifts in outcomes
		Political: political, social, cultural and ecological actions consistent with reducing vulnerability and risk and supporting adaptation, mitigation and sustainable development
		Personal: individual and collective assumptions, beliefs, values and world views influencing climate-change responses

Source: Adapted from IPCC (2014d), table SPM 1.

Chapter III
Bringing inequalities to the forefront of climate assessments

Key messages

- Natural and social scientists are addressing the complexity of climate impacts and policies using integrated climate impact assessments. They integrate different models to capture the multiple interlinkages across the environmental, economic and social dimensions of development as they relate to climate. This generates a cascade of scenarios on the potential impacts of climate projections and policy options for addressing them within a well-structured science-policy interface.

- The focus of these assessments needs to be sharpened in order to broaden the analysis to include both policy options for climate adaptation and resilience and a broader analysis of the economic and financial feasibility of those options. Importantly, the analysis of inequalities should be at the forefront.

- Existing modelling frameworks are useful for addressing inequalities from different perspectives by: analysing impacts on livelihoods that rely on climate-sensitive natural resources; addressing income distribution on the basis of ownership and employment of production factors; assessing options for building human capital and access to public services; and identifying the vulnerability of households based on their socioeconomic characteristics. The analysis is improved considerably if stakeholders participate in designing and developing an understanding of the results.

- Countries have much to gain from enhancing capacities to develop and use integrated climate impact assessments through which they gather a robust range of estimates of impacts and policy options for informed policy decision-making. Improved communication of results and engagement of stakeholders in the discussion of policy options derived from integrated assessments will improve collaboration and strengthen governance.

[Integrated Assessment Models combine] key elements of biophysical and economic systems into one integrated system. They provide convenient frameworks to combine knowledge from a wide range of disciplines. These models strip down the laws of nature and human behaviour to their essentials to depict how increased GHGs in the atmosphere affect temperature, and how temperature change causes quantifiable economic losses.

IPCC, *Climate Change 2001: Mitigation*
Contribution of Working Group III to the
Third Assessment Report of the
Intergovernmental Panel on Climate Change,
p. 490, sect. 7.6.4

Introduction

It is important to bring together the different methodologies available to support integrated assessments in informing sustainable development policy

One of the major challenges in the implementation of the 2030 Agenda for Sustainable Development[1] is integrating the various facets of the environment into development policies. Based on the experience of the past decades, there is better understanding of the links between the economic and social dimensions of development. It took several years and improved data and analytical capacities to move away from the narrow focus on economic growth as the main source of development. There is a better understanding of the characteristics of households and the sources of people's vulnerability to economic shocks. The policy frameworks that enhance consistency between economic and social policies have also been strengthened. Environmental concerns, in general, and the impact of climate hazards on people's livelihoods, in particular, need to be better understood. Addressing these challenges requires improved policy frameworks and analytical capacities to assist in the design and implementation of coherent policies across the economic, social and environmental dimensions of development. More broadly, and as is consistent with the 2030 Agenda, it is important to strengthen the science-policy interface and the development of strong evidence-based instruments so as to support policymakers in promoting poverty eradication and sustainable development.[2] It is thus important to bring together the different methodologies available to support integrated assessments of development challenges, including building climate resilience.

Consideration of options for achieving climate resilience for sustainable development is a complex task. It requires good information systems which provide the data and statistics necessary to identify people at risk in their (often very local) geographical contexts. It also requires improved integrated assessments of possible impacts of climate hazards on people and their livelihoods, including sound analysis of policy options for building resilience in anticipation of such impacts or, when they occur, for providing assistance in coping with and recovering from them. These assessments, in turn, require knowledge across disciplines belonging to the natural and social sciences, as well as local knowledge; in fact, they extend beyond the traditional expertise of the development community and the scientists working within their own disciplines.

Integrated assessments of climate impacts and policies are informing international climate discussions and policymaking...

Faced with such complexity, the international community of natural and social scientists has adopted an integrated approach to climate impact assessments. This approach seeks to generate scenarios on potential impacts of climate projections and the policies available to address them, for the world as a whole and for smaller geographical levels.

Scenarios from integrated climate impact assessments rely on various models to evaluate impacts of climate change on different aspects of development. Model-based analyses have been informing international climate discussions and feature prominently among the tools used in assessment reports of the Intergovernmental Panel on Climate Change (IPCC) to support conclusions and recommendations (see, e.g., the IPCC Fifth Assessment Report, 2014). Scenarios from these assessments are also being used by countries to develop narrative storylines which help decision makers plan policy interventions for reducing adverse impacts arising from a changing climate.

---

1   General Assembly resolution 70/1.

2   Ibid., para. 83.

At the same time, the members of the international community of scientists and local researchers developing integrated climate impact assessments have taken note of the limitations of the approach and, not least, of the uncertainty surrounding the results obtained from model-based scenarios. The climate projections upon which assessments rely are themselves uncertain. There is also an awareness that since even the most sophisticated models represent an imperfect simplification of complex realities, their results need to be utilized with caution. These imperfections notwithstanding, integrated climate impact assessments seem to be the most reliable mechanism available for establishing a range of plausible impact scenarios which are critical for achieving an understanding of the magnitude of potential risks and policy responses. Other approaches to assessments that are more qualitative in nature—and sometimes even entirely theoretical—cannot fully replace the key functionality of integrated climate impact assessments (i.e., numerical estimation across the different dimensions of development), although they are a highly important complement. In fact, new methodologies designed to incorporate systematically the opinions of relevant stakeholders in modelling specifications, including scenario-building, are helping to improve the interpretation of, and reduce the uncertainty surrounding, the outcomes of climate impact assessments. This practice can be critical in helping to build consensus around development priorities and strengthen policy coordination and the governance of decision-making processes.

Through its holistic character, the 2030 Agenda for Sustainable Development is increasing the demand for integrated assessment approaches with the engagement of stakeholders, as the basis for coherent policy formulation. However, the use of integrated impact assessments as a tool for policymaking is in its infancy in developing countries and needs to be nurtured through capacity-building. In many countries, there are data and technical capacity constraints on the use of modelling tools as part of routine policymaking assessments. Those countries therefore rely on partial quantitative assessments, qualitative evaluations or value judgments. While these partial approaches are useful and necessary, they do not fully capture the interlinkages among the different dimensions of development. Developing capacity to design and use integrated impact assessments will enable them to provide the policy dialogue with scientific evidence within the margin of uncertainty surrounding these methodologies.

In strengthening the capacity of countries to use integrated impact assessments for climate resilience, it is necessary to sharpen the focus of analysis in various areas, three of which are discussed in the present chapter. In this regard:

- It is important to expand the narrow focus on long-term climate change and mitigation to include assessments on the impact of climate hazards that are caused by climate variability and extreme weather events, and expand the assessment of policy questions to include adaptation and resilience.
- There is a need to expand beyond a limited accounting of the costs and benefits of single climate policies by deepening the analysis of the broader economic and financial feasibility of development policies for climate resilience.
- Importantly, integrated climate impact assessments have not systematically addressed the way in which inequalities exacerbate vulnerability to climate hazards and the policy options that would contribute to addressing structural inequalities with a view to building climate resilience.

...through helping to establish a range of plausible impact scenarios, which is critical for understanding the magnitude of risks and policy responses

The use of integrated impact assessments as a tool for policymaking in developing countries needs to be nurtured through capacity-building

Sharpening the development focus of assessments and bringing inequalities to the forefront of the analysis enhances their relevance in decision-making

Without a doubt, it is of critical importance for data and statistical capacity to be improved before we can even begin to think about the construction of integrated climate impact assessments, particularly in developing countries, and this challenge will be discussed in depth in chapter V. In addressing the three areas of improvement listed above, this chapter focuses attention on the need to bring inequalities to the forefront of analysis. In doing so, it examines different ways in which existing modelling frameworks can be used to trace effects of climate hazards on vulnerable populations and assess policy options for addressing different sources of inequality. Through improvements in these three areas (as well as in data and statistical capacity), integrated climate impact assessments can respond to such questions as:

- What are the potential impacts of climate hazards on livelihoods? Do existing inequalities exacerbate these impacts or the risk of experiencing them? What are the dimensions of inequality that make people vulnerable to climate hazards? Are inequalities aggravated by climate hazards?

- Which are the policy options that, by addressing existing inequalities, contribute to building climate resilience? Are these policies economically feasible in view of the challenging financial gaps, not least in the area of adaptation?

The following section describes the integrated approach to climate impact assessments in the form in which it is mostly applied in practice, focusing on the analytical steps it entails and its strengths and weaknesses. This description lays the ground work for achieving an understanding, in the subsequent section, of the ways in which modelling frameworks are used to explore different dimensions of inequality. The final section sets out the key challenges going forward to making the integrated approach to climate impact assessments more accessible and more applicable, particularly in developing countries where the urgency of adaptation and building resilience to climate hazards is greatest.

The integrated approach to climate impact assessments

The different models that are featured at present in integrated climate impact assessments can be used to bring inequalities to the forefront of the analysis. Before elaborating on this possibility, it is first necessary to understand the analytical steps and the strengths and weaknesses of the integrated approach as it is typically implemented in practice. It is particularly important to understand the extent to which inequalities have or have not featured in integrated climate impact assessments.

Analytical steps and strengths of the integrated approach

Climate impact assessments integrate different modelling tools to facilitate an understanding of the interlinkages across the various dimensions of development...

The integrated approach to climate impact assessments has a number of strengths: It relies on the expertise of natural and social scientists from across different disciplines; integrates modelling tools to facilitate an understanding of the multiple interlinkages across and within the environmental, economic and social dimensions of development; and aids in the estimation of climate-related impacts and deliberations on alternative policy responses. While this approach has been used mainly in assessing long-term climate impacts, it is also well suited (as shown below) to assessing short-term risks and it is thus useful to assess policy options for climate resilience.³

Figure III.1 provides a simplified representation of the cascade of analytical steps taken in this approach, and also depicts the extensions needed to incorporate climate variability and extreme weather events within the analysis, as well as the possible engagement of stakeholders in the assessment process.

Figure III.1
Simplified representation of the integrated approach to climate impact assessments

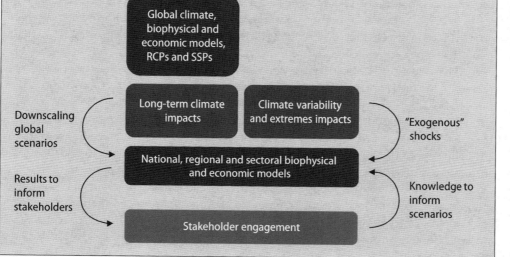

Source: UN/DESA.

Global climate models are generally used by natural scientists, to project climate changes, typically changes of temperature and precipitation patterns, over relatively large spatial and temporal scales.⁴ These projections are influenced by different scenarios, for the world, of greenhouse gas emissions and concentration pathways, under different levels of mitigation, as given by so-called representative concentration pathways (RCPs). Projections derived from these climate models, under different degrees of confidence, feature prominently in the IPCC assessment reports and have been utilized as a tool for informing international climate negotiations.

Climate projections are subsequently downscaled through global biophysical models to simulate how they affect natural resource systems (land, energy and water). At this stage, an objective of the analysis may be to determine, without much socioeconomic detail, how changes in natural resource systems affect a particular area or sector. The IPCC Fifth Assessment Report, which is also the most recent, presents evidence emanating from biophysical models suggesting that climate change impacts are strongest and most comprehensive for natural systems (IPCC, 2014d, p. 4).

---

3   For a more detailed description of this approach, as typically taken in assessments of long-term climate change impacts, see Sánchez (2016).

4   These models are also known as global circulation models (GCMs).

More recently, there has been an incorporation of global economic models, generally by social scientists working with natural scientists in a multidisciplinary context, as a means of generating scenarios that translate changes in natural resource systems into changes in socioeconomic ones. At this step, shared socioeconomic pathways (SSPs), which were introduced in appendix I.1 of chapter I, are used to inform the scenarios through addition of details on population growth (disaggregated by age, sex and education), urbanization and economic development (proxied generally by growth of gross domestic product (GDP)), which are otherwise not specified in global economic models.

...thereby helping to generate a cascade of scenarios of potential climate impacts and vulnerabilities at different geographical levels

The cascade of global impact scenarios that are generated from these models is further downscaled if the purpose is to understand potential impacts and vulnerabilities at lower geographical levels. In this case, additional biophysical and economic models are used for countries, regions or sectors. Once all of the scenarios of impacts and vulnerabilities associated with climate projections have been assessed at global and lower geographical levels, additional scenarios can be run at different geographical scales to assess alternative policy responses for reducing adverse impacts.

The results of the scenarios generated are characterized by uncertainty and must therefore be interpreted with caution. Major sources of uncertainty include, among others, climate change projections under different levels of mitigation; climate variability; socioeconomic projections; model simplifications; and data constraints, particularly at the local level. With regard to simplifications of complex realities, the results from models critically depend on assumptions made in relation to people's behaviour. If modellers fail to incorporate plausible behaviours, model results may lead to the wrong conclusions.

Working with policymakers and relevant stakeholders is important when designing scenarios and interpreting results

Scientists and researchers who are developing integrated climate impact assessments have adopted certain practices in response to these limitations. In the field of climate, for example, uncertainty tends to be "deep",[5] which accounts for their recent practice of working closely with policymakers and relevant stakeholders to improve the estimation of parameters and the interpretation of results (see figure III.1, bottom right). In the context of such uncertainty, it is widely recognized that rather than offer predictions of the future, integrated climate impact assessments provide information on a plausible range of future outcomes that policymakers need to keep in mind.

Emphasis on mitigation and long-term climate change

Climate impact assessments have been focused more on mitigation and long-term climate change and less attention has been paid to the impact of climate hazards arising from climate variability and extreme weather events and on the policy options for adaptation and resilience. The focus on mitigation can be accounted for by the difficulty inherent in measuring adaptation. The concepts of adaptation and resilience have no common reference metrics comparable to the ones that exist for mitigation, namely, tons of greenhouse gases and radiative forcing values. Measuring adaptation would require a larger number of indicators relevant to each country and specific local context (Noble and others, 2014; see also chap. I).

---

5   Deep uncertainly arises when analysts do not know, or cannot agree on, how the climate system may change, how models represent possible changes or how to value the desirability of different outcomes (Jiménez Cisneros and others, 2014).

Nevertheless, the lack of common reference metrics for adaptation and resilience need not hinder analysis of those processes. By their very nature, adaptation and resilience are interwoven with broad development goals (i.e., reducing vulnerability to climate hazards requires livelihood improvements, food security, improved health systems, infrastructure development and better educational services). As meeting such goals requires a continuum of policies, planning and practices leading to transformative change and sustainable development (see chaps. I and II), any analysis that integrates those goals and policies will be multi-metric in nature. Integrated climate impact assessments are well suited to performing this function precisely because the multiplicity of models used makes it possible to integrate the different facets of development. The tools being used in integrated climate impact assessments also make it possible to analyse adaptation and resilience in the context not only of long-term climate change but also of climate hazards resulting from climate variability and extreme weather events.[6]

> **By virtue of their multi-metric nature, climate impact assessments help to integrate different dimensions of development, including adaptation and resilience**

Insufficient analysis of the macroeconomic feasibility of policies

In integrated climate impact assessments, the impacts detected in climate and biophysical models are translated into socioeconomic impacts using economic models in order to produce a standard accounting of the costs and benefits of climate policy, typically the costs and benefits of a single project or intervention. There has been a tendency to use economic models that are aggregated and simple in terms of their data requirements and estimation techniques.[7] However, it is important to broaden the scope of the analysis to encompass not just a simple cost-benefit analysis of a single invention, but also the economy-wide repercussions and macroeconomic feasibility of policies, which requires the use of more comprehensive modelling approaches. This is particularly important given both the existing gaps in the financing of adaptation and the need to scale up investments in order to build climate resilience as discussed below and in greater depth in chapter V.

> **It is important to consider the economy-wide repercussions and macroeconomic feasibility of policies for climate resilience**

Some of the most frequently used economic models (e.g., reduced-form econometric models) take prices as given, which means that they cannot trace changes in the allocation of resources resulting from price changes.[8] Other economic models (e.g., microeconomic structural and land-use models) do allow for changes in resource allocation but lack details

---

[6] From a methodological point of view, there is ample evidence of the severity of impacts from climate extremes and variability on people and livelihoods (see chaps. I and II). This evidence provides an order of magnitude of potential shocks inflicted on natural resources and socioeconomic systems. Such information can be used in designing scenarios for integrated climate impact assessments. The sequence of analytical steps may begin with imposing an exogenous change (i.e., a "shock") on national, regional or sectoral models, without necessarily linking this with global models (see figure III.1, upper right). This makes it possible to estimate the sensitivity of outcomes to climate variability and extreme weather events as well as evaluate policy options.

[7] However, it is not clear whether, on the contrary, the tendency to use the standard accounting of the costs and benefits of climate policy is actually due to a deliberate choice — that of using the simplest (albeit not the most useful) models available.

[8] Reduced-form econometric models are based on the notion that adaptive responses to climate change can be represented by equations that relate climate variables directly to economic outcomes. These models are estimated econometrically using cross-sectional or panel data (pooled cross-sectional and time series) and are then simulated using projected future climate variables to determine the impacts of climate change on the dependent variable in the model.

on how prices are determined in different markets. In practice, however, prices in the different markets of the economy change over time, particularly in contexts characterized by changing climatic conditions: some agents may allocate resources differently in response to these changes.[9] Not allowing for resource allocation effects in economic modelling also makes it difficult to evaluate the macroeconomic and financial feasibility of policies. The allocation of funds to finance the implementation of policies aimed at climate resilience can, for example, crowd out other climate and non-climate investments and have unintended consequences for the economy. This would represent a case of policy incoherence or maladaptation (see chap. IV).

It is important that these considerations be kept in mind when the wider costs and benefits of climate policies are being assessed for the national economy as a whole. This presupposes the use of economy-wide models that are well suited to assessing the economic and financial feasibility of policies for climate resilience while taking into consideration the macroeconomic constraints.[10]

The tendency to exclude inequalities or address them inadequately

Few climate impact assessments address inequalities, with their methodologies being generally unsuited to tracing impacts on vulnerable groups

Even though inequalities exacerbate the vulnerability and exposure of disadvantaged groups to climate hazards, as noted in chapters I and II, they are often overlooked in integrated climate impact assessments. Their methodologies are generally not suited to tracing impacts on specific groups that are particularly vulnerable and only a few of those assessments incorporate equality considerations. As noted in chapter II, this explains both why the discussion on the social impact of climate change has been limited and why the interlinkages between climate change and inequality have yet to be fully explored.

Equality considerations in relevant studies are limited to the analysis of the "social cost of carbon" — the expected present-value damages arising from carbon dioxide (CO_2) emissions.[11] This type of analysis provides estimates for socially desirable mitigation policies; however, those policies are difficult to implement because the analysis assumes that people who benefit from them will be better off if they compensate those negatively impacted by the policy, which may not be the case in practice.

Another important assumption in these studies is that a dollar given to a poor person is the same as a dollar given to a rich one, so that it is then possible to add up monetized welfare losses across disparate incomes. "Equity weights" have been introduced to "relax"

---

9   For example, the prices of internationally traded food commodities interact with climate change (Porter and others, 2014). Changes in these prices tend to have a greater effect, in particular, on the welfare of households that use a large income share to purchase staple crops (Olsson and others, 2014). As a consequence, these households may adapt by shifting their consumption habits, which would have implications for their vulnerability and well-being.

10   Economy-wide models are also known as computable general equilibrium (CGE) models. Partial equilibrium (PE) models and CGE models belong to the family of market equilibrium models. Both types of models help simulate the effects of "shocks" or changes in productivity, policy or other factors such as climate on various economic outcomes, including market equilibrium prices, production, productivity, consumption, trade and land use. CGE models are particularly suited to tracing effects that work through the different markets of the economy (e.g., factors, commodities and foreign exchange), under given macroeconomic constraints.

11   Present values in these assessments are estimated based on a discount rate. The lower the discount rate, the higher the estimates of climate-related costs. There is considerable disagreement among economists regarding the rate (or rates) at which future costs and benefits should be discounted.

this unrealistic assumption, which has significantly changed the results of calculating the social cost of an incremental emission (Anthoff, Hepburn and Tol, 2009). This has represented an important step towards accepting the suggestion that equality should be a prime concern in climate policy. However, owing to data restrictions, equity weights tend to be constructed based on average per capita income of regions rather than of individuals.[12] Furthermore, approaches to equity weighing may not be appropriate from the point of view of a national decision maker because domestic impacts of global emissions are not valued at domestic prices (Anthoff and Tol, 2010).

Not only is mitigation the focus of the studies cited above, but their approaches to equality (i.e., entailing the social cost of carbon and equity weights) are inadequate for the purpose of tracing impacts on the specific groups that are particularly vulnerable to climate hazards. Thus, there is a serious gap in addressing inequalities in the literature on integrated climate impact assessments, even in the few existing assessments that focus on adaptation.

The IPCC Fifth Assessment Report suggests that few assessments examine how inequalities shape differential vulnerabilities to climate change (see Olsson and others, 2014). A review of 13 economic assessments of adaptation options in the Fifth Assessment Report, spanning the period from 2006 to 2013, corroborates this observation (table III.1). Only two of the studies addressed health issues that matter for inequality, and in both, inequality was not a central theme. One analysis, whose focus was diarrhoeal diseases, placed emphasis on the major burdens among the poor and evaluated different policy options for addressing this vulnerability. The other study evaluated adaptation options that reduce undernourishment, a potentially serious public-health problem which can deprive generations of opportunities. While some of the studies provided an analysis of the effects of climate change on food security and the livelihoods of the rural poor, or considered different types of farms, they did so without making any explicit reference to inequalities; and another study considered inequalities only contextually. It is also noteworthy that few of the studies addressed the macroeconomic repercussions of adaptation policies.

> Only 2 of the 13 economic assessments of adaptation options reviewed in the IPCC Fifth Assessment Report addressed issues that matter for inequality

Analytical dimensions of inequalities in climate impact assessments

It is possible to use different combinations of modelling tools to explore the four analytical dimensions of inequalities as part of an integrated climate impact assessment that addresses adaptation, resilience, climate variability and extreme weather events. Existing modelling frameworks can be integrated to enable an exploration of four analytical dimensions of inequalities. The role of stakeholders in providing information and expertise is critical both to improving modelling results in general and to providing insights regarding vulnerabilities to climate hazards.

Table III.2 summarizes the four analytical dimensions of inequalities, and the different modelling frameworks that can be used to address each one of them. The present section discusses each dimension in detail with regard to its relevance for integrated climate impact assessments. It also presents the findings derived from existing analyses that help to explain the strengths and weaknesses of those modelling frameworks and show the kind of policy options that may function as enablers of climate resilience in a specific country context.

> Inequalities can be featured more prominently in integrated climate impact assessments through the combining of modelling tools

---

12   It has recently been shown that a more fine-grained representation of economic inequalities within regions is an important consideration for the estimation of the social cost of carbon (Dennig and others, 2015).

Table III.1
Consideration of inequalities in economic evaluations of adaptation options

Sector	Study, scope and methodology	Consideration of inequalities[a]
Agriculture, forestry and livestock	Seo and Mendelsohn (2008). Seo and others (2009). Economic choices of livestock owners to maintain production in the face of climate change in African countries. Econometric analysis	Different farm types, without analysis of inequalities
	Butt, McCarl and Kergna (2006). Economic implications of potential adaptation possibilities in cropping systems in Mali. Simulation analysis	The analysis shows that adaptation reduces climate change-related economic losses and undernourishment
	Sutton, Srivastava and Neumann (2013). Climate effects and adaptation for the crop sector in four Eastern European and Central Asian countries. Simulation with cost-benefit analysis. Considers non-market and socially contingent effects through the stakeholder consultation process	The analysis addresses the effects of climate change on food security and livelihoods of the rural poor. No explicit reference to inequalities is made
Sea-level rise and coastal systems	Nicholls and Tol (2006). Coastal regions at a global scale. Simulated adaptation options for coastal regions at the global scale (i.e., construction of sea walls and levees, beach nourishment and migration)	No
	Neumann (2009). Risks of sea-level rise for a portion of the coastal United States of America. Simulated adaptation options, including sea walls, bulkheads, elevation of structures, beach nourishment and strategic retreat	No
	Purvis, Bates and Hayes (2008). Risks of coastal flooding in Somerset, England. Simulation using a probabilistic representation to characterize uncertainty in future sea-level rise and other factors that could affect coastal land-use planning and development investment decisions	No
Water	Ward and others (2010). Water investments at the municipal level across the world, scaling down to national and local scales. Analysis through an optimization algorithm. Costs with and without climate change of reaching a water-supply target in 2050 are assessed	No
Urban flooding	Ranger and others (2011). Direct and indirect impacts of flooding in Mumbai, India. Global climate change downscaled to city level to investigate the consequences of floods and simulate improved housing quality and drainage and access to insurance	No
Energy	Pereira de Lucena and others (2010). Energy production in Brazil under future climate conditions, focusing on hydropower. Simulation of multiple adaptation options, including substitution of energy sources. Uses an optimization model of energy production	No
Health	Ebi (2008). Climate scenarios to address costs and policy responses. Global adaptation costs of treatment of diarrhoeal diseases, malnutrition, and malaria, downscaled for analysis in Indonesia and South Africa	Inequality is not the central theme but the analysis of diarrhoeal diseases places emphasis on the major burdens among the poor. Policy options include breastfeeding promotion, rotavirus immunization, measles immunization and improvement of water supply and sanitation
Macroeconomic analysis	De Bruin, Dellink and Tol (2009). Adaptation strategies compared with mitigation strategies for the world. Adaptation options include investments in infrastructure and market responses. Use of an integrated assessment model with refined adaptation functions to analyse policy options	No
	Margulis, Dubeux and Marcovitch (2011). Impacts of climate change trends on Brazil's economy. Socioeconomic trends approximate adaptation. Global trends downscaled to a general equilibrium model to quantify impacts on agricultural, livestock and energy sectors	Reference to inequalities is essentially contextual

Source: UN/DESA, adapted from Chambwera and others (2014), table 17-4. Last column has been added.

a There is deemed to be a consideration of inequalities if the study addresses inequalities in respect of access to basic public services, climate-related effects on human development, or income inequality.

Table III.2
Sources of inequality in modelling frameworks

Sources of inequality	Modelling approach	Strengths of modelling approach	Weaknesses of modelling approach
Livelihoods relying on climate-sensitive natural resources	Biophysical modelling	Detects impacts on livelihoods that depend on climate-sensitive natural resources	Relies on assumptions about behaviour without incorporating behavioural change, which is critical for adaptation
		Detects how changes in one natural resource may impact other natural resources	Changes in natural resources are not fully translated into socioeconomic changes
		Suggests how natural resources can be allocated more efficiently for adaptation	Does not specify effects on the livelihoods of disadvantaged groups in particular
			Data-intensive
Ownership and employment of production factors	Economy-wide modelling	Allows for estimation of indirect impacts of climate hazards and policies, detecting losers and winners; factor income distribution; resource allocation and thus some aspects of adaptation; and policy feasibility	Relies on assumptions regarding behaviour without incorporating behavioural change, which is critical for adaptation
		Can include human development indicators as a function of socio-economic determinants, including public investments in social sectors and infrastructure	Because of the aggregation of representative household groups, estimates of changes in income distribution may be biased
Human capital and access to public services and resources			Limited with respect to addressing other forms of primary inequality beyond income
			Data-intensive
Socioeconomic characteristics at the household level	Microsimulation modelling (with household surveys, prefereably linked to economy-wide model)	Adds value in identifying vulnerability associated with socioeconomic characteristics (e.g., gender, age, race, religion and ethnicity) whose intersection defines inequalities	Relies on assumptions about behaviour without incorporating behavioural change, which is critical for adaptation
		Points to possible policy options for reducing vulnerability	Limited analysis of financial feasibility of policies
		Less data-intensive when at least one household survey is available	Depends on the quality and coverage of household surveys

Source: UN/DESA.

Livelihoods and climate-sensitive natural resources

Livelihoods that depend on climate-sensitive natural resources, such as land, water and energy, are exposed to climate hazards (see chap. II). Amid poverty and structural inequalities, large groups of people and communities whose members secure a living in climate-sensitive environments also face high vulnerability to climate hazards. Understanding how such vulnerability translates into actual impacts on the economy and inequality first requires an analysis of the impacts of climate hazards on climate-sensitive natural resources.

Climate projections can be translated into changes in natural resource systems that support the livelihoods of vulnerable populations

This type of analysis begins with biophysical models (models for land, water and energy systems) which help translate climate projections (derived from climate models) into changes in natural resource systems. The analysis can be designed to assess adaptation options, too. For example, Bhave and others (2016) have downscaled regional scenarios of future climatic change through a water systems model in order to estimate impacts on water availability in India's Kangsabati river basin. In assessing policy options, they found that increasing forest cover is more suitable for addressing adaptation requirements than constructing check dams. Different studies in Cervigni and others, eds. (2015) use an energy systems model to channel the impacts of a wide range of future climate scenarios on hydropower and irrigation expansion plans in Africa's main river basins (Congo, Niger, Nile, Orange, Senegal, Volta and Zambezi). Those studies suggest that hydropower infrastructure needs to be developed irrespective of the scenario for water availability.[13]

Integration of climate, land, energy and water models facilitates an understanding of how natural resources can be allocated more efficiently for adaptation

Each natural resource systems model (whether for land, water or energy) is useful in its own right. However, a more holistic approach, through which those systems models are integrated, is better suited to facilitating an understanding of how changes in one resource resulting from a climate hazard may impact other resources, as well as how natural resources can be allocated more efficiently to meet the demands for crops, water and energy services, or to achieve a broader form of adaptation. A number of favourable studies present the advantages of using the Water-Energy-Food Security Nexus and Climate, Land, Energy and Water Systems (CLEWS) frameworks, which integrate different natural resource systems models.[14]

The International Renewable Energy Agency (IRENA) (2015) has reported the noteworthy findings derived from a number of exploratory case studies on the Water-Energy-Food Security Nexus. One study showed that half of China's proposed coal-fired power plants, which require significant water for cooling, are located in areas already affected by water stress, leading to potential conflicts between power plant operators and other water users. Another study demonstrated that, in India, where nearly 20 per cent of electricity-generation capacity is used for agricultural water pumping, lower-than-usual rainfall accompanied by decreasing water tables is putting tremendous stress on the electricity system during peak seasons. These two examples underline the functionality of the Water-Energy-Food Security Nexus approach in yielding important policy insights centred around the fact that water, which is constrained by climate change, faces competing allocations between energy generation and other uses such as in farming. The scarcity of water can hamper farmers in their pursuit of a livelihood and it may not be easy for them to find alternative means of coping with these changes.

Another example is provided by the island of Mauritius, where important policy concerns have been addressed using the CLEWS framework (Howells and others, 2013). Facing the recent loss of the sugar industry's export competitiveness, the Government has considered two policy objectives: developing bioethanol production to reduce greenhouse gas emissions and cutting energy imports. These objectives may have important implications for livelihoods because achieving them entails diverting sugarcane production away from export markets towards the domestic processing of bioethanol on an island where sugarcane plantations cover 80-90 per cent of cultivated land. The CLEWS analysis showed that

---

13 The studies find that under the driest climate scenarios, there could be significant losses of hydro-power revenues and increases in consumer expenditure for energy. Alternatively, under the wettest climate scenarios, substantial revenues could be forgone if the larger volume of precipitation was not utilized to expand hydropower production.

14 Using the CLEWS framework for Mauritius, Welsch and others (2014) have demonstrated the advantages of integrating natural resource systems instead of using an energy systems model alone to analyse energy pathways, given the importance of decreasing rainfall and future land-use changes.

the two policy objectives can be achieved, but not without important trade-offs. In recent years, lower rainfall has led to water shortages on the island which, under scenarios of climate change, implies that the water needed for sugarcane production would be supplied through irrigation so as to maintain bioethanol production. This would ultimately lead to a gradual drawdown of storage levels in reservoirs; and if the demand for more energy needed to desalinate water for irrigation is met with coal-fired power generation, as planned, then the greenhouse gas-related benefits of the bioethanol policy will be eroded by increased emissions from the power sector. Higher coal imports would also have a negative impact on energy security. Hence, the benefits of the policy are vulnerable to the impacts of climate change.

As a result, the island faces two possibilities. Either sugarcane producers will eventually have to scale back production (which would jeopardize the livelihood of populations that rely on that production) or they will have to resort to expensive water desalination (which would have detrimental environmental impacts). The CLEWS analysis has prompted the Government of Mauritius to start thinking about how to adapt to these challenges.[15]

This holistic approach to natural resource systems analysis offers a first point of entry into the area of analysing inequalities in integrated climate impact assessments. It allows for an understanding, with some precision, of how climate-sensitive natural resources are affected by climate hazards, with and without the presence of adaptation policies, and provides information on how, as a result, the livelihoods that depend on those resources are affected. However, identification of the specific distributional impacts of climate hazards and the policy options available to offset them would require additional socioeconomic analysis.

In the CLEWS analysis for Mauritius, for example, under the scenario where sugar cane producers scaled back production owing to climate change, unemployment, welfare and perhaps income distribution would likely be affected. The population that owns factors of production employed in the bioethanol industry, whether labour, capital or land, could be adversely affected in the process. However, these impacts are not quantifiable by applying the CLEWS methodology (nor by applying the Water-Energy-Food Security Nexus approach for that matter). They would require the complementary use of socioeconomic modelling tools to bridge this methodological gap. Economy-wide models are particularly well suited to initiating understanding on how changes in climate-sensitive natural resources, as identified through natural resource systems models, affect the economy. In addition, household survey analysis would be particularly useful in capturing the distributional impacts of shocks, including those affecting livelihoods in climate-sensitive environments.

Ownership of production factors and income distribution

Channelling the physical impacts of climate hazards on natural resources throughout the economy provides useful information on the income gains and losses of people with

> The holistic approach to natural resource systems analysis offers a first point of entry into the area of analysing inequalities in integrated climate impact assessments...

> ...but socioeconomic modelling frameworks are still necessary to assess changes in climate-sensitive natural resources throughout the economy

---

15   In his address delivered at the 3rd plenary meeting of the United Nations Conference on Sustainable Development, held in Rio de Janeiro, Brazil, from 20 to 22 June 2012, the Minister of Environment and Sustainable Development of Mauritius, Devan and Virahsawmy, pointed out that the government programme for 2012-2015 already provided for the appointment of a high-level CLEWS panel to ensure an integrated approach to all climate, land, energy and water strategies (see http://webtv. un.org/search/mauritius-general-debate-3rd-plenary-meeting-rio20/1700992573001?term=Devanand%20Virahsawmy).

different factor endowments, these being labour, land and capital. Climate hazards have disproportionate impacts on the assets of vulnerable groups owing to the disruption of economic activity and the resulting unemployment of production factors. For disadvantaged groups, a small but adverse change in the employment of the production factors upon which their livelihoods rely (generally labour and land) will likely exacerbate their vulnerability and exposure to climate hazards. However, the impact of climate hazards propagates throughout the entire economy: poverty and distributional impacts will be the result of the multiple direct and indirect effects of the initial shock. This multiplicity of transmission mechanisms emerging from the direct impact of climate hazards justifies the use of economy-wide models in integrated climate impact assessments.

Economy-wide modelling analysis can transmit the impacts of climate hazards through the employment of production factors...

Several examples help illustrate the functionality of the economy-wide modelling framework. Sánchez (2016) shows that, within the context of the Plurinational State of Bolivia, a reduction in labour productivity as a result of the impact of rising temperature on workers' health, or a destruction of public infrastructure after an extreme weather event, can result in lower labour wages, both in absolute terms and relative to capital. Household members whose livelihoods rely on labour income, and who generally belong to vulnerable groups, lose out in the process. While additional scenarios show that public investment options would help in coping with the simulated climate shocks, further analysis indicates that, under existing fiscal constraints, financial options for these investments may jeopardize macroeconomic stability and economic growth. The fact that some policy options may thus have unintended consequences points to the importance of analysing the macroeconomic feasibility of policies for climate resilience.

...enabling the identification of "winners" and "losers" with and without adaptation options

This type of economy-wide analysis also permits identification of situations where there may be winners from changing climate conditions, which could result in a reduction of inequality and poverty. The same analysis for the Plurinational State of Bolivia (Sánchez, 2016) shows that, in an alternative scenario where the world price of food increased, presumably as a result of climate change, farmers and food producers would win relative to producers in other sectors. Unskilled non-salaried workers would benefit most from the food price shock because of the large presence in food production of small-scale farmers and self-employed workers, who constitute an important share of the total population. In the face of a situation such as this, public policies would have an important role to play in strengthening the capacity of small-scale food producers to benefit from the price hike by facilitating market access and the eventual increase in production. In addition, policy options would have to be considered for reducing the burden imposed by the price shock on vulnerable consumers.

Another interesting example in this regard is provided by a recent integrated climate impact assessment, undertaken under the auspices of the International Food Policy Research Institute (IFPRI) (Andersen and others, 2016). The analysis estimates the impact of crop-yield losses in the order of 10-30 per cent over the next half century owing to the impact of climate change. The study finds that such a significant shock would not necessarily translate into proportional income losses for farmers or the population in general if farmers were to find ways to adapt autonomously. It was found that this would indeed be the case within the contexts of Brazil and Mexico if farmers in these countries had the capacity to modify planting dates in order to maximize crop yields, shift towards climate-resilient crops or migrate to different agro-climatic zones. As a result, the final effects of climate change would tend to be smaller than that of the initial crop-yield shock and the net effects on income of different household groups would be modest in either direction. In Mexico, 80 different household types were analysed (differentiated by gender of household head, agroecological zone and income decile), with impacts being very similar for them all, i.e., there were tiny losses in welfare between 0.1 and 0.3 per cent. Interestingly, this small effect on income across income deciles is robust to the choice of climate model (figure III.2).

Figure III.2

Combined impacts of global price and local yield changes on net present value of household welfare in Mexico, by income decile, under a climate change scenario relative to a perfect mitigation scenario

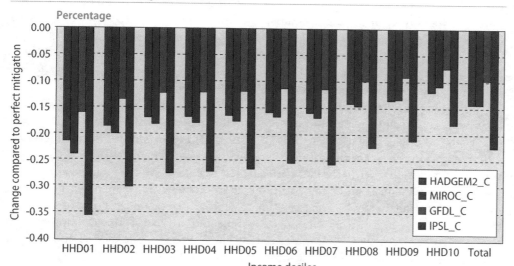

Source: Andersen and others (2016), figure 28.
Note: HHD01 to HHD10 = first to tenth income decile, _C = combined scenario of global price changes and local yield changes, resulting from climate changes simulated through four global climate models (GFDL, HADGEM2, IPSL and MIROC). These scenarios are passed on to an economy-wide model for Mexico so that income effects can be analysed.

While the IFPRI study was not intended to analyse adaptation policies per se, the results of such a study are useful in informing policymaking aimed at climate resilience. It suggests that the capacity of farmers to adapt autonomously to climate change is critical in the long run. Policy options with a focus on inequality and poverty should thus accelerate this adaptation process through, for example, public investments in infrastructure that boost productivity and incentives for adopting climate-resilient technologies. Further analysis of planned adaptation strategies, in farming, for example, might be explored by integrating more disaggregated models, such as crop and livestock models as explained further below.

Albeit a necessary step, the analysis of income generated (mostly through employment of production factors) and its distribution across different household groups is insufficient. It is useful because households located at the lowest deciles of a distribution are those that tend to exercise relatively less ownership over production factors and assets in general. They are generally vulnerable and understanding how their income changes in the face of climate hazards is important. Changes in the income of these households can be compared with changes in the income of households located in higher income brackets. However, this approach to distributive analysis is still highly aggregative, even if households groups are classified according to income decile, and misses out on the details of income distribution within household groups, which can ultimately affect the well-being of vulnerable

Assessments need to be taken one step further — to the microlevel — to facilitate an understanding of impacts across households

households.[16] Nor is economy-wide analysis alone well suited to addressing other forms of inequality, including those that are determined by certain configurations of socioeconomic characteristics such as gender, age, race, religion and ethnicity. Analysis at a level that is more micro in nature helps surmount these methodological limitations, but before describing that form of analysis, it is important to understand another useful feature of the economy-wide modelling approach.

Human capital, public services and resources

Exploring human development policy options for the resilience of disadvantaged groups is a necessary facet of climate impact assessments

In coping with climate hazards, the poor and disadvantaged groups often face the difficult choice between protecting their human capital (health and education) and preserving their physical capital or even their consumption levels (see chap. II). Those groups face such choices because they are under an income constraint and may also have insufficient access to basic public services and resources. These are factors that act as important determinants of vulnerability to climate hazards. Exploring human development policy options for the climate resilience of these groups is a necessary facet of climate impact assessments.

The long-term effects of climate change on human development have been estimated mainly through using (reduced-form) econometric models, which found that climate change, for example, would reduce life expectancy, in Peru (Andersen, Suxo and Verner, 2009); depress people's incomes, in Chile (Andersen and Verner, 2010); and encourage within-country migration, in the Plurinational State of Bolivia (Andersen, Lund and Verner, 2010). Some economists argue that such long-term econometric estimations constitute a means of capturing the various economic adjustments or adaptations that occur in response to climate change and can be interpreted as reflecting a type of "analog" approach to climate impact assessment (Antle and Valdivia, 2016). Econometric models, however, do not provide information on the feasibility of human development policy options within a consistent macroeconomic framework.

Human development options can be addressed within the contours of economy-wide modelling. In this case, the models have the potential to specify human development indicators as a function of socioeconomic determinants such as household income; private and public spending on education, health, water and sanitation; and public infrastructure.[17] These indicators enhance the multi-metric character of integrated climate impact assessments and bring inequality in access to basic services to the forefront of the analysis. However, while economy-wide analyses with these characteristics do exist, they have not featured prominently in climate impact assessments.

For example, an economy-wide analysis for Bolivia (Plurinational State of), Costa Rica and Uganda presenting such characteristics has explored the scope for scaling up public investments in human development by raising public revenue through an implicit carbon tax (Sánchez and Zepeda, 2016). Scenarios show that the direct impact of imposing a carbon tax will be to reduce economic growth, but that this unintended consequence could

---

16   Even an approach that introduces a function to represent the income distribution within each household group is limited by the assumption that the variance of the distribution within each group is fixed.

17   It is important to underline that economy-wide models may in this case still necessitate an econometric approach, through which the elasticities of human development indicators with respect to socioeconomic determinants are estimated. Using econometrically estimated parameters is an accepted practice, particularly in an assessment approach that relies on the integration of modelling tools.

be offset by increasing investments in public infrastructure. The overall economy-wide impact of a carbon tax to finance public investments will be increasing economic growth, improved primary completion rates and reduced child mortality rates. The improvement in social indicators is the result of more equal access to basic public services in education and health. The construction of this type of scenario can inform decision-making processes through exploration of options for building development policy coherence by pursuing the simultaneous objectives of reducing greenhouse gas emissions and building climate resilience through reduction of inequalities in the access to basic services.

Additional examples in this regard are found in economy-wide modelling analyses for 27 countries from different developing regions which demonstrated that scaling up public spending in primary education, health, and water and sanitation would have allowed for faster progress towards achieving the Millennium Development Goals (Sánchez and others, 2010; Sánchez and Vos, 2013).[18] However, these analyses also illustrate the importance of giving full consideration to the financial sources for investment, as fiscal sustainability and economic growth were found to be in peril when particular financing options were utilized. Again, this type of analysis is useful in assessing trade-offs associated with building resilience through improved access to basic public services without jeopardizing economic growth and macroeconomic stability.

Socioeconomic characteristics at the household level

Alone or combined, gender, race, ethnicity, religion and other socioeconomic attributes of people, can, depending on context, generate inequalities with important roles in defining exposure and vulnerability to climate hazards (see chap. II). Analysis conducted at the micro level making better use of household surveys adds value in terms of identifying households whose exposure and vulnerability are determined by specific socioeconomic characteristics.

Such an analysis need not be complex: it can rely on a single household survey and a simple definition of vulnerability. Andersen and Cardona (2013), for example, used the household survey for 2011 of the Plurinational State of Bolivia to construct indicators of vulnerability (and resilience) on the basis of level and diversification of income. Using these indicators to identify the types of households most likely to be vulnerable to shocks according to different socioeconomic attributes (see appendix III.1), they found that the households that were particularly at risk of being vulnerable were young households with high dependency burdens, large households, urban households (given that, in the Plurinational State of Bolivia, it is income in rural areas that is more diversified) and households in indigenous communities. Importantly, how socioeconomic characteristics shape vulnerabilities is context-specific. Using a panel of data from the Ethiopian Rural Household Survey (1994-2004), Dercon, Hoddinott and Woldehanna (2005) found that female-headed households were particularly vulnerable to drought-induced shocks.

This kind of analysis utilizing household surveys provides useful information for policy analysis through the simple microsimulation of counterfactual scenarios. For example, a microsimulation of an evenly distributed cash transfer in the Plurinational State of Bolivia in the amount of 80 bolivianos (Bs) per person per month (equivalent to US$ 0.38 per day), using the same 2011 household survey mentioned above, showed that, although

Analysis using household surveys helps identify households whose exposure and vulnerability are determined by specific socioeconomic characteristics...

...and provides useful information for policy analysis through the simple microsimulation of counterfactual scenarios

---

18 For a combined analysis of the public spending and economic growth results for all 27 developing countries, see United Nations (2016, chap. II).

the transfer was not sufficient to ensure survival, it did reduce vulnerability and increased resilience (table III.3). When the monthly transfer was targeted specifically at people living in poverty, the transfer increased substantially (to Bs 175) without, however, increasing the total costs of the programme. Although the exercise considered neither the feasibility of financing such a programme nor the complexities of targeting, it did point to the potential effectiveness of that programme in reducing vulnerability and increasing resilience.

Table III.3

Effects of policies on per capita income, vulnerability and resilience under microsimulation scenarios in the Plurinational State of Bolivia

Baseline scenario and alternative scenarios	Income per capita (Bs per month per person)	Share of households that are highly vulnerable (percentage)	Share of households that are highly resilient (percentage)
Baseline situation, Plurinational State of Bolivia, 2011	1 360	14.9	33.5
Citizen salary of Bs 80 per month per person	1 440	6.3	45.3
Cash transfer of Bs 175 per month to all poor persons	1 428	3.7	44.1
Prevention of all teenage pregnancies	1 464	11.3	38.7

Source: Microsimulations based on the vulnerability methodology of Andersen and Cardona (2013).
Note: Vulnerable households have low levels of income and of income diversification. Resilient households do not live in poverty and their income is diversified. The thresholds that determine when a household is "highly vulnerable" or "highly resilient" are defined in appendix III.1.

More complex policy microsimulation scenarios can be evaluated. For example, consider a scenario where, rather than bear children before they are 20 years of age, young Bolivian women work for a minimum wage (Bs 815 per month). It is assumed implicitly that instead of raising children in their teens, those women were able to receive more of an education and have more time to work. The results of this scenario show an increase in per capita income and a reduction in the share of vulnerable households. Although this policy does not yield results as impressive as those achieved under the simulated programme of cash transfers to all people living in poverty, as described above, it requires a much lower investment of public resources (less than 1 per cent of the costs of the cash transfer programme). In contrast, the simulated universal cash transfer requires public spending in the order of 5 per cent of gross domestic product (GDP).

Supplementing household survey analysis with economy-wide analysis is necessary when putting the economic feasibility of social policies under scrutiny

Complementing such microsimulation analysis with the use of an economy-wide model helps determine if such social protection policies would be economically feasible in practice. Typically, the analysis begins by developing an understanding of the macroeconomic repercussions of the policy and its financial and macroeconomic feasibility through the use of an economy-wide model. Subsequently, key information on employment and income changes emanating from this analysis is passed on to the household survey to determine distributive impacts through microsimulation (Vos and Sánchez, 2010). The strength of this approach lies in the fact that effects are quantified for the "full" income distribution (i.e., at a disaggregated level) and not across different types of household groups, as would be the case if an economy-wide model was used alone. Combining these two methodologies is highly useful in integrated climate impact assessments.

It was not until recently that methods for including income distribution in economy-wide models for long-term climate change research began to be reviewed (see van Ruijven, O'Neill and Chateau, 2015). On the other hand, some already existing studies have provided interesting illustrations of the usefulness of this approach. Cicowiez and Sánchez (2011), for example, applied the approach to assess the impacts and feasibility of cash transfer programmes targeting households living in poverty in Latin American countries. They found that while these transfers led unambiguously to a reduction in income inequality, financing and sustaining them under existing fiscal constraints depended largely on sustained economic growth.

Vulnerability through the lens of stakeholders

The modelling frameworks described above can generate scenarios for climate resilience that are useful in informing policymaking, particularly when they are integrated. As noted in the introduction to the present chapter, those scenarios are characterized by uncertainty and by the intrinsic limitations of modelling, which is what has prompted analysts and researchers to work with stakeholders. Feedback from stakeholders on the ground is proving useful in the design and reassessment of scenarios, and the incorporation of the detailed information provided has helped reduce uncertainties.[19] This feedback is in fact critical because stakeholders provide information and share knowledge regarding factors that exacerbate their exposure and vulnerability to climate hazards, on one hand, and adaptation options that are relevant to increasing their resilience, on the other.

The benefits of engaging stakeholders in scenario design and policy dialogue are well documented. In its consideration of adaptation to future flood risk in the Thames Estuary, the United Kingdom Environment Agency applied four scenarios over three time periods to flood management. Based on the outcome of a wide consultation process, it was determined that improving the current infrastructure would continue to be the preferred strategy until 2070, when construction of an outer barrage might become justifiable, especially as economic and climate change conditions changed over time (O'Brien and others, 2012). To facilitate the analysis centred on water availability and climate change in India's Kangsabati river basin, as mentioned above, the authors organized multilevel stakeholder workshops to identify and prioritize adaptation options which were subsequently evaluated using a water systems model (Bhave and others, 2016). Another study entailed an examination of climate impacts and adaptation within the context of the crop sector in four countries in the region of Eastern Europe and Central Asia. The scenarios considered non-market and socially contingent effects, including information derived from a stakeholder consultation process (Sutton, Srivastava and Neumann, 2013).

The Agricultural Model Intercomparison and Improvement Project (AgMIP) is perhaps one of the best examples of an initiative relying on stakeholders for scenario-building. The Inter-comparison and Improvement Project developed the regional integrated assessment (RIA) framework and the concept of representative agricultural pathways (RAPs). While the RIA framework links global and regional scenarios essentially along the

Uncertainty and the intrinsic limitations of modelling require stakeholders' engagement in building scenarios and discussing results

---

19   From a modelling point of view, this feedback helps to improve model "parametrization" and calibration (Jiménez Cisneros and others, 2014), among other benefits.

lines of the integrated approach discussed above, a number of features of this framework stand out.[20] Using farm survey data for regions, the framework enables the study of heterogeneous populations of farm households whose livelihoods depend on agricultural systems. Representative agricultural pathways are one of the outstanding features: they add further details about the future socioeconomic (non-climate) conditions to which farm households may be exposed and also help project a level of detail on inputs that generally does not exist in models.

Engaging decision makers, experts and farmers has proved critical in modelling climate change impacts and adaptation options...

In developing their regional studies with the AgMIP-RIA framework, research teams engage in ongoing interactions and activities with stakeholders over the life of the project (figure III.3). Specific milestones are reached by or during the AgMIP regional workshops. Two groups of stakeholders participate: higher-level decision makers and experts, and communities of farmers. The interactions with these stakeholders are particularly important for scenario design; they follow several cycles, with each cycle encompassing the several steps needed to develop the representative agricultural pathways (starting in the midterm workshops).

The AgMIP-RIA framework is being applied by regional teams (researchers and stakeholders) in sub-Saharan Africa and South Asia to assess climate change impacts, vulnerability and the potential for adaptation strategies. For these assessments, the regional

Figure III.3
The AgMIP national and regional engagement process

Ongoing team/stakeholder meetings to identify interested stakeholders and important regional issues → Ongoing collaboration between teams and stakeholders to create representative agricultural pathways and identify adaptations

Kick-off workshops	Midterm workshops	Finish line workshop
• Stakeholders learn about AgMIP overall • Stakeholders provide research teams with regional priorities, key climate-related decisions and questions • Stakeholders familiarized with initial AgMIP plans for regional integrated assessments • Stakeholders provide feedback on initial methods and tools	• Teams share findings of ongoing research • Stakeholders give feedback on research • Stakeholders and research teams co-generate representative agricultural pathways (RAPs) and identify set of adaptation strategies • Stakeholder interviews establish decision-making context, information needs, driving motivations for encouragement with AgMIP • Stakeholder panel provides feedback on current process and future challenges	• Teams present research highlights and key messages • Stakeholder panel responds, including on challenges not yet addressed • Stakeholders assess how they can interact with AgMIP research outputs • Stakeholders and research teams co-draft climate risk information • Stakeholders share perspectives and ongoing priorities • Teams and stakeholders stake out a path for longer collaboration

Source: Antle and Valdivia (2016).

20 Crop and livestock models are used to translate the biophysical consequences of climate change into economic impacts at the regional level. These impacts are further understood through simulations using the microeconomic structural model known as the Trade-off Analysis model for Multidimensional impact assessment (TOA-MD). For a stylized representation of the linkages between models and data for climate impact, adaptation, mitigation and vulnerability assessment in the AgMIP-RIA framework, see Antle and Valdivia (2016), figure 5.

teams devise representative agricultural pathways for each of the regions providing region-specific information that supports the construction of several key indicators describing future biophysical and socioeconomic conditions (Valdivia and others, 2015). The knowledge shared by stakeholders has been critical for capturing the large degree of heterogeneity in the key indicators and trends among the regions' farm population.[21] This is a key factor in modelling the way in which systems are impacted by climate change and how they can adapt to it.

Because it is heterogeneous populations that are under study, unsurprisingly, the AgMIP regional studies demonstrate that there is a wide range of vulnerability to climate change under current socioeconomic conditions. About 60 per cent of farmers, across study sites, are currently vulnerable to net income losses due to climate change (figure III.4). Results also show that under a scenario characterized by more favourable future socioeconomic conditions (as defined by the regional representative agricultural pathways), 40 per cent of farmers (not 60 per cent, as under current conditions) would be vulnerable to climate change, which means both an avoidance of potential income losses and the experiencing of less poverty. This demonstrates the importance of accelerated socioeconomic developments in reducing vulnerability to climate change and poverty.

Figure III.4

Current and future climate change impacts on farms located in agricultural regions of Africa and South Asia, 2005 and 2050

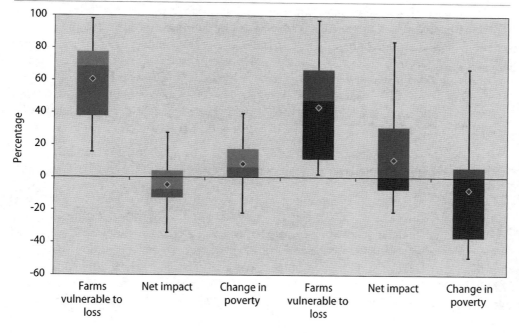

Source: Antle and Valdivia (2016), based on data in Rosenzweig and Hillel, eds. (2015).
Note: Impacts are estimated from a climate change scenario using the integrated climate impact assessment approach described above (adding a crop model). This scenario was generated under current conditions and more favourable socioeconomic conditions in the future, as perceived by farmers (and captured by representative agricultural pathways). The results for current and future conditions are presented for 2005 and 2050, respectively. Bars include the results for all farms in the areas of study; within the bars, boxes represent quartiles and diamonds represent averages. Boxes in light blue (left side) and dark blue (right side) indicate current and future socio-economic conditions, respectively. Net impact represents the net effect on farm returns.

21   For example, a trend towards increased soil degradation has been identified as a major issue by researchers working with stakeholders. However, the magnitude of soil degradation is not as large in regions where there is more government investment in agriculture, promotion of better soil conservation activities, and increased fertilizer use.

...and has helped reduce uncertainty in scenario results and produce a more realistic assessment of options

A comparison of AgMIP studies analysing impacts of climate change in regions in Senegal and Zimbabwe attests to the importance of engaging stakeholders so as to reduce uncertainty in scenario results. The Senegal team used model-based projections of price and productivity trends, while the Zimbabwe team used price and productivity trends estimated from interactions with stakeholders and local experts. The results for Senegal show a larger variability in the range of net economic impacts and also a much larger positive impact of improved socioeconomic conditions in the future. In the case of Zimbabwe, direct interaction with farmers improved the precision of estimates (i.e., it reduced uncertainty) and facilitated a more realistic assessment of the possibilities of improved socioeconomic conditions.[22]

Preliminary analyses of adaptation strategies for some of these regions also show that there are substantial opportunities to offset the adverse impacts and enhance the beneficial effects of climate change (Rosenzweig and Hillel, eds., 2015), pointing further to the usefulness of integrated climate impact assessments when they are designed in collaboration with stakeholders. With regard to the Nkayi region of Zimbabwe, scenarios built in collaboration with stakeholders have made it clear that asset ownership is an important contributor to an understanding of the unequal effects of climate change and the effectiveness of adaptation strategies (box III.1). Scenario results show that without adaptation measures, farmers possessing cattle are more exposed, inasmuch as the main adverse impact of climate change is not on crops but on livestock feed availability and livestock productivity. However, farms without cattle are poorer and more dependent on a single source of farm income, and are thus more vulnerable to climate change. Indeed, in the absence of adaptation, the impact of climate change will be relatively greater on farms with no cattle. With adequate adaptations in farming, and once account is taken of the factors that determine differential levels of exposure and vulnerability across the spectrum of farmers, the simulated scenarios yield substantial impacts on per capita incomes, significantly increasing the incomes of the poorest farmers. These results point to the importance of engaging with stakeholders, particularly communities (in this case, farm communities), to uncover the aspects of poverty and inequalities that are relevant for modelling analysis and for consideration of policy options.

Challenges going forward

Inequality analysis is a central component of climate impact assessments; and feedback from stakeholders is critical to design and assessment of the scenarios that underpin it

This chapter has described how integrated climate impact assessments can assemble different modelling frameworks to generate an understanding of the economic, social and environmental challenges posed by climate hazards to exposed and vulnerable people and the policy options available to confront those challenges. Several suggestions have been made on how to broaden the analytical scope of those assessments along different lines, for example, through incorporation of adaptation, resilience, and climate hazards (including extreme events). It is also critical to consider the economy-wide feasibility of policies for climate resilience, especially given that, as discussed further in chapter V, bridging the financial gaps in adaptation presents a particular challenge going forward. Putting inequalities at the forefront of these assessments is an essential means of shifting the focus of attention towards the very core of the climate change adaptation challenge. To this end,

---

22   See Antle and Valdivia (2016) for an integrated presentation of results derived from the regional studies presented in Masikati and others (2015) and Adiku and others (2015).

Box III.1

Climate change and adaptation strategies in the Nkayi region of Zimbabwe

The regional integrated assessment (RIA) framework of the Agricultural Model Intercomparison and Improvement Project (AgMIP) was applied by a research team in Zimbabwe, with the aim of generating information on adaptation strategies for crop-livestock systems in the Nkayi region (Masikati and others, 2015). The research process was conceptualized as a long-term dialogue for co-learning, where researchers interacted with stakeholders in exploring and designing alternative sets of plausible future scenarios and climate change adaptation packages for integrated modelling (Homman-Kee and others, 2016; and Homman-Kee and others, forthcoming). Different adaptation options in maize farming for particular farm types and entire communities were assessed through integrated modelling.

Table III.1.1 summarizes research results that have been used in an economic analysis of climate change impacts for the Nkayi farm population, as stratified into three groups: farms without cattle; farms with less than eight heads of cattle (small herd); and farms with more than eight heads of cattle (large herd). Without adaptation, vulnerability to loss from climate change ranges from 45 per cent of farm households without cattle to 61 per cent and 71 per cent of households with small and large herds, respectively. The households with cattle are more exposed because the main adverse impact of climate change is found to fall on livestock feed availability and livestock productivity. Losses range from 25 to 57 per cent of mean farm net returns before climate change, which is a substantial figure for the vulnerable households. However, some farms benefit from favourable biophysical and economic conditions, with gains ranging from 28 to 34 per cent of mean returns before climate change. The net impacts aggregated across all farms are positive but small for farms without livestock, and much larger but negative for farms with large herds. Even though the losses represent a larger proportion of farm income for the farms with cattle, the farms without cattle are much poorer. Thus, with climate change, the negatively impacted farms without cattle will be in an even worse-off condition than before climate change and much poorer than the farms with cattle.

"Adopters" generally reap greater farm net returns compared with "non-adopters". Farms without cattle are very likely to adopt the adaptation measures being considered, with adoption rates of about 96 per cent under the rapid adaptation scenario and over 75 per cent under the transitional adaptation scenario, where the benefits are realized more gradually, over 10 years. While these farms gain relatively more (as a percentage of their farm income) than farms with cattle, they do not necessarily gain more in absolute terms because of their much lower incomes. The reason for the relatively smaller impact of climate change on farms without livestock and their greater benefit from adaptation is that the adaptations under analysis result in a greater improvement in crop productivity than in livestock productivity. The adaptations have substantial impacts on per capita incomes, more than doubling the farm incomes of the poorest households.

In this analysis, resilience is defined as the capability of a system to minimize the magnitude of adverse impacts or enhance positive effects. Resilience analysis considered two adaptation scenarios: transitional adaptation, where farmers need five years to realize the full benefits of the practices (owing, for example, to learning requirements) and rapid adaptation, where farmers realize the full benefits immediately. As the rapid adaptation scenario is interpreted as entailing minimum loss, resilience is in this case 100 per cent. The no-adaptation and transitional adaptation cases are evaluated relative to the rapid adaptation case. The analysis considers the benefits over a 10-year period, using a discount rate of 10 per cent.

Under these assumptions, the no-adaptation scenario assigns to the farms without cattle a resilience of 91 per cent, a figure that is somewhat higher than that for the resilience of the systems with cattle (both small and large herds) (79 per cent). With the adaptation package,

(continued)

Box III.1 (*continued*)

Table III.1.1
Vulnerability, resilience and net economic impacts of climate change projected until 2050 for crop-livestock systems in Nkayi, Zimbabwe, without and with adaptation scenarios

Percentage								
			Climate impact on net returns				Adoption of adaptations	
Stratum	Adaptation	Vulnerability	Gains	Losses	Net impact	Resilience	Adoption rate	Adopter gain
No cattle	None	45	28	-25	3	91	-	-
No cattle	Transition	18	73	-32	41	93	75	60.5
No cattle	Rapid	1	139	-20	119	100	96	136
Small herd	None	61	32	-41	-9	79	-	-
Small herd	Transition	39	42	-33	9	93	80	20
Small herd	Rapid	25	51	-27	24	100	98	51
Large herd	None	71	34	-57	-23	79	-	-
Large herd	Transition	46	47	-42	5	98	64	43
Large herd	Rapid	42	48	-40	8	100	80	87

Source: Antle and Valdivia (2016).
Note: Transitional adaptation occurs over five growing seasons, rapid adaptation in the first growing season. Gains, losses and gains to adopters are expressed as a percentage of mean farm net returns before climate change. Vulnerability is defined in terms of the proportion of households that are at risk of losing net returns and resilience in terms of the proportion capable of minimizing the magnitude of adverse impacts or enhancing positive effects. Antle and Valdivia offer more precise definitions.

these resilience factors are improved substantially. This analysis thus illustrates the potential benefits of enhancing the adaptive capability of farmers, thereby enabling them — when effective adaptation options are available and can be readily adopted — to reduce vulnerability substantially and enhance resilience.

it has been suggested that different modelling frameworks should be integrated in response to the specific policy questions confronting each country, depending on data availability. Improved use of integrated modelling frameworks along these lines will contribute to the assessment of the impacts of climate hazards and policies relating to:

- Climate-sensitive natural resources upon which livelihoods rely, using biophysical models
- Distribution of income on the basis of ownership and employment of production factors (land, capital, labour), using economy-wide models
- Human capital and access to basic public services and resources (education, health, sanitation, infrastructure), using economy-wide models
- Vulnerabilities of disadvantaged groups that are defined based on a configuration of socioeconomic attributes, explored through more intensive use of household surveys and microsimulation analysis

In view of the inherent limitations of any modelling exercise, engaging different stakeholders (including policymakers, experts and communities) is an important means of procuring the sort of detailed information and feedback that are critical to the design of model-based scenarios and reassessment of those scenarios and their results. The meaningful participation of stakeholders assures the input of local political and expert judgment. The feedback of vulnerable population groups and communities is particularly important for achieving an understanding of the factors that exacerbate people's exposure and vulnerability to climate hazards, including how those factors may relate to structural inequalities as people experience them. It is also important when assessing adaptation options to ensure that they are made relevant to the building of climate resilience among people and communities.

It is indeed regrettable that not all developing countries are in a position to apply integrated climate impact assessments at the level of detail needed to inform policy. Some countries are using partial quantitative assessments, qualitative evaluations and expert judgment to promote an understanding of the links between climate and socioeconomic conditions, which represents a good starting point. Many countries conduct at least a household survey which, as noted, can be highly instrumental in identifying drivers of households' exposure and vulnerability which provide a basis for analysing policy options. However, these partial approaches, unlike integrated climate impact assessments, cannot fully capture the interlinkages among the different aspects of development that are important in assessing the policy options for building climate resilience and achieving sustainable development that are available to countries. Extending the use of integrated climate impact assessments to inform policy in developing countries requires dedicated efforts in three areas: (a) improving basic information systems and statistics, (b) building countries' capacity to construct and use modelling tools for integrated assessments and (c) strengthening institutional capacities to support evidenced-based policymaking and implementation, including the use of integrated assessments as part of policy decision-making processes, with proper dissemination of results, and stakeholders' engagement in the assessment of policy options.

Extending the use of climate impact assessments requires improved information systems, improved technical expertise and strengthened governance...

With regard to data and statistics at a level that is more macro in character, there is a gap in environmental accounting and climate-related statistics and indicators. Nevertheless, the United Nations, other multilateral institutions and countries themselves have already started making headway in this area. It is at the micro level, however, that the most critical information gap exists. Information to help identify characteristics of vulnerable populations at the local level in developing regions, where adaptation is most needed, is lacking (see chap. V). The regional studies developed by the AgMIP project, as noted above, relied on their own farm surveys in different regions because that type of information is not collected under standardized processes. There is also limited access to other important sources of information (e.g., global climate projections, geographic information systems, visualization of sea level and forest coverage). Collaboration with the international statistical community will play a fundamental role in building new and assessing existing data and statistical capacity (see chap. V).

...which in turn requires international collaboration on bridging gaps at the country level

Building capacity to construct and use integrated assessments at the country level is also important. While greater efforts are needed to improve the production of data and statistics, it is also true that existing information is underutilized. As noted above, a large number of countries have at least one household survey which can be used to address issues related to vulnerability and inequality at some levels of disaggregation that are relevant to support of development policies (United Nations, 2016). Modelling capacities should also be strengthened in areas where information exists. For example, crop simulation models, which are used extensively in climate change studies, are not widely used in developing countries. White and others (2011) examined 211 peer-reviewed papers that used crop simulation models to examine different facets of the question of how climate change might affect agricultural systems. The main focus of those papers (approximately 170) was the response to climate change of producers of wheat, maize, soybean and rice. The United States of America (with 55 papers) and Europe (with 64 papers) were the dominant regions studied.

Scenario-building that supports policymaking and implementation requires procedural stability, and permanent yet flexible institutional and governance structures which build the trust and experience needed to take advantage of new insights for effective and fair risk management (Volkery and Ribeiro, 2009). This includes institutionalizing the use of the integrated analytical framework within government, using scenario results to inform policymaking and propel policy implementation; coordinating and mobilizing technical expertise across sectoral ministries; and working with stakeholders and researchers at all levels. In other words, what is required are changes in the policy system (see chap. IV).

Timely, fluent and effective communication of climate impact assessment results improves understanding of the policy options available for building resilience

Communicating the results of integrated climate impact assessments, within government and to stakeholders at large, is another area where improvement is needed. Timely, fluent and effective communication of those results is critical to improving understanding of the multiple interlinkages that exist across the different dimensions of development and the policy options available for building resilience. A wider communication of results is an instrument that is useful in engaging multiple stakeholders in policy dialogues oriented towards identifying priorities based on informed options. Finding adequate communication mechanisms that help influence behaviour for reducing the risk of maladaptation is also important (see chap. IV).

Translating, reporting and communicating results through user-friendly visualizations are grounded in statistical techniques, which also require capacity-building efforts. Along the same lines, broad dissemination channels (e.g., television, radio and Internet broadcasts, blogs and high-level summits) constitute a useful means of creating widespread awareness among the general public. Evidence from the Advancing Capacity for Climate Change Adaptation (ACCCA) project, UKCIP (formerly known as the United Kingdom Climate Impacts Programme) and IPCC (2012) suggests that these broad communication channels do work. Indeed, interactive strategies, group discussions, workshops and user-friendly and visually appealing documentation will be critical tools for communicating and working with stakeholders and researchers at the local level. Such outreach mechanisms for communicating scenario results are learning and discussion platforms which serve to facilitate knowledge exchange and adaptation. Information can then be shared through wider networks and in turn exert an influence on action, thereby enabling the conduct of new experiments and engagement in new practices which can in turn strengthen systemic resilience (Ospina and Heeks, 2010).

The support of the international modelling community for the process of strengthening the use of integrated climate impact assessments will be important with regard to improving coordination across the spectrum of communities involved in the generation of those assessments at the global level, so as to make them more accessible to Governments and researchers in developing countries. This will include the development and transfer of new modelling tools and climate data as well as protocols, based on rigorously documented methodologies, that are available to the public. These protocols will be critical to replicating and comparing results, improving methods over time, linking results to "knowledge products" that improve their usability among policymakers and stakeholders, and increasing the credibility of assessments.

Consistent with the commitment under the 2030 Agenda for Sustainable Development to the strengthening of the science-policy interface and the development of evidence-based instruments to support sustainable development policymaking, United Nations entities and other multilateral and bilateral organizations can play an important role in improving coordination among the members of the international modelling community and in strengthening countries' capacities to bridge modelling-related gaps. At the same time, it is important that Governments themselves liaise more with the researchers engaged in smaller, often community-based integrated assessment projects, where results can be gathered within relatively short time frames and direct interactions among researchers, stakeholders and policy implementation agencies are a common practice.

Appendix III.1

Determinants of vulnerability and resilience: a household survey-based analysis

The identification of vulnerable households can be made through household surveys, with the starting point being a concrete and practical definition of vulnerability. The work of Andersen and Cardona (2013) is drawn upon here for purposes of illustration. The most vulnerable households are those that, simultaneously, have low levels of per capita income and low levels of diversification as a result of which any adverse shock will threaten their entire income base. A household that has a per capita income below the national poverty line and a diversification index (DI) of less than 0.5 is classified as highly vulnerable; households above these thresholds are classified as highly resilient (figure A.III.1).

Figure A.III.1
The four main vulnerability types as constructed by Andersen and Cardona (2013)

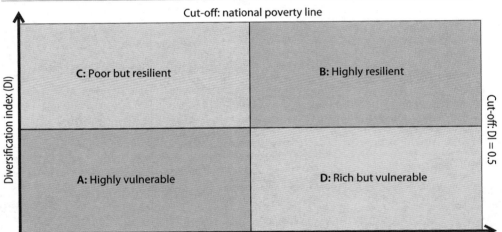

Source: Andersen and Cardona (2013).

Abbreviations: DI, diversification index.

Since diversification is the opposite of income concentration, a simple and logical way of constructing the diversification index is simply as 1 minus the widely used Herfindahl-Hirschman index of concentration, whereby

$$DI = 1 - \sum_{i=1}^{N} p_i^2,$$

where N is the total number of income sources and p_i represents the income proportion of the ith income source. The value of the index is 0 when there is complete specialization (100 per cent of total household income comes from one source only) and approaches 1 as the number of income sources increases and no single source dominates household incomes.

Both measures of vulnerability—the diversification index and per capita household income—can be calculated for each household using a standard household survey and can be aggregated to any group or socioeconomic characteristics of interest. This makes it possible, through econometric analyses, to establish the determinants of vulnerability and resilience which in turn allows the types of households most likely to be vulnerable to shocks to be identified.

This type of analysis has been applied using the 2011 household survey carried out by the National Statistical Institute of the Plurinational State of Bolivia. Income per capita and the diversification index are estimated for each household. Based on these two variables, two dummy variables are constructed to indicate whether a household belongs to the highly vulnerable group (incomes below the poverty level and DI<0.5) or the highly resilient group (incomes above the poverty level and DI>0.5). The factors and characteristics most strongly associated with vulnerability and resilience are determined through probabilistic (probit) regression.

This analysis shows that the most important determinant of vulnerability and resilience in the Plurinational State of Bolivia is the presence of a working spouse in the household (table A.III.1). This reduces the probability of being highly vulnerable by 12.2 percentage points and increases the probability of being highly resilient by 31.2 percentage

Table A.III.1

Probit regressions demonstrating the factors associated with vulnerability and resilience in the Plurinational State of Bolivia, 2011

Independent variable	Vulnerability regression	Resilience regression
Years of education of head of household	-0.004 (-5.15)	0.002 -2.14
Number of persons in household	0.027 -15.7	0.012 -4.34
Urban dummy	0.043 -5.65	0.026 -2.06
Age of head of household	-0.005 (-19.85)	0.01 -26.3
Female head of household dummy	-0.005 (-0.52)	0.016 -1.25
Indigenous dummy	0.027 -3.31	-0.077 (-6.61)
Dependency ratio	0.019 -7.9	-0.015 (-4.69)
Remittance dummy	-0.07 (-6.69)	0.12 -5.04
Public sector dummy	-0.059 (-6.37)	0.087 -5.37
Working spouse dummy	-0.122 (-18.21)	0.312 -27.39
Number of observations	*8848*	*8848*
R^2	*0.148*	*0.1747*

Source: Andersen and Cardona (2013).

Note: The numbers in parentheses are z-values.

points. However, only about one third of Bolivian households use this strategy, as there is still a strong traditional belief that married women should dedicate their time to child-rearing and domestic chores. According to the analysis, this is the single most important factor associated with high vulnerability in the Plurinational State of Bolivia.

The age of the head of household is the second most important determinant of vulnerability and resilience. The older the head, the lower the probability of being vulnerable, and the higher the probability of being resilient. Adding 20 years reduces the probability of being in the highly vulnerable category by 10 percentage points and increases the probability of being highly resilient by 20 percentage points. This is a natural life-cycle effect: young families have not had time to build a supply of assets which can provide supplementary income (such as rental income) and at the same time they often have young children to care for. In this context, very young families are of particular concern. According to the survey, there are more than 30,000 families with children in which the head of household is no more than 20 years old, of which 46 per cent are highly vulnerable. In more than 11,000 of these very young households, there are already two or more children. The probability of being highly vulnerable is 59 per cent for this group and the probability of being highly resilient is less than 2 per cent. This kind of situation can be prevented by better family planning education and support.

The next most important determinants of vulnerability are remittances and having a public sector job, both of which reduce the probability of falling into vulnerability by about 6 or 7 percentage points. Other important determinants include number of persons in the household and belonging to an indigenous population group.

Chapter IV
Coherent, participatory and adaptive policymaking for climate resilience

Key messages

- Building resilience to climate change, an essential component of sustainable development, is a challenge with multiple dimensions, which increases the need for substantive coordination and integration of policy interventions. Designing integrated and coherent policies will strengthen the resilience to climate hazards of the most vulnerable, not only by addressing issues crucial to their livelihoods, but also by taking advantage of potential co-benefits, while avoiding unintended consequences and maladaptation.

- The most intense and direct effects of climate events are experienced at the local level, with a disproportionate impact on the poorest and marginalized groups. The success of interventions aimed at building resilience depends on the participation of all stakeholders, especially stakeholders representing those groups. A broader participation can help policymakers identify development objectives and assess how to achieve them through building synergies and addressing the underlying causes of vulnerability.

- Climate hazards and their effects are characterized by significant uncertainties, which introduce new challenges for policymakers in designing adequate adaptation strategies, with inclusion. Policymakers must fully embed uncertainty into their long-term plans, using iterative and adaptive processes. This requires a more flexible policy process, capable of incorporating the new information and emerging knowledge needed to scope, assess, implement and monitor policy interventions.

The 2030 Agenda elevated the importance of policy coherence. Integration implies vastly different policy frameworks, policies, institutions and capacities. Development cooperation partners need to take a holistic approach to their partnerships, pursuing policies in different sectors that are complementary rather than contradictory...The 2030 Agenda is new to all of us. There is no paved way to follow. Every country needs to find the solution that fits its own national context. This leaves space for innovation in policies, institutions and practices.

Wu Hongbo, Under-Secretary-General
for Economic and Social Affairs,
6 November 2015

Introduction

Socioeconomic systems stumble in the face of climate hazards because some people are particularly exposed and vulnerable. Public policies have an important role to play in addressing people's vulnerability and building climate resilience but they have to be consistent with interventions for mitigation and adaptation within the larger context of policies for sustainable development.

To be successful, mitigation and adaptation policies must be part of the larger sustainable development policy framework

Mitigation policies that aim to reduce the anthropogenic sources of climate change focus on reducing risk over a long-term horizon extending as far as 2100, while adaptation policies focus on reducing current exposure and vulnerabilities so as to strengthen people's capacity to cope and adapt to climate hazards in the present and the medium term. Mitigation and adaptation policies are complementary and need to be strategically crafted to strengthen the overall resilience of socioeconomic systems along a continuum of development policies.

Other policies extending beyond mitigation and adaptation are also needed because, as noted in previous chapters, vulnerability and exposure to climate hazards are closely linked to existing underlying (structural) inequalities. Differences in access to physical and financial assets; unequal opportunities to access quality health services, education and employment; and unequal voice and political representation, as well as the perpetuation of discrimination under cultural and institutional norms, are structural conditions that aggravate the exposure and vulnerability of large population groups to climate hazards. The disproportionate impact of climate hazards further aggravates existing socioeconomic inequalities and may actually undermine the capacity of people to cope and adapt.

Breaking the vicious cycle of vulnerability and climate hazards requires well-integrated policies designed to reduce current underlying structural inequalities

Breaking this vicious cycle requires well-integrated and coherent policies designed to reduce current well-known vulnerabilities, including policies targeting poverty eradication, income diversification and improved access to basic social services such as education, health, and water and sanitation, among many others. Not only is closing the development gaps that leave people vulnerable to climate hazards a goal of sound development policies, but it is also essential to reducing the risk posed by climate change. Investing, for example, in prevention to halt the spread of malaria and other debilitating diseases to improve the quality of life of the most disadvantaged population groups, is both a sound development policy and part and parcel of a sound adaptation policy: healthier and potentially wealthier people will be more resilient to future climate hazards.

There is a clear role for public policies to play in addressing the structural inequalities that underlie vulnerability. Disadvantaged groups typically possess few options for diversifying their income sources, gaining access to insurance and financial markets and improving their education and health status. A continuum of well-integrated economic, social and environmental policies for building climate resilience, as discussed in chapter II, would help harmonize present adaptation efforts within short-term political and funding cycles with longer-term development objectives. Addressing the root causes of poor outcomes requires transformative policies that change the fundamental attributes of systems, particularly the existing governance systems and norms that perpetuate inequalities. Transformative policies should aim towards generating shifts in production and consumption behaviours to encourage sustainable practices, in line with some of the goals set out in the 2030 Agenda for Sustainable Development.[1]

---

1   General Assembly resolution 70/1.

Effective and coherent implementation of such policies necessitates a sound policy process. The present chapter discusses some of the key features that such a policy process must possess in order for policy decision-making to succeed in building climate resilience. The discussion centres around three principles which, when applied to the policy process, can prove helpful in facilitating adaptation and development, with particular benefits to disadvantaged groups. The underlying uncertainty of climate change, the locality in which its effects materialize, and the interconnected nature of various sectors require a policymaking system that is (1) coherent[2] and integrated, (2) participatory and (3) flexible.

Policy coherence is important for achieving climate resilience, particularly because of the need to integrate (or mainstream) adaptation objectives into longer-term development processes. The present *Survey* has noted, more broadly, that building consistency across the economic, social and environmental dimensions of development policy is a core challenge that building climate resilience and achieving sustainable development will have to confront.

Direct consultation with and participation of multiple stakeholders in policy decision-making improves understanding of specific risks and vulnerability at the local level. Further, application of a better understanding of risks and priorities achieved through the engagement of local communities improves both policy design and implementation as well as development outcomes.

In the context of a changing climate and greater weather variability, policymakers, using iterative and adaptive processes, must also fully embed uncertainty into policy planning. This requires a more flexible policy process, capable of incorporating lessons derived from each step of the process, with a view to improving knowledge and outcomes. Within the context of uncertainty, no-regret and low-regret policies constitute a good starting point for adaptation, as they can address immediate vulnerabilities and structural inequalities, without compromising the foundations of future resilience.

A policy process based on the principles of coherence and integration, participation and flexibility should help address underlying inequalities by identifying vulnerable populations, particular intersecting inequalities, and concrete actions for strengthening resilience. These three principles are discussed in greater detail and applied to concrete situations in the following three sections. The final section provides a summary of the requirements that must be met in order for the goals considered in this chapter to be realized.

> **Building climate resilience requires strengthened policymaking systems which are coherent, integrated, participatory and flexible...**

> **...through which to address the underlying inequalities that make some people disproportionately vulnerable to climate hazards**

Increasing policy coherence and integration across sectors

As already discussed, sustainable development and resilience are multidimensional challenges, which, as this chapter argues, defy single definitions or solutions. The objectives to be pursued in building climate resilience alone encompass multiple sectors, thereby increasing the need for substantive coordination and integration of policy interventions. Particularly within the context of climate hazards, resilience requires that instead of focusing on individual risks, the policymaking process take a more integrated approach to management of change and uncertainty (Arup, 2014).

It is through the integration and coherence of policies across sectors that the root causes of vulnerability, which are often interrelated and cumulative, can be addressed most

> **Policy integration across sectors is needed to address the root causes of vulnerability, which are often interrelated and cumulative**

---

2   Policy coherence can be defined as the systematic promotion of mutually reinforcing policies across government departments to create synergies towards achieving agreed objectives and to avoid or minimize negative spillovers in other policy areas.

effectively. While poverty and development status, for example, are obvious determinants of the capacity of people to cope with and adapt to shocks, there is also an underlying connection between vulnerabilities and multiple inequities in access, for example, to assets, land, work and political processes. Addressing these inequities requires simultaneous actions, as they all play a role in determining exposure to climate hazards and the capacity to cope and adapt. Designing policies that are coherent and adequately integrated is a critical facet of strengthening the resilience to climate of the most vulnerable groups: such policies will not only help strengthen their livelihoods but also make it possible for potential co-benefits to be taken advantage of and for unintended consequences including maladaptation to be avoided.

Integration in support of a multisectoral approach

The challenge lies in achieving an effective coordination across multisectoral policies that is consistent with long-term objectives without losing sight of immediate needs

Many countries are formulating plans for adaptation to climate change and for development in general. However, it is the building of coherent and integrated policies which take into account the multidimensional nature of livelihoods and address the multiple sources of inequality that is the biggest challenge. Adaptation policies must be an integral part of sustainable development strategies in order to minimize the current and future impacts of climate hazards on livelihoods. The challenge lies in determining how to effectively coordinate and integrate multi-sectoral policies under the aegis of a single overarching vision which is consistent with long-term objectives and does not lose sight of immediate needs and relevant priorities at the sectoral level.

The case of food security attests to the magnitude of the challenge. Food production, which is one of the most critical sectors affected by climate change, requires a multisectoral approach, given the number of interrelated dimensions that need to be simultaneously addressed in order to minimize current and future impacts of climate change on food systems and livelihoods in general. Agricultural practices, for instance, need to change in order not only to improve yields and ensure sufficient food production, but also to preserve ecosystems and natural resources in the long term. The preservation of ecosystems, through new management responses regarding natural resources, is also a determinant in ensuring sustainable livelihoods and food security. Thus, policies to stimulate agricultural productivity should be designed not in parallel with environmental policies but in such a way as to integrate goals of ecosystem preservation.

A community-based project on forest rehabilitation for slope stability in the Bolivian Altiplano offers a concrete example of the successful integration of natural resources management and adaptation objectives. The project was implemented over the course of 15 years using a community forestry approach both to generate income and to stabilize slopes that had become exposed as a result of environmental degradation and were consequently at risk of landslides. The assessment of the project was conducted in close consultation with communities and the results encompassed a greater diversification of livelihoods and improved watersheds, together with a decrease in the risks from landslides. This highlights the importance of management of ecosystems and livelihoods as the basis for an integrated strategy for climate change adaptation and development (Renaud, Sudmeier-Rieux and Estrella, eds., 2013).

Evidence shows that the right combination of policies has greater impacts on livelihoods and people

The importance of integrating policies is also illustrated by a study on the impact of three adaptation options used by farmers in Ethiopia's Nile Basin — changing crops, water conservation and soil conservation. Veronesi and Di Falco (2012) have found that, when each of the options is taken in isolation, it has no effect on improving net revenues for farmers. However, when adaptation options are combined, the gains for farmers are significant. For example, the authors found that changing crops, when combined with water conservation strategies, delivers the largest gains of any of the adaptation options. The study concludes that, while adaptation to climate change based upon a portfolio of strategies is superior to single-option strategies, finding the right combination of interventions requires experimentation with different options to iterate the optimal course of action. The study also sheds light on the need to remove the structural barriers encountered by some groups when they attempted to access the full range of strategies, either because of poor socioeconomic status or weak access to financial resources, or owing to an absence of knowledge attributable to low levels of education or lack of information.

A number of broader social and economic policies can contribute to stabilizing and increasing the income levels of the most disadvantaged groups, thereby ensuring that their livelihoods are more resilient. Social protection systems, for instance, including safety nets, can protect lower-income groups against short-term economic and food price shocks, enhancing their coping capacity and maybe even their capacity to contribute to transformative change in the future. Instruments or policies that promote access to insurance and capital markets can, when integrated, complement those protection schemes, thereby helping local small landholders cope with possible negative consequences of extreme weather events and encouraging them to invest in new crops or any other relevant input to facilitate the process of adaptation to future climate hazards.

Complementing policies designed specifically for the agricultural sector with other interventions which improve rural-urban linkages (e.g., transport infrastructure) can promote the production of alternative sources of income, enhance food security for both rural and urban households and reduce poverty, especially in countries where the process of urbanization is accelerating (United Nations, 2013). In China, for example, the existence of areas of high population density areas that are also well served by transportation infrastructure has encouraged the engagement of a rural labour force in labour-intensive manufacturing. Evidence for agriculture-based economies demonstrates that non-farm sources of income account for about 20–30 per cent of total income for rural households, a significant portion of which could consist of remittances from household members who migrated to urban areas (Food and Agriculture Organization of the United Nations, World Food Programme and International Fund for Agricultural Development, 2012). Policies that facilitate the transfer of such remittances would then come to be considered highly necessary for stabilizing and increasing income levels of the most disadvantaged groups.

A main challenge is to ensure that multisectoral approaches lead to transformative adaptation strategies which can enhance resilience to climate hazards rather than provide just temporary relief against short-term shocks. How to cope with and adapt to the impact of higher temperatures on human health is a relevant issue in this regard. Increasingly, national heat wave plans are being implemented to deal with extreme heat, especially in countries where temperatures can reach unbearable levels. In response to the devastating heat wave that killed at least 2,500 people across India in 2015, the government is launching a programme designed to protect people from extreme heat in two high-risk regions. In preparation for the onset of summer, the cities involved in the programme will have spent months educating children about heat risk, stocking hospitals with ice packs and extra water, and training medical workers to identify heat stress, dehydration and heat stroke. These plans, which are geared towards reducing health risks incrementally, present a unique opportunity to achieve policy integration. Adequate execution of these plans would require a strengthening of the health system as a whole and the building of closer links with policies

The challenge is to develop transformative adaptation strategies through which to build resilience to climate hazards

in other sectors, such as transportation, building design, and urban land-use management (World Health Organization, 2009). For instance, the so-called urban heat island[3] effect, a major source of aggressive heat injurious to human health, can be reduced by creating more green spaces or utilizing different materials in construction[4] (Silva, Phelan and Golden, 2010), which could contribute to building climate resilience and more sustainable cities. Further, policies that improve roads, rules and signals for bicyclists, pedestrians and other alternative road users in urban areas not only help improve safety but also, by incentivizing the uptake of these means of transportation, yield health and climate benefits as air pollution is curbed and physical activity is promoted.

Integrated policies that promote co-benefits

Integrated policies are needed to explore synergies between policies for building resilience to climate hazards and sustainable development objectives

Resilience-enhancing policies can yield benefits for development objectives, and vice versa. The potential for such co-benefits has important implications for designing and implementing adaptation and development policies and needs to be properly assessed. It should therefore be mentioned that while policies with potential co-benefits offer cost-effectiveness advantages, which may encourage policymakers to implement them, they are not in all cases easy to devise. In this regard, an integrated approach can both take advantage of and encourage the development of policies that provide co-benefits for resilience to climate hazards and sustainable development.

A good example within the context of food security is the introduction of social protection systems. As already noted, social protection systems, including safety nets, as well as broader social protection policies and programmes, are designed to protect the most vulnerable against short-term economic and food price shocks, thereby enhancing their coping capacity. At the same time, they can also contribute to long-term resilience, by strengthening the ability of small-scale farmers to manage risks and adapt. Evidence has shown that climate change reduces investment incentives in agriculture and the ability to adopt better adaptation strategies, with negative effects on food production. As observed in Ethiopia's Nile Basin, which has been affected by changes in temperatures and rainfall over the past 20 years, farmers experiencing financial constraints were less likely to introduce recommended adaptation methods, while those who could afford to adapt undertook soil conservation, used different crop varieties and irrigated their farms (Deressa and others, 2009). Thus, predictable social security programmes that target the most vulnerable, particularly small landholders, by providing a robust safety net, can stimulate investment in more productive human capital and technologies. By ensuring a basic level of consumption, such safety nets enable small landholders to engage in production strategies that are higher-return, albeit riskier from a subsistence-related point of view. Along similar lines, access to insurance and capital markets can assist local small landholders in coping with the possible negative consequences of extreme weather events and investing in new crops or in any relevant input that can help foster the process of adaptation to climate hazards.

The degrees of uncertainty are particularly high at the local level, making it difficult to predict the impact of climate hazards on the agricultural sector. In the face

---

3   An urban heat island is a city or metropolitan area that, owing to human activities, is significantly warmer than surrounding rural areas.

4   For example, concrete or more heat-reflective substances could be substituted for bitumen, typically used in road surfacing and roofing.

of such uncertainty, more diversified livelihoods can broaden the options for adaptation, particularly for the most vulnerable population groups. A diversified farming system can also have co-benefits: integrating horticulture and livestock, for instance, can enhance nutritional outcomes by improving rural households' access to food from different sources. In Viet Nam, a diversified farming system at the household level integrating vegetation, aquaculture and use of cages in animal husbandry has contributed to improvements in both income and nutritional outcomes (Food and Agriculture Organization of the United Nations, 2013).

The health sector is another domain where spillover effects from a number of policies in other sectors can yield benefits. For instance, improving fuel and combustion efficiency for the purpose of decreasing greenhouse gas emissions requires actions which may generate co-benefits in the health sector if they succeed in curbing air pollution and thereby ameliorate its health-related consequences and reduce the demand for health services. Air pollution is a classic example where public policy is required to enable environmental and health risks to be reduced at the same time.[5] In a significant number of countries, mostly in sub-Saharan Africa, more than 95 per cent of the population uses solid fuels for cooking (Forouzanfar and others, 2015). Poor households, women and children in particular are exposed to indoor air pollution (Smith and others, 2014; World Health Organization, 2014). Relatively simple yet extremely efficient measures, such as using improved cook stoves in households, could have averted many of the 2.9 million deaths that occurred in 2013 as a result of indoor air pollution, while decreasing greenhouse gas and pollutant emissions. Several initiatives are already in place, including the ambitious pledge by the Global Alliance for Clean Cookstoves (a public-private partnership hosted by the UN Foundation) to foster the adoption of clean cook stoves and fuels in 100 million households by 2020.

A need for coherent policies to prevent maladaptation

A sectoral adaptation policy will generally address unidimensional issues, such as vulnerability arising from a specific source. Such a policy would not be designed for integration and coordination with sectoral adaptation policies addressing other sources of vulnerability. Maladaptation (entailing further environmental deterioration, increased vulnerability or decreased welfare) may arise owing to inconsistency among these sectoral adaptation policies, or among short-term solutions and long-term adaptation needs. Maladaptation may then result in greater vulnerability in the future or in negative effects on other communities or sectors. An integrated policy approach, in contrast, possesses the advantage of taking into consideration different priorities and various sources of information, which are crucial in the policymaking process, in order to prevent maladaptation.

The case of the Morogoro region of the United Republic of Tanzania is often invoked to illustrate the maladaptation that may arise from local adaptation strategies (Paavola, 2008). As discussed above, livelihood diversification in agriculture-based economies that incorporates non-farm income activities is considered an effective adaptation strategy. Many

Maladaptation may arise from short-term solutions or narrow adaptation policies which end up increasing vulnerability or inflicting further environmental damage in the longer term

---

5   Indoor air pollution arises from exposure to particulate matter (comprising small solid particles containing sulphur and other toxic elements mixed with liquid droplets), which is released into the air through the burning of solid fuels (such as wood, dung, crop wastes, charcoal and coal) for cooking, heating, illumination and waste management, and by power plants, industrial manufacturing and vehicle exhaust.

farmers in Morogoro, however, have tapped to a greater extent into natural resources for subsistence and alternative income through, for example, their increased access to mining and development of new artisanal activities. While these strategies have helped them respond to short-term needs, in the long term they pose a number of new challenges arising from natural resources degradation, in particular deforestation and land cover change, which has negative consequences for the condition of land and water. This environmental degradation will likely hamper adaptive capacity in the long term.

At the same time, efficiency in the use of natural resources can also lead to maladaptation. Governments tend to create incentives for farmers to conserve water use through access to more efficient irrigations options. However, irrigation that is more efficient can prompt farmers to use more water through their expansion of the size of the cropland to be irrigated. In some cases, greater efficiency results in greater total water use (Food and Agriculture Organization of the United Nations, 2015a, chap. 3). In another typical example of maladaptation, which occurs more often in richer countries, policies to protect the population from heat waves and avert excessive demand on urgent health services result in greater use of private air conditioning and consequently a greater demand for energy (O'Brien and others, 2012). This type of adaptation initiative is in fact a form of maladaptation, since it shifts the pressure from one sector to another. The overall vulnerability of the system is not reduced: instead, one source of vulnerability is simply replaced by another.

> The existence of some trade-offs notwithstanding, an integrated policy approach should be able to implement compensation mechanisms for dealing with the negative effects of specific policies

An integrated approach can avert some of these unintended consequences. In coastal areas, the challenge often exists of preventing the destruction of sand dunes owing to the construction of tourism facilities close to the water. The degradation of sand dunes not only alters the coastal ecosystem but, in the long run, also increases those facilities' exposure to storms and water rise (Magnan, 2014). This situation entails a typical trade-off between economic development and environmental challenges. Ideally, an integrated approach would attenuate the impact of the trade-off by limiting habitat degradation and consequently the collateral effect on assets in terms of their exposure to climate-related hazards. Such an approach may not completely eliminate the trade-off, but, by taking into account the negative effects, it can put in place compensation mechanisms, such as for protecting marine ecosystems so as to allow them to maintain their natural resilience and adaptive capacities, and then ensuring that their buffering function against waves is maintained (ibid.).

Overcoming constraints on integration

> Policy integration, in practice, remains an immense challenge

Designing and implementing an integrated approach is not an easy task owing to the complex nature of the policymaking process and the divergent priorities of stakeholders. Notwithstanding the fact that an integrated policy process can benefit greatly from the recognition of diverse interests, circumstances, sociocultural contexts and expectations, in practice integration remains an immense challenge (IPCC, 2014d). The effective integration of policies and agendas entails addressing the following concrete difficulties:

- Complexity of the problems and the options
- Uncertainties regarding policy impacts
- Existence of institutions with specific mandates
- Difficulties created by short-term funding cycles

Adaptation initiatives must be sensitive to social characteristics and cultural values at the local level. While improvement of women's livelihoods, for example, is undeniably a necessary condition for inclusive and sustainable development, such an initiative sometimes clashes with social norms and cultural values. In some communities in India, for example, participation of women in the labour force has decreased, in spite of rapid economic growth in recent years. Multiple factors explain this decline. In some areas, there are social constraints deeply rooted in local culture that determine what constitute "suitable jobs for women" based on which, women are allowed to work outside the home only under certain conditions (Chatterjee, Murgai and Rama, 2015; 2016). Even when laws are in place to ensure equal rights in labour markets for women and men, cultural barriers prevent women from exercising their rights (Barry, 2016). For communities that are exposed to climate and economic hazards, lack of work opportunities for women further increases existing vulnerabilities. Thus, to ensure that the desired outcomes are achieved, policies designed to build climate change resilience, including through economic empowerment of women, must be sensitive to the cultural context (Le Masson and others, 2016).

Policy integration and coherence require complex coordination processes across different sectoral priorities and stakeholder interests. Disregarding these complexities for the sake of a cross-sectoral ideal bespeaks an overly simplistic perspective. In a recent study of the European experience, it was found that "comprehensive policy integration cannot be achieved through a single multisectoral strategy" (Nordbeck and Steurer, 2015). Through an examination of how each of the countries that are members of the European Union put into practice its sustainable development agenda, the study identified at least two common problems. First, the strategies emphasized a breadth of topics and sectors rather than priorities. This allowed policymakers in each area of government (or sector) to focus on those dimensions that interested them to the detriment both of other dimensions and of overall coordination. Second, the call for a balanced approach across the three dimensions of sustainable development was often undermined by the fact that economic and social priorities prevailed over environmental concerns.

Policy integration requires multisectoral governance arrangements for developing a shared vision and overarching priorities; but as each stakeholder has its own mandates, specific priorities and funding, political dialogue and negotiation are required for policy coordination. The lesson in this regard is that effective strategies for policy integration require clearly defined sectoral action plans which focus on well-defined priorities. More importantly, the challenge lies in building synergies across other sectoral strategies: political dialogue and negotiation are indispensable in cases where conflicting objectives are identified. In their review of the European experience, Nordbeck and Steurer found that "better policies usually emerge from conflicts between specialists advocating competing solutions, not from a vague consensus" (p. 14). Nonetheless, the coordinating agency has an important role to play in ensuring that all relevant actors are integrated in the policy process and in fostering synergies with their own sectoral needs.

In short, effective policy integration must sustain a balance between a vision that is holistic and coherent and existing sectoral and local contexts, including political and cultural considerations. The opportunities to strengthen policy integration must be explored through ex ante assessments which take into account the specific mandates of sectoral ministries and institutions as well as the local context within which policies are to be implemented. The institutions involved in coordinating multisectoral programmes confront the challenge of building synergies among sectoral mandates, each operating within the framework of its own financial resources, political power structures and implementation mechanisms.

Adaptation initiatives must be sensitive to social characteristics and cultural values at the local level

Effective strategies for achieving policy integration require a shared vision of development with clearly defined sectoral action plans focused on well-defined priorities

Involving all stakeholders in identifying risks and implementing solutions

Building climate change resilience requires policymaking based on the participation of all relevant stakeholders, including local experts and existing social networks

The importance of consultation and participation in policy decision-making has long been acknowledged. Yet, even if respectfully accommodating diverse perspectives is not an easy task, it is indispensable for building climate resilience. That people's opinions and interests differ and often clash is the result of a multiplicity of factors, including differences related to wealth and educational and cultural backgrounds. Very often, public institutions lack the experience and capacity that they need to be able to interact with the local communities. In most countries, the functioning of institutional mechanisms established to provide broad access to information and enable public engagement is less than optimal; and the resources needed to facilitate engagement in costly and time-consuming consultative processes are often lacking.

To the extent that the impacts of climate hazards are largely local, stakeholder engagement is critical both in identifying the challenges of adaptation vis-à-vis the needs of communities and in formulating alternative solutions that are relevant to the community and effective in building resilience. However, to be effective, stakeholder engagement must meet three criteria: (i) it must include the participation of all relevant stakeholders on an equitable basis; (ii) it must encompass a process open to incorporating local knowledge so as to improve the identification of problems and alternative policy options and (iii) it must engage communities' existing social networks in order to improve project implementation.

Why involve all stakeholders?

Processes characterized by an imbalance in the representation of stakeholders reinforce inequalities and may result in the adoption of inefficient and ineffective policies

The complexity of the process of building climate resilience with a focus on reducing vulnerability and structural inequalities demands the participation of all relevant stakeholders. Imbalances in representation in policymaking may prevent the identification of and attention to critical problems and may potentially have dire consequences, since those who could have identified those problems and offered suggestions on how to resolve them were not present. Even if problems have been identified correctly, the solutions chosen may have unintended consequences for the groups that did not participate in the consultations and negotiations. Also, owing to the lack of a diversity of viewpoints, analyses may be constrained and the range of solutions less inventive. Lastly, the solutions may turn out to be — or may be perceived as being — non-representative of the very community whose problems they have been chosen to address, or they may not be adopted owing to their irrelevance and/or the lack of consensus, or, if adopted, they may ultimately turn out to be ineffective. Involvement of all stakeholders is essential to improving the outcomes at each stage of the policymaking process. And, within the context of climate change, it is critical that negative trade-offs, unintended consequences and maladaptation be avoided.

As noted in chapter II, inequality in political participation and representation in policy decision-making is a key determinant of vulnerability and exposure to climate hazards. Regrettably, those most vulnerable to climate hazards are often excluded from policy discussions or are inadequately represented. This is an issue well recognized in the Rio Declaration on Environment and Development, which includes a provision on guaranteeing citizens' rights to information, participation and environmental justice (principle 10) (see box IV.1). Under the 2030 Agenda for Sustainable Development (United Nations (1993), the importance of ensuring full and effective participation and equal opportunities for leadership at all levels of decision-making in political, economic and public life for those traditionally excluded is reiterated.[6] There exist well-known instruments designed to make such participation part of policy practice. In the context of climate change, new tools for engaging stakeholders in the design of climate impact assessments and consideration of policy options are emerging, including at the local level as discussed in chapter III.

Box IV.1

Access to information, participation and justice in environmental matters: key instruments in ensuring equality in adaptation and resilience-building strategies

Adopted on 14 June 1992 by the United Nations Conference on Environment and Development, the Rio Declaration on Environment and Development,[a] comprising 27 principles, laid the foundations for national and international efforts towards achieving sustainable development. According to principle 10:

> Environmental issues are best handled with the participation of all concerned citizens, at the relevant level. At the national level, each individual shall have appropriate access to information concerning the environment that is held by public authorities, including information on hazardous materials and activities in their communities, and the opportunity to participate in decision-making processes. States shall facilitate and encourage public awareness and participation by making information widely available. Effective access to judicial and administrative proceedings, including redress and remedy, shall be provided.

The three provisions under principle 10 — access to information, participation in decision-making processes, and access to justice in environmental matters, also referred to as "access rights" — serve as key instruments. They ensure both that the environmental problems affecting disadvantaged groups and vulnerable communities are adequately addressed and that policy decisions, either on environmental issues or as affecting the environment, take into consideration the needs of those groups. In so doing, those provisions also serve as key instruments in ensuring that climate change adaptation and resilience-building strategies (as well as mitigation measures) promote equality.

Access rights, as defined above, are enshrined in the legislation in many countries, both developed and developing. Yet, even in countries that have enacted such legislation, challenges to implementation remain. International agreements and cooperation are important means of supporting implementation. Through the Economic Commission for Europe Convention on Access to Information, Public Participation in Decision-making and Access to Justice in Environmental Matters (Aarhus Convention),[b] which was adopted on 25 June 1998 and entered into force on 30 October 2001, countries have been engaged in ensuring that access rights become effective. In Latin America and the Caribbean, a regional instrument whose aim is to ensure the full implementation of access rights and to promote international cooperation in that regard, is currently under negotiation, with the support of the Economic Commission for Latin America and the Caribbean. Further, at the eleventh special session of the United Nations Environment Programme (UNEP) Governing Council/Global Ministerial Environment Forum, held in Bali, Indonesia, from 24 to 26 February 2010, the Governing Council of UNEP adopted the Guidelines for the Development of National Legislation on Access to Information, Public Participation and Access to Justice in Environmental Matters (Bali Guidelines).[c]

a Report of the United Nations Conference on Environment and Development, Rio de Janeiro, 3-24 June 1992, vol. I, Resolutions Adopted by the Conference (United Nations publication, Sales No. E.93.I.8 and corrigendum), resolution 1, annex I.
b United Nations, Treaty Series, vol. 2161, No. 37770.
c Official Records of the General Assembly, Sixty-fifth Session, Supplement No. 25 (A/65/25), annex I, decision SS.XI/5 A, annex.

---

7 Several targets under the Sustainable Development Goals refer directly to the importance of expanding participation and political representation of groups traditionally excluded. This is also amply recognized in the preamble and principles of the 2030 Agenda.

Adaptation requires the mobilization of collective action in many different areas to implement integrated and coherent initiatives which are efficient, sustainable and equitable; and as building climate resilience is an objective most likely to be in competition with other priorities, early recognition of diverse interests, sociocultural contexts and expectations will facilitate effective policy decision-making processes. Governments, which have a unique capacity to convene all relevant stakeholders from the private sector, civil society and the scientific community, have an important role to play in facilitating consultations with, interactions among and the participation of those stakeholders so as to enhance reciprocal trust. Governments also have an important role to play in ensuring the balanced representation needed to facilitate equitable and inclusive processes and outcomes.[7]

Ensuring equitable participation

Building climate resilience is a particularly complex endeavour and defies any simple solution. As highlighted above, actions in multiple sectors (including energy, health, agriculture, transportation and technology, among many others) and at different levels of governance are therefore required to provide coordinated and coherent policy support. An additional layer of complexity is imposed by the fact that the negative impact of climate hazards is usually localized. Further, improving coordination and policy coherence between national and local governments is particularly important in this regard.

Both national and local governments have a role to play in ensuring equitable participation of all stakeholders in building climate change resilience

National Governments have a role to play in creating the policy space—involving legal frameworks, information and financial resources—required to strengthen policy decision-making and policy implementation among local governments, which are closer to communities and have a better understanding of risks and local needs. Coordination across sectors for coherent programme/project implementation is also made easier at the local level, where there is closer interaction across sectors and among stakeholders.

However, the legitimacy of actions frequently depends on the capacity of local governments to engage all stakeholders in the process. Vulnerabilities are usually more visible at the local level, where structural inequalities such as differences in social status and political power, among others, critically shape them. Giving voice and agency to those who are otherwise invisible to the process would serve to address vulnerabilities and inequalities at their source and create the conditions for building consensus and mobilizing collective actions towards resilient development.

The occurrence of climate hazards usually exposes deep inequalities in political participation, representation and decision-making

Many factors—including economic status, political voice, religion, culture, tradition and disability—have the potential to limit the participation of individuals and groups in the process. In many cases, those with greater experience in decision-making processes and greater social and political capital may dominate those processes. The case of Hurricane Katrina, referred to in chapter II, provides a good example in this regard. It has been argued that the Industrial Canal, bounding the Lower Ninth Ward to the west, which failed and flooded the city of New Orleans, was constructed in that area partly owing to the limited political power of its residents. During the recovery period, those same residents had less access to the political resources needed to draw attention to their specific needs. Even when the key groups are included, interests and priorities may be irreconcilable, with outcomes

---

[7]   Chap. V of *Report on the World Social Situation 2016* (United Nations, forthcoming) elaborates on the policy areas that are relevant for equitable and inclusive societies.

often reflecting an imbalance in political resources and power (Few, Brown and Tompkins, 2007).

Thus, without participation of *all* stakeholders, there is the risk that existing inequalities will remain, owing to the differentials in political influence of various groups of people. In this regard, public institutions have a major role to play in strengthening the capacity of key local stakeholders to deliberate and engage in the decision-making processes. Achieving this in practice requires identification of key local stakeholders at the beginning of the policy cycle or of any given project.

Involving local communities in the management of funds, including those for climate adaptation projects, could be a means of improving transparency in the use of those funds, especially in areas, such as forestry and water resources management, where there is a particular proneness to misuse of public resources. The implementation of participatory budgeting programmes is a potentially effective mechanism in this regard, through which ordinary citizens become involved in budget meetings with local government officials and have the opportunity to vote on how the budget (or, as is usually the case, part of it) will be spent. In Brazil, for example, where participatory budgeting was first adopted (in 1989), municipalities utilizing such programmes appear to manage their public finances with a significantly greater effectiveness than those where the programmes have not been implemented (Petherick, 2014). Concerned experts might wish to keep decision-making power out of the hands of local stakeholders in cases where more complex matters such as climate adaptation need to be confronted, not recognizing that local stakeholders can provide different but complementary forms of expertise (ibid.). While local buy-in and ownership do contribute to successful project implementation, participatory budgeting is sometimes not sufficient to deter corruption, as vulnerable groups may become victims of elite capture or bribing. Therefore, a participatory accountability framework must be implemented alongside participatory decision-making.

Participatory budgeting in the allocation of climate funds can help reduce fund mismanagement while also reducing inequalities

Taking advantage of local knowledge

Because the most intense and direct effects of climate events are experienced at the local level, scoping (or identifying) objectives and risks can benefit tremendously from the knowledge accumulated by local communities. There is an obvious role for this knowledge in tailoring interventions to the local context and conditions; for example, local knowledge can inform technical assessments of adaptation options while those assessments can inform local communities on how to better deal with climate change (see chap. III). As stated in the Sendai Framework for Disaster Risk Reduction 2015–2030:[8] "Indigenous peoples, through their experience and traditional knowledge, provide an important contribution to the development and implementation of plans and mechanisms, including for early warning" (para. 36 (a) (v)). Furthermore, local experience and knowledge may help reduce inequalities, as they can provide particular insights regarding the causes of vulnerability and exposure as well as insights applicable in the search for solutions. Tapping into local knowledge has brought significant benefits in terms of climate resilience to the citizens of the city of Gorakhpur in India, where communities are constantly challenged by floods, heat waves, storms and other climate-related shocks (see box IV.2).

Incorporating the voice of people in their local context contributes to an increase in policy effectiveness and a decrease in inequalities

---

8   General Assembly resolution 69/283, annex II.

Box IV.2

Building resilience of local communities in the city of Gorakhpur, India

Hydro-meteorological disasters have been a part of life in the city of Gorakhpur in northern India, where the population has had to cope with constant floods, heat waves, storms and other shocks. In response, the city embarked on a resilience-building project which integrates climate vulnerability assessments and micro planning and implementation. It was designed, implemented and monitored using a community-led bottom-up approach which began with the identification of climate vulnerabilities. Some key lessons have been derived from that experience.

The project defined resilience as a desired characteristic of a system (economic, political, infrastructure, ecological, social and institutional) that includes multiple activities, interactions and relationships. The focus of the interventions was on local communities that were well positioned to participate in the process. Engagement was driven by four main principles:

- Engagement of local communities and individuals is key to the formulation of a realistic and effective resilience plan
- The resilience plan should be based on practical experiences gained through pilot programmes
- A facilitator (or "champion") is required to lead the process
- The process needs to be flexible and to evolve, since building resilience is a dynamic process

The project found that the administrative systems in the ward were ill suited to providing basic services and sustaining the residents' quality of life. To redress this, the project started by defining the baseline conditions in the ward and then assessed vulnerabilities to climate hazards using the local knowledge provided by the community and its own perceptions regarding the relevance of development interventions.

The community was instrumental in generating an understanding of local climate threshold risks derived from historical events. These were compared with climate projections to estimate how often those thresholds would be reached in the future. Progress on resilience was monitored using indicators created to track the performance of the system, actors and institutions, which facilitated fulfilment of one of the most important requirements under this model: continuous review of the implementation of interventions to ensure that they contributed to producing the expected results. This kind of process of iteration helps to identify problems as they arise and to ensure the incorporation of new information so as to improve project implementation, which is particularly important as new information on climate impacts is continuously evolving.

This project illustrates the usefulness and applicability of a bottom-up approach and offers a template for identifying key elements and their nuances which are important for local implementation of resilience interventions by focusing on local communities in planning, implementation and monitoring. Such an example also sets out a clear-cut path towards integration of disaster risk, climate change adaptation and implementation of sustainable development agendas in such a way as to reduce inequalities and build climate-resilient livelihoods.

Source: Gorakhpur Environmental Action Group (2014).

Understanding local impacts and contexts also helps to eliminate actions that may lead to maladaptation. In Sri Lanka, for example, while the introduction of high-yielding hybrid varieties of rice seeds had initially had a beneficial effect on yields, support for their use led to an undermining of the ability of farmers to adapt to changing conditions.

Indigenous knowledge of the almost 2,000 existing traditional varieties was eroded and the operation of local seed banks undermined. Further, to the detriment of the livelihood of small farmers in Sri Lanka, those new, fertilizer-dependent seeds proved less able to cope with the increasing water salinity in the region caused by higher temperatures, the rise of sea level and the failure of irrigation systems (Weragoda, Ensor and Berger, 2009, chap. 5).

Studies have shown that choice of type of adaptation and its implementation are facilitated when there is constructive and transparent engagement with the communities at risk (Nurse and others, 2014). Such engagement can help prevent the outcomes described above. A study of Fiji's tourism sector concluded that "approaches that explicitly integrate stakeholders into each step of the process from vulnerability assessment right through to consideration of alternative measures can provide a sound basis for assisting…the implementation of appropriate adaptation interventions" (Moreno and Becken, 2009). The study also concluded that stakeholder participation can better incorporate people's priorities and expectations when there are multiple adaptation options available.

Maladaptation can best be avoided through constructive and transparent engagement with the local community

Taking advantage of local social networks

Policy implementation benefits largely from closer interaction between public implementing agencies and local communities. The effort to engage communities at the stage of policy implementation will benefit from the presence of existing social networks which can be effectively mobilized to disseminate information, for example, health messages (Frumkin and McMichael, 2008) and to improve monitoring of results. Sharing of information derived from climate impact assessments can be a means of influencing action and strengthening systemic resilience (see chap. III).

Policy implementation benefits from tapping into existing social structures to enable dissemination of information and monitoring of results

In the context of food security, such fruitful interaction is exemplified by the Southern Agricultural Growth Corridor of the United Republic of Tanzania (SAGCOT). The Growth Corridor integrates several stakeholders—the private sector, government and civil society—within a common platform in order to achieve the multiple objectives of increasing agricultural productivity, improving food security and protecting local livelihoods and ecosystems (United Nations, 2013, p. 100). The participation of all relevant stakeholders, including at the local level, has helped to improve the use not only of natural resources but of the ecosystem as a whole. This is considered an important determinant of the sustainability of the entire agricultural and food system.

Timely information and support for mobilizing communities are also important. In the city of Manizales in Colombia, for instance, national and regional authorities worked together with local communities and leaders to discourage settlements on slopes characterized by instability, which posed a threaten to people's lives and livelihoods. A public awareness campaign provided information on the risks of living in areas deemed dangerous, and a scheme was put in place for those willing to relocate. In addition, women in the community received training, involving the participation of local institutions including the municipal government, academic institutions, technical specialists and non-governmental organizations, on how to stabilize slopes in their respective locations. Further, a local committee representing all actors was called upon to review the new plans for urban relocation (Arup, 2014).

The need for an iterative and flexible policy process to cope with uncertainties

Flexibility and adaptability of policy processes are fundamental to building climate-resilient development

Achieving climate-resilient development, under scenarios of climate uncertainty and taking into account the complexities of policy implementation, requires policy processes that are flexible and adaptable. Moreover, addressing the structural inequalities that perpetuate social exclusion and vulnerability requires integrated and coherent policies which are consistent over time. Policymakers increasingly recognize this challenge and the need to focus on immediate and near-future decisions that have longer-term impacts, while maintaining the flexibility needed to adjust to changing conditions and information.

Uncertainty

The uncertainty of climate and weather predictions and the complex interaction between environment and socioeconomic conditions have implications for policymakers

Determinations of the magnitude of the impacts of climate change are being constantly revised as new climate projections and impact assessments are generated and new information becomes available through improvement in environment statistics and those data provided, albeit more limitedly, by local stakeholders. A recent report on the melting of the West Antarctic ice sheet, for example, found that sea levels will possibly have risen by as much as three feet by the end of the century, with severe implications for the world's coastal cities (Gillis, 2016). This new estimate of the speed of sea-level rise yields roughly twice the increase expected under the plausible worst-case scenario produced by IPCC in 2013 (Church and others, 2013). Rapid improvements in climate technologies is facilitating new assessments, better environment statistics and more information, although important gaps do remain (see chaps. III and V).

Owing to the nature of the problem, climate and weather predictions, despite continuous improvements, are characterized by large margins of uncertainty (National Academies of Sciences, Engineering, and Medicine, 2016). At the same time, long-term trends in inequality, population growth, urbanization, economic globalization, technological change and other socioeconomic processes will exert profound impacts on the changing climate which are difficult to envisage (see chap. I). In addition, future climate trends will depend on national and international actions aimed at mitigation over the next few decades.

Policymakers require information on the local impact of larger trends

All of these uncertainties have profound implications for policymaking. The uncertainty associated with forecasting long-term climate trends and their effect on weather patterns is complicated by the need to be geographically precise, since the effects of climate hazards are felt at the local level. Policymakers need information not only on global and regional climate trends, but also on their expected effect on local weather and local communities. The uncertainty of climate trends and the need to incorporate the new information that is becoming available demand that policymaking be responsive and relevant to the needs of people through short-term actions which are coherent with longer-term sustainable development objectives and actions.

Implementation requires proper monitoring and assessment

The multiple actions required to achieve adaptation should be viewed as steps on an evolving pathway along which implementation is properly monitored and repeatedly assessed and revised (Reisinger and others, 2014) to enable the incorporation of new information and changing priorities (Davoudi, Brooks and Mehmood, 2013). Incorporating uncertainty within policy action day by day through iterative and adaptive policy processes helps to reduce the risks of lock-in solutions and path dependency. Those processes also enable

Figure IV.1
The four stages of the decision-making process

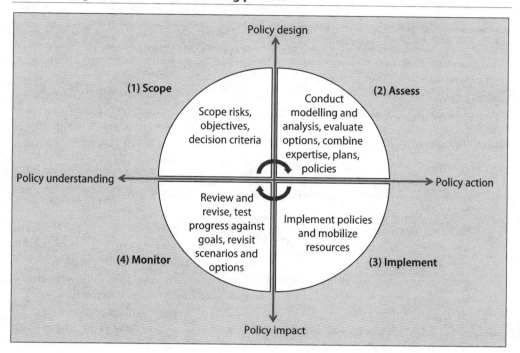

Source: UN/DESA, adapted from Jones and others (2014), fig. 2-3.

policymakers to benefit from flexibility and risk diversification and to adopt a portfolio approach encompassing complementary policy options.

An iterative policy process

A decision-making process comprises a series of activities, starting from policy design, followed by implementation, monitoring and evaluation of impacts. Sometimes referred to as iterative risk management, the process can be divided into four stages, as illustrated in figure IV.1. Each quadrant represents one of the steps of the policy cycle, which encompasses formulation of objectives and assessment of risks, assessments of the effect of policy options-related decisions on the course of action, policy implementation, and monitoring and review of outcomes. At each stage, progress can be measured in terms of the quantity and quality of outcomes along each of the four axes: policy design, policy action, policy impact and policy understanding.

Acquisition of learning at the various stages of the decision-making process and review of results are important for tracking progress and improving outcomes. Lessons learned from practical experiences and from pilot programmes need to be reinvested in the decision-making process. Within the context of hazards caused by climate change and the need for resilient sustainable development, flexibility must be a key characteristic of the policymaking process if it is to be useful in situations characterized by persistent uncertainties, long time frames, emergence of new information, and the multidimensionality of the problem. Maintaining both flexibility through the various stages of the policy process and the capacity to change and iterate towards improved outcomes is crucial to ensuring that policy interventions are properly informed by the knowledge gained in the process.

Improving outcomes requires a process of continuous evaluation and learning

Flexibility and adaptability constitute an integral component of continuous improvement

Flexibility and adaptability underpin the ability to incorporate lessons derived at each step of the policymaking process. They are integral contributors to the continuous process of improving existing policy frameworks (Watkiss, 2015). The capacity to change as new knowledge and information are gathered is important for delivering on the multiple objectives of effective climate change adaptation (Arup, 2014).

The static picture of the decision-making process as presented in figure IV.1 belies the fact that underlying the structure are dynamic forces in constant change. If, for example, as circumstances change, intended outcomes are not achieved or if unintended consequences are identified, a flexible policymaking system will have the capacity to adjust the scope, the implementation modalities, or the expected outcomes when necessary. This iteration is strengthened by the participation of stakeholders, which begins with the identification of policy objectives and the scoping of options and continues with contributions to the design of policy interventions and follow-up of implementation. It is important that, throughout the process, the scope and assumptions of the project be revisited based on experience (Jones and others, 2014).

An iterative policy cycle is one in constant evolution

Building on the illustration of the policy cycle in figure IV.1, figure IV.2 presents the circuitry encompassing policy design, assessments, implementation, monitoring and evaluation as constituting a dynamic system. An ideal iterative policy cycle is one in constant evolution, adjusting to new information and learning throughout the process. A flexible policymaking process will have the capacity to iterate best possible outcomes when it is sensitive to the context, involves all stakeholders, leverages expert and local knowledge, and establishes clear pathway connecting knowledge-generation, decision-making and action.

Active participation of stakeholders is important in all stages of the policy cycle

At each stage, leveraging other resources and benefiting from the participation of stakeholders also play a role. For example, during the stage of design of policy options, the process will be well served by the decision to involve stakeholders, representing many different organizations, communities and government agencies, which can present their priorities and concerns (see the sect. on participation). When assessing policy options, policymakers may benefit from the interactions of members of academia and experts in the area of quantitative modelling, as well as from local knowledge and experiences (see chap. III). When implementing policies, there is a need to mobilize the resources that will impact outcomes. When policy outcomes are being monitored, participation of multiple stakeholders will improve transparency and accountability. As the process benefits from more information and from greater participation, a virtuous cycle should lead to successive improvements in development outcomes, including strengthened accountability and improved governance (represented by the movement along the red arrows away from the origin in figure IV.2). Some of the key characteristics of such an iterative policy process aimed towards achieving adaptation and climate resilience are better understood using specific examples, as shown below.

Iterative improvement in practice: three examples

The three examples provided below highlight the practical advantages derived from incorporating an iterative process of learning as part of the policy decision-making process. The Sustainable Water Management Improves Tomorrow's Cities' Health (SWITCH) project in Lima was designed was designed to enable continuous learning from local experience and from the experience of stakeholders, and to build on small-scale experiments. In Chicago, the city's Climate Action Plan recognizes the uncertain nature of the challenge and is expected to evolve as new information from assessments and changing priorities comes to light. In London, plans to deal with sea-level rise include contingent actions which are

Figure IV.2
The iterative decision-making process

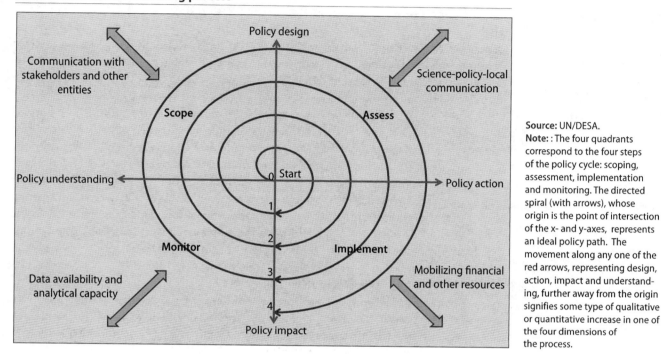

Source: UN/DESA.
Note: : The four quadrants correspond to the four steps of the policy cycle: scoping, assessment, implementation and monitoring. The directed spiral (with arrows), whose origin is the point of intersection of the x- and y-axes, represents an ideal policy path. The movement along any one of the red arrows, representing design, action, impact and understanding, further away from the origin signifies some type of qualitative or quantitative increase in one of the four dimensions of the process.

activated based on different forecasts of sea-level rise. All three initiatives exemplify clear-cut approaches to avoidance of path dependence, constant re-evaluation of information and redesign of policy interventions so as to improve outcomes.

Sustainable water management in Lima[9]

The aim of the SWITCH action research project was to catalyse change directed towards more sustainable urban water management in the "city of the future". Under the programme, research was conducted and pilot projects were implemented which demonstrated the importance of learning from experiences and from stakeholder dialogue and knowledge exchange. The objective of SWITCH was to develop new solutions with regard to increasing the efficiency of urban water systems and their resilience to a range of future climate change scenarios. The project's approach was one of strengthening the connections between experts and stakeholders, and decision makers, so as to facilitate knowledge-sharing. The project's major outcome was the development of the SWITCH approach, encompassing the following four key features:

- Creation of a strategic planning process which encourages all city stakeholders to view the city's water cycle as an integrated system, so as to promote integrated and coherent solutions for water management
- Building on pilot experiences that are designed for upscaling
- Creation of learning alliance platforms which involve all relevant stakeholders during the process of research, design and implementation of activities

Building connections among all stakeholders and decision makers to facilitate knowledge-sharing can have profound impacts

9   Based on information published on the project's website (www.switchurbanwater.eu), and Arup (2014).

- Development of a training toolkit in partnership with members of the learning alliance platform

In Lima, the SWITCH project aimed at transforming a region where annual rainfall is scarce into one of green sustainable areas through the development of innovative approaches to the reuse of wastewater. The SWITCH project built on the lessons derived from previous efforts to reuse treated wastewater for urban agriculture and city greening. One major barrier to the reuse of treated water, however, is the lack of a proper institutional setting and relevant legislation.

The SWITCH project was able to identify means of surmounting those barriers by involving national and local authorities, ranging from the water authority in national ministries to local governments and non-governmental organizations. The focus of the contributions of the learning alliances ranged from national policy issues related to water treatment to local issues derived from the lessons learned during the pilot projects. The project was able to present ways of reusing treated wastewater effectively for irrigation of green areas and meeting the needs of the local population. This experience led to the development of national policy guidelines on the safe reuse of wastewater, increased public awareness on water recycling and created incentives for the development of new financial mechanisms for promoting small-scale wastewater treatment initiatives.

The SWITCH approach enabled the project to learn from local knowledge and to leverage that knowledge in the identification, development and implementation of relevant solutions. The project has also provided new projects with a template for improving governance and financial management structures, identifying new uses for water and incorporating natural systems in water treatment cycles.

Chicago Climate Action Plan

Long-term plans which recognize the uncertain nature of the challenge can adjust more easily to changing information and priorities

The Chicago Climate Action Plan is another example of an approach that embraces the uncertainty and risks of climate change by building flexibility into decision-making processes. Based on existing future scenarios, the Plan aims at adapting to future conditions instead of trying to build resilience on the basis of the status quo (City of Chicago, 2016). More importantly, the Plan acknowledges the inherent uncertainty associated with forecasting tools. It uses projections and scenarios of climate change and its likely effects on the city to propose specific actions under five main rubrics: energy-efficient buildings, clean and renewable energy sources, improved transportation options, reduced waste and industrial pollution, and adaptation. In the case of adaptation, the Plan calls for achievement of nine specific goals, ranging from management of heat and improvement of cooling capacities to monitoring of air quality with the engagement of multiple stakeholders.

To prepare for the possibility of hotter summers and more intense heat waves, for example, the city has worked with other organizations to identify populations at risk and to update emergency response plans. In this regard, the Plan also calls for the introduction of new ideas and anticipates that new knowledge derived from research on how to eliminate *urban heat islands* will lead to new initiatives. The city uses satellite imagery to identify hotspots and targets for policy interventions and has also identified the link connecting heat, respiratory illnesses and smog. With regard to smog, the Climate Action Plan calls for lower emissions from power plants and the modes of transportation that cause it.

Chicago's Climate Action Plan is expected to evolve as new information emerges. Progress is continuously monitored against goals and the results of such monitoring will inform the possible changes to be made to goals, targets and indicators. Those responsible for the Plan are aware that strategies may become obsolete and that new technologies may be utilized to address expected future challenges. For this purpose, the city has created a Green Steering Committee whose function is to gather the information and acquire the knowledge needed to inform future policy actions. Introducing flexibility as an integral part of the Climate Action Plan helps policymakers avoid path dependence and will enable the cost of future adjustments in response to unexpected events and the emergence of new information to be lowered.

Thames Estuary protection plan (London)

The plan to protect London's Thames Estuary, a subject mentioned in chapter III, offers a more clear-cut example of an iterative and flexible adaptation policy designed to meet the uncertain long-term risks arising from climate change. The plan was developed by the United Kingdom Environment Agency as a means of addressing sea-level rise and the threat of flooding that it poses to London. Since engineering projects for protecting the city entail lead times for planning and construction that are measured in decades, the acceleration of sea-level rise presents a difficult policy challenge. The protection plan addresses this challenge through an iterative approach which builds incrementally upon the existing system, selectively raising defences and taking other measures to elevate the protection standards of the current system (see figure IV.3). If sea-level rise accelerates, the plan calls for measures that are more substantial in the longer term, including the construction of a

Addressing contingencies under a range of scenarios helps build a fully adaptable system

Figure IV.3
Adaptation measures and pathways in the Thames Estuary 2100 plan

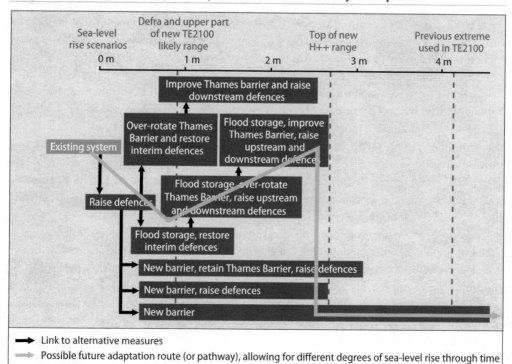

Source: Wong and others (2014), box 5-1.
Note: Each measure is drawn according to the range of sea-level rise over which it is considered effective. The black arrows point to alternative measures which may be applied once a measure is no longer effective. The red dotted lines signify three sea-level scenarios used in the analysis. The green line signifies a possible adaptation pathway as the forecasts on sea-level rising change. Note that the recently revised forecast of sea-level rise (three feet) (Gillis, 2016) is within the likely range of 0.9 metres which is used in this analysis.

new barrier or a coastal barrage. The plan will be adjusted based on careful monitoring of the drivers of risk to obviate the need for emergency measures (Wong and others, 2014, box 5-1). It may be noted that the newly revised estimates of the speed of melting of the West Antarctic ice sheet highlighted above has implications for the options under the plan.

Low- or no-regret interventions

Policymaking aimed at building climate resilience entails a high level of complexity. This stems from the fact that incremental policies designed to address immediate needs must be consistent with longer-term investments and initiatives aimed at facilitating the more substantial transformative changes required to address the underlying determinants of poverty, marginalization and vulnerability to climate hazards. Policymakers are confronted with the challenge of delivering immediate responses to current risks and adaptation deficits while ensuring that short-term interventions are consistent with longer-term strategies for building resilience and sustainable development (see discussion in chap. II and table A-II.1). While some problems require long-term horizons for analysis and planning, others must be addressed within the framework of the present. In the absence of a flexible and comprehensive plan which lays out the strategic objectives and their internal consistency with more immediate interventions, there is a tendency to focus on the middle ground, or on intermediate solutions, which, as time elapses, prove to be either insufficient for addressing extreme shocks or inefficient, should the shock not materialize. At the same time, policy action must aim for transformative solutions, which address the underlying structural inequalities that perpetuate the vulnerabilities of certain groups. All these challenges must be tackled within a context of climate uncertainty, which poses its own particular problems with respect to the assessment of policy options: different climate scenarios may require different policy options. Making decisions under scenarios characterized by uncertainty may increase the risk of path dependence and under- or overinvestment, depending on whether or not the climate hazards actually materialize and if they do, on their characteristics.

Achieving a balanced solution which takes into account all of the above challenges is a difficult task, but not an impossible one. Proper timing and phasing of actions, including the separation of those requiring immediate attention from those that can be deferred or that cannot be pursued without additional information, is a first step towards incorporating uncertainties into the process of designing and implementing policy interventions (Watkiss, 2015; Wong and others, 2014). Giving priority to low- or no-regret interventions provides policymakers with the space required for responding to immediate needs without incurring the risk of maladaptation or of being faced with unintended consequences.

Low- or no-regret interventions are those that can be justified from an economic, social or environmental perspective even if the climate hazard does not occur. The health sector provides a vast number of examples of low-regret actions, such as distributing mosquito nets, improving child nutrition, extending the coverage of health services, developing hygiene education campaigns, and improving water and sanitation facilities, among many others. Early warning systems constitute another example, as they grant authorities the flexibility to act pre-emptively and adjust civil security plans to the expected weather conditions, thereby reducing the number of lives at risk and/or the quantity of resources used. They include heat-wave early warning systems and early warning systems for vector- and food-borne infections, such as malaria and dengue, and (more recently)

Zika. Low-regret interventions reduce people's vulnerability, including to climate hazards, while contributing to the closure of development gaps that remain.

Final considerations

In order to ensure climate change-resilient livelihoods and advance towards achieving the goals set out in the 2030 Agenda for Sustainable Development, it is critical that public policy address the structural inequalities that perpetuate poverty and increase the vulnerability and exposure of people and communities to climate hazards. This could generate a virtuous cycle of lower vulnerabilities and exposure, better socioeconomic opportunities and outcomes, and a greater resilience of livelihoods to climate. The various facets of these objectives are well reflected in the Sustainable Development Goals, which constitute an important global framework for national policy decision-making. However, meeting the goals of sustainable development and climate resilience will require a systemic improvement in policymaking systems, particularly in those countries where population groups are most exposed and most vulnerable to climate hazards.

This chapter has provided a thoroughgoing description of the characteristics that policymaking systems need to possess if they are to be up to the task of building climate resilience while reducing inequalities. First, there is the need to integrate (or mainstream) adaptation objectives into longer-term development processes, with careful consideration given to the uncertainties inherent in forecasting under the climate change scenarios and the hazards created by a changing climate. Second, a participatory approach is fundamental to acquiring a better understanding of risks and vulnerability and the various priorities and interests of stakeholders, particularly at the local level. Direct engagement of local communities and stakeholders leads to a better identification of problems and an improved policy design in accordance with people's needs, and allows local problems to be addressed through local solutions, thereby increasing policy ownership and implementation. Third, in the context of a changing climate, policymakers must fully embed uncertainty into their long-term plans, using iterative and adaptive processes. This requires a more flexible policy process, capable of incorporating lessons derived from each step of the process, for improved outcomes.

A policy process that meets these three core criteria should be able to help address underlying inequalities through identification of vulnerable populations, particular intersecting vulnerabilities and relevant actions. However, as mentioned above, there are deeper underlying reasons why vulnerable groups are disproportionately at risk from climate hazards, which must not be left unexamined. Building greater resilience for long-term sustainable development requires addressing those underlying factors through transformative policies capable of closing the remaining development gaps which leave people exposed and vulnerable to shocks. This will benefit from a more flexible, participatory and integrated policy process.

Realizing a transformative agenda requires a longer-term strategic vision of development, an integrated approach across the economic, social and environmental dimensions of development, and support of policy planning and implementation through the effective inclusion of stakeholders. While the 2030 Agenda for Sustainable Development conveys a respect for the mechanisms through which countries formulate their policies in order to achieve the transformations that sustainable development demands, it also emphasizes the importance of strengthened development cooperation, which is particularly important

Addressing underlying structural inequalities is at the heart of the challenge of ensuring climate-resilient development

To have a better chance of succeeding, policy processes must be integrated, participatory and flexible

for those countries at higher risk from a changing climate. The mobilization of financial resources as well as capacity-building at many levels, not least of all in the area of data and statistics, will constitute important elements of support to countries in their efforts to build resilience to climate change, as further discussed in chapter V.

Enhanced cooperation for climate-resilient development

Key messages

- Delivering on the commitments set out in the 2030 Agenda for Sustainable Development to revitalize the Global Partnership for Sustainable Development will be critical to strengthening resilience to climate change among the most vulnerable countries and population groups. Improving access to stable and adequate sources of finance for adaptation and contributing to the building of the information systems needed to guide policy-making for climate resilience are two concrete actions where greater international cooperation is needed.

- Funding for adaptation projects lags behind funding for mitigation efforts by a significant margin. Public domestic and international efforts are needed to mobilize sufficient resources and provide incentives to the private sector to invest in adaptation. This is especially important for building the resilience and adaptive capacity of the most marginalized areas and population groups.

- Identifying vulnerable people, understanding the risks they incur and designing policies aimed at building climate resilience require intensive collaboration, among a wide range of data programmes and across disciplines, on uncovering the interlinkages between vulnerability and climate hazards. Efforts in this direction require unprecedented levels of cooperation at the global and national levels as the foundation for a new form of data development.

Introduction

The 2030 Agenda for Sustainable Development[1] is a universal instrument that recognizes the importance of the contribution of all countries to achieving the goal of sustainable development, including through support to developing countries, particularly the most vulnerable among them. As discussed in chapter I of the present *Survey*, a significant component of the vulnerability of many developing countries, in particular low-income countries, is associated with their exposure and susceptibility to climate hazards. Left unattended, this vulnerability will make it difficult to achieve climate resilience as well as other development goals, especially those related to poverty and inequality reduction, food security, and improved nutrition and health.

The global annual average cost of climatic disasters, including floods, storms, droughts and heat waves, is estimated to have risen from $64 billion during the period 1985-1994 to $154 billion in the period 2005-2014.[2] A more complete estimate of global

---

1   General Assembly resolution 70/1.

2   Calculations of UN/DESA, based on data from the Centre for Research on the Epidemiology of Disasters (CRED) International Disaster Database (EM-DAT). Available from http://www.emdat.be.

costs, taking into account the loss associated with slow-onset climate events (e.g., sea-level rise and desertification), is likely to yield a larger figure. Slow-onset events have particularly devastating effects on climate-sensitive livelihoods such as agriculture, fisheries and forestry. It is developing countries which have fewer resources and less capacity to adapt to a changing climate — in particular small island developing States, and countries where livelihoods depend on climate-sensitive natural resources — that are the most exposed (see chap. I).

A Global Partnership for Sustainable Development can harness development capacities for building climate-resilience in the countries that are the most in need of it

Against this backdrop, a strengthened Global Partnership for Sustainable Development has an important role to play in supporting and harnessing development capacities for building climate-resilience in countries that are the most in need of it. The historical agreements adopted by the members of the international community in 2015, including the 2030 Agenda for Sustainable Development and the Addis Ababa Action Agenda of the Third International Conference on Financing for Development,[3] usher in a unique opportunity to solidify effective global cooperation and coordination in support of global, regional and national efforts towards achieving sustainable development in general and climate-resilient development more specifically.

The imperative of limiting global warming to less than 2° C above pre-industrial levels and pursuing efforts to limit the temperature increase to 1.5° C, together with the task of effectively reducing the impact of climate hazards on vulnerable populations, requires a profound transformation of international cooperation. Much of the previous focus of climate action has been on mitigating the effects of anthropogenic activity so as to limit global temperature rise. In addition to this effort, unprecedented levels of cooperation are needed for the specific purpose of achieving climate change adaptation. This cooperation must facilitate the complex task of assessing needs and policy options for meeting those needs as well as supporting actual implementation of interventions towards achieving climate resilience, including the kind of transformative policies that would help address the structural inequalities underlying climate change vulnerability, as discussed in previous chapters. Such an accomplishment demands that cooperation be strengthened in a number of critical areas, two of which are discussed in detail below.

The first critical area of support encompasses provision of stable and sufficient sources of financing for climate-resilient development. The second encompasses improvement in capacities to produce and utilize large and complex sources of data and information, which, within the context of adaptation and climate resilience, need to cover local and even more highly specific geographical resolutions.

The next section emphasizes a key point, namely, that funding for adaptation projects lags behind that for mitigation efforts by a significant margin. This reflects in part the general emphasis in climate discussions on mitigation, as noted in chapter I. While the challenges of adaptation are recognized in international forums, that recognition has not yet generated the resources and level of support required for climate-resilient development. Part of the adaptation gap in financing can be explained by four specific characteristics of interventions directed towards adaptation that impact risk and return and limit the interest of private sector investors: (a) adaptation projects are difficult to separate from other types of development investments, particularly those aimed at reducing the vulnerability of people to climate hazards; (b) based on (a), an operational definition of adaptation does not exist, which prevents an explicit focus on adaptation; (c) adaptation projects are public

---

3   General Assembly resolution 69/313, annex.

goods, whose benefits accrue mainly to local communities; and (d) adaptation impacts are difficult to quantify, which complicates investment decisions.

A large part of the challenge of mobilizing resources to build resilience and adaptive capacity derives from the need to identify the vulnerable, understand the risk they incur and monitor the effect of interventions on reducing their vulnerability. Understanding the socioeconomic attributes of vulnerable groups and further assessing the potential impacts of climate hazards and policies on their livelihoods requires sound data and information, at the lowest possible geographical resolutions, with respect to where people live and where adaptation must take place. This is critical for enabling policymakers and population groups and communities to be better informed and acquire an understanding of the true nature of the problems to be confronted, as well as the expected impact of policy alternatives. When such fine-grained data and information are missing, rigorous climate impact assessments (chap. III) and the capacity of policy systems to respond (chap. IV) are seriously challenged. A discussion in a later section of this chapter will focus on the ways in which international cooperation can facilitate the building of capacity to collect and effectively use fine-grained data and information in support of policymaking processes aimed at building climate resilience.

Increasing financial flows for adaptation and supporting the construction of sound information systems for climate resilience require stronger global partnerships

Financing local climate adaptation at a global scale

At its twenty-first session, held in Paris from 30 November to 13 December 2015, the Conference of the Parties to the United Nations Framework Convention on Climate Change adopted the Paris Agreement.[4] The 195 States parties to the Convention and the European Union achieved a historic partnership through the adoption of the Agreement, which is the first universal, binding global climate agreement to put the world on track towards mitigating global warming by limiting it to well below 2° C and pursuing efforts to limit the increase in temperature to 1.5° C.[5] As of 29 June 2016, there were 178 signatories to the Paris Agreement.[6] The process of confronting the challenge of implementation has already begun: to curb warming by limiting it to 1.5° C-2° C above pre-industrial levels will require a profound shift in the pathways of industrialization. The pursuit of efforts to achieve this shift offers new opportunities to address previously entrenched socioeconomic inequalities while building more sustainable economies.

The challenge is a formidable one and will be met only through a global partnership that includes all levels of government, in addition to the private sector and civil society. Prior to negotiations held at the twenty-first session of the Conference of the Parties to the Convention, 160 States submitted intended nationally determined contributions (INDCs) which laid out plans for reducing greenhouse gas emissions (Ecofys, Climate Analytics, New Climate Institute and Potsdam Institute for Climate Impact Research, 2014). The United Nations Environment Programme (UNEP) Emissions Gap Report 2015 (UNEP, 2015) estimates, however, that full implementation of the INDCs would achieve only half of the emissions reduction required for there to be a reasonable chance of keeping below

---

4   FCCC/CP/2015/10/Add.1, decision 1/CP.21, annex.

5   Limiting the temperature rise to 1.5° C is considered a much safer defence against the worst impacts of a changing climate.

6   The Paris Agreement was opened for signature on 22 April 2016 and will remain open for signature for one year.

The Paris Agreement calls for a road map for achieving the goal of $100 billion dollars per year by 2020 for the financing of climate change mitigation and adaptation

the 2° C target in 2100 (Olhoff and Christensen, 2015). Accordingly, the Paris Agreement formally recognizes a significant gap between the current level of emissions reduction pledges contained in the intended nationally determined contributions and the 2° C pathway.

In order to help encourage bolder action towards a low carbon emissions economy, the Paris Agreement calls for developed countries to create a road map for ratcheting up financing for climate change mitigation and adaptation activities in developing countries to $100 billion per year by 2020 (decision l/CP.21, para. 114). This goal is feasible: government measures in support of fossil fuels are conservatively valued at $160 billion-$200 billion per year (OECD, 2015a);[7] and total new investment in renewable energy alone was valued at $286 billion in 2015 (REN21 Renewable Energy Policy for the 21st Century, 2016).[8] Raising $100 billion in climate finance per year is safely within the realm of possibility. But will it be enough?

According to the Fifth Assessment Report of the Intergovernmental Panel on Climate Change (Chambwera and others, 2014), adaptation costs within the developing countries alone will range from $70 billion to $100 billion per year by 2050. An updated review by UNEP indicates that these figures are very likely to represent an underestimate. Further, the $100 billion climate finance pledge is for both mitigation and adaptation finance.[9] Put simply, climate finance streams will need to far exceed the Paris Agreement target if climate change needs are to be met.

Current estimates of climate finance flows are aggregated and reported on by the UNFCCC Standing Committee on Finance. According to its most recent report, the outlay of funds for climate change mitigation dominates the climate finance portfolio (United Nations Framework Convention on Climate Change secretariat, 2014). Some estimates suggest that mitigation accounted for 93 per cent of total climate finance in 2014 (Climate Policy Initiative, 2014).

The present section addresses the factors that explain the vast difference between mitigation and adaptation financing. The first part presents a brief summary of the state of and prospects for climate finance, arguing that adaptation needs are currently underserved. In the second part, the discussion turns to an analytical assessment of the barriers to adaptation finance. By unpacking the black box of those project barriers, the analysis reveals that some areas of adaptation are better funded than others. The third part, which focuses on closing the gap, zeroes in on the notion that different types of adaptation activities require different types of support. Case studies bolster the argument that the public sector will have a continuing and strengthened role to play in all areas of adaptation programme implementation. This section also puts forward three policy scenarios, or leverage points, for ramping up private sector assistance in adaptation. Finally, an analysis

---

7   This figure can be considered conservative because it includes subsidies only from OECD partner countries and key developing-country partners (Brazil, China, India, Indonesia, the Russian Federation and South Africa). Further, only direct subsidies are included. The International Monetary Fund (IMF) estimates, which include indirect subsidies (e.g., non-taxation of externalities), are much higher.

8   Investments include all biomass, geothermal and wind power generation projects of more than 1 megawatt (MW); all hydro projects of between 1 and 50 MW; all solar power projects, with those less than 1 MW estimated separately and referred to as small-scale projects or of small distributed capacity; all ocean energy projects; and all biofuel projects with an annual production capacity of 1 million litres or more.

9   The Paris Agreement has called for a working group to draft a formal — and urgently needed — definition of what constitutes climate finance.

of the lessons learned from these cases yields some principles applicable to the question of how partnerships and policy interventions may be used to promote effective, locally appropriate and scalable adaptation measures.

The many ways to count to $100 billion

In 2009, under the Copenhagen Accord (para. 8),[10] agreed by Heads of State, Heads of Government, Ministers and heads of other delegations at the fifteenth session of the Conference of the Parties to the United Nations Framework Convention on Climate Change, held in Copenhagen from 7 to 19 December 2009, developed countries committed to mobilizing $100 billion per year for financing climate action in developing countries by 2020.[11] In the lead-up to the climate negotiations in Paris at the Conference of the Parties to the Convention at its twenty-first session, developed and developing countries sought greater clarity on the sources and quantity of flows for climate change mitigation and adaptation, as well as on the creation of policies designed to address recovery for loss and damage from climate change impacts.

The UNFCCC Standing Committee on Finance, which provides an operational definition of climate finance as "all finance that specifically targets low-carbon or climate-resilient development" (UNFCCC secretariat, 2014), estimates that climate finance mobilized by developed for developing countries ranges from $40 billion to $175 billion per year. In 2015, the Organization for Economic Cooperation and Development (OECD) and the Climate Policy Initiative reported that those flows had reached $52 billion in 2013 and $62 billion in 2014 (OECD, 2015a).[12] The total, including public finance provided by donor Governments, including non-concessional loans, did not include the value of capacity-building, policy interventions and the creation of enabling environments (ibid.), which, as seen in previous chapters, are critical facets of building climate resilience.

Even if only climate finance flows from developed to developing countries qualify as being part of the $100 billion pledge, a larger estimate is still useful in providing some idea of other, additional funds from other sources. All global climate finance, including public and private resources devoted to addressing climate change in all countries, yields a much larger estimate. According to the "Global landscape of climate finance", total global climate finance, including available estimates of domestic financing, amounted to $391 billion in 2014 (Climate Policy Initiative, 2015; and figure V.2).[13]

Under the United Nations Framework Convention on Climate Change, it is estimated that climate finance mobilized by developed for developing countries ranges from $40 billion to $175 billion per year

---

10   FCCC/CP/2009/11/Add.1, decision 2/CP.15.

11   This would come from bilateral or multilateral public or private sources, including innovative financing sources. Public financing may take several forms: financing by multilateral funds such as the Green Climate Fund; financing from multilateral or regional institutions such as the World Bank; government contributions; and financing from bilateral institutions.

12   It should be noted that those figures have not been immune to criticism. Developing countries, for example, argue that official development assistance (ODA) flows may be double-counted and that the methodology for calculating mobilized private finance needs improvement. The figures exclude finance for high-efficiency coal plants, which Japan and Australia argue should be considered a form of climate finance. Japan has provided $3 billion for such projects over the period 2013-2014.

13   The Climate Policy Initiative estimates that the domestic public budget for climate-related development not captured in the report could reach at least $60 billion per year.

Figure V.1
**Mobilized climate finance from developed to developing countries,
by funding source, 2013–2014**

Billions of United States dollars

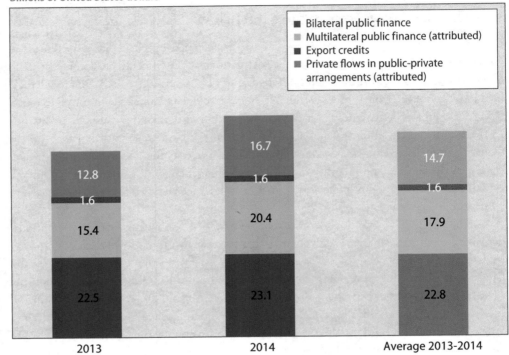

■ Bilateral public finance
■ Multilateral public finance (attributed)
■ Export credits
■ Private flows in public-private
arrangements (attributed)

Source: OECD (2015a, 2015b).

**Of the global total of
financial resources
channelled to developing
countries, more than
11 per cent represents
South-South cooperation**

Developed countries are not the only contributors of financial resources to developing countries. The smaller figures reported by the Standing Committee on Finance and OECD/ Climate Policy Initiative are limited to cross-border financial flows from developed to developing countries (i.e., South-South cooperation is not included). On the other hand, of the global total, more than 11 per cent represents South-South cooperation (OECD, 2015). Both methods of accounting for climate finance flows fill in part of the overall picture, but each has its limitations, as recognized under the United Nations Framework Convention on Climate Change[14] and by relevant institutions. For example, the fact that there is no central accounting mechanism for climate finance flows makes it particularly difficult to quantify beyond those resources channelled through multilateral development banks and other public institutions. There is therefore a need for a comprehensive definition of and monitoring system for climate finance.

A further complication is revealed through discussion on the mainstreaming of private investments into climate finance. Taking into account private flows, resources for climate-related finance are reaching record highs each year, owing in large part to investments in renewables and energy-efficient technologies by the private sector. Global private investment in renewable energy grew to $243 billion in 2014, up 26 per cent, from

14   United Nations, *Treaty Series*, vol. 1771, No. 30822.

Figure V.2
Climate finance flows along their life cycle, for latest year available (mostly 2014)

Billions of United States dollars

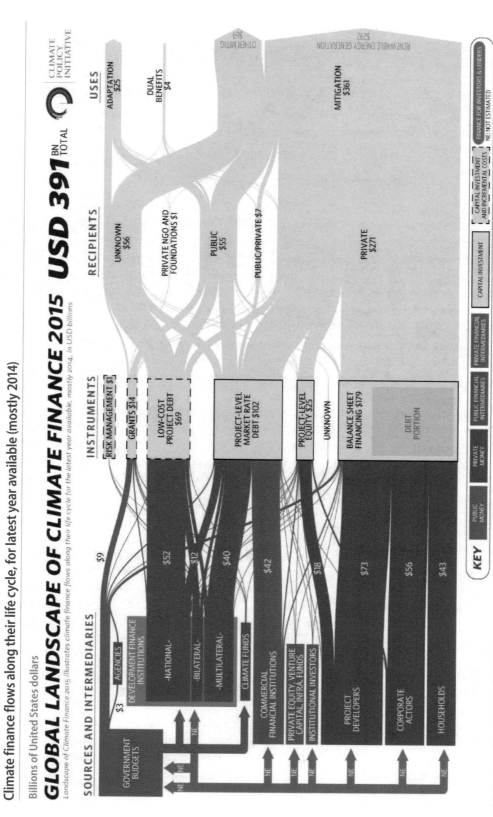

2013 (Climate Policy Initiative, 2015).[15] Again, achievements in mainstreaming climate-compatible technology into the global economy render the current $100 billion dollar metric misleading in some instances. Negotiations therefore continue on how climate finance accounting can be clarified and made more informative operationally for all.

Finally, while the Paris Agreement promises to strengthen efforts to provide $100 billion in climate finance from developed countries as a floor, the salient issue for developing countries is likely not only the volume but also the quality and predictability of the financial flows.

Official development assistance and climate finance

Developing countries have argued that financing for climate objectives should be offered in addition to official development assistance

Ambiguities associated with the definition of climate finance are symptomatic of the tension and ambivalence displayed within the political context of the climate negotiations themselves. While there have been efforts to further integrate climate considerations into the greater development agenda, developing countries have argued that finance for climate objectives should be offered in addition to official development assistance (ODA). In order to scale up ambition prior to 2020, the Conference of the Parties to the United Nations Framework Convention on Climate Change, in its decision 1/CP.21, entitled "Adoption of the Paris Agreement": "*strongly urge(d)* developed country Parties to scale up their level of financial support, with a concrete road map to achieve the goal of jointly providing USD 100 billion annually by 2020 for mitigation and adaptation while significantly increasing adaptation finance from current levels and to further provide appropriate technology and capacity-building support" (para. 114).

It is significant that the operational language of the Paris Agreement focuses on the purpose of the $100 billion promise but does not provide a clarification of the relationship between climate finance and regular ODA budgets, which is critical going forward. Without clear distinctions and definitions, cases where development projects are also considered climate-compatible projects can lead to the double-counting or under-counting of flows offered for ODA and/or climate finance.

Current financing trends in adaptation

Up to 77 per cent of climate finance is allocated to climate change mitigation compared with 16 per cent for climate change adaptation

Even given the constraints of current accounting possibilities, the OECD/Climate Policy Initiative is able to estimate that 77 per cent of climate finance from developed to developing countries is allocated towards climate change mitigation objectives, compared with the 16 per cent allocated for climate change adaptation (the remaining 7 per cent is allocated for activities that target both mitigation and adaptation in combined form). These results are driven by the dominance of mobilized private climate finance which leans towards mitigation-related activities (over 90 per cent). While the financing gap between mitigation and adaptation activities is significant, the public sector is slightly more amenable than the private sector to slating climate finance flows for adaptation. This may be explained in part by the public good nature of some adaptation projects, as discussed in chapter I. The Climate Funds Update (Heinrich Böll Stiftung (HBF) and Overseas Development Institute, 2016) estimates that 81 per cent of multilateral development bank funding goes for mitigation. It also reports that OECD members channel 53 per cent of their overall climate contributions to mitigation projects (when REDD+ funds are included, this share

---

15   See http://climatepolicyinitiative.org/press-release/global-climate-finance-increases-to-usd-391-billion/.

rises to 69 per cent), while 31 per cent is directed to adaptation projects and projects that combine mitigation and adaptation efforts (ibid).[16]

In response to pressure from developing countries on narrowing the gap between mitigation and adaptation resources, the Green Climate Fund, established as the principle mechanism for the financing of agreements adopted by the Conference of the Parties to the United Nations Framework Convention on Climate Change, committed to directing 50 per cent of its funds to adaptation, with half of that amount going to least developed countries, small island developing States and African States—which are, as was seen in chapter I, among the countries most vulnerable to changing climate conditions. Five years after its launch, the Green Climate Fund has so far given away $168 million to eight projects. In line with the Fund's mandate, the majority of those eight projects include an adaptation component (Green Climate Fund, 2015).

Five years after its launch, the Green Climate Fund has given $168 million to eight projects

Other formal acknowledgements of the gap between adaptation and mitigation financing exist at the highest level of international climate policy. In its decision 1/CP.21, the Conference of the Parties to the Convention requested the Adaptation Committee and the Least Developed Countries Expert Group, in collaboration with the Standing Committee on Finance and other relevant institutions, to make recommendations for consideration and adoption by the Conference of the Parties serving as the meeting of the parties to the Paris Agreement on the necessary steps towards facilitating the mobilization of support for adaptation in developing countries and on reviewing the adequacy and effectiveness of adaptation and support (para. 45). In addition, long-standing efforts have been directed towards responding to the special needs of least developed countries. As early as its seventh session, held at Marrakesh from 29 October to 10 November 2001, the Conference of the Parties to the Convention decided that support should be provided for the development, by the least developed countries, of national adaptation programmes of action (NAPAs), with funds from the Least Developed Countries Fund allocated to finance the preparation of the programmes of action and the implementation of the plans proposed.[17] A NAPA Project Database was established and is maintained at the UNFCCC website. The Least Developed Countries Fund is currently financed at $415 million, and it is estimated that an additional $550 million has been raised in co-financing for the 47 projects that have been approved for funding (Heinrich, 2016).

Explaining the adaptation financing gap

The adaptation financing gap is defined by UNEP (2016, p. 2) as the difference between the costs of meeting an adaptation target and the funds available to do so. Adaptation targets are themselves subjective: the act of "adapting" implies that there is a baseline of needs that can be safeguarded within a changing climate. It is also assumed that beyond a certain level of climate change, no amount of expenditure on adaptation will be sufficient

---

[16] Dedicated adaptation funds data are compared with those for general climate funds on the Climate Funds Update website, a joint initiative of Heinrich Böll Stiftung (HBF) and the Overseas Development Institute (ODI). REDD+ stands for countries' efforts to reduce emissions from deforestation and forest degradation and foster conservation, sustainable management of forests, and enhancement of forest carbon stocks.

[17] See FCCC/CP/2001/13/Add.1 and Corr.1 and Add.4 and Corr.1 for the relevant decisions adopted by the Conference of the Parties to the Convention at its seventh session, namely, decisions 4/CP.7, 7/CP.7 and 28/CP.7.

to maintain conditions suitable for human life, which means that the gap would be even larger. This fact, together with the priorities of high-income countries, partially explains the prioritization of mitigation activities, given that mitigation is the first and most fundamental action required in an effective response to climate change. Moreover, as noted in previous chapters, the fact that mitigation is easier to measure using common reference metrics (e.g., tons of greenhouse gases and radiative forcing values) makes it easier to estimate the resources needed for progress in mitigation compared with adaptation, which, owing to its intrinsic association with the multiple dimensions of development, is multi-metric in nature. These and other barriers to financing of adaptation projects (e.g., their public good nature and the difficulties inherent in separating adaptation investments from other development investments and therefore in creating incentives for adaptation) are discussed further below.

Given that global mean temperature is already 0.85° C above pre-industrial levels, adaptation expenditure is particularly urgent in countries where there is greater exposure and where infrastructure and health services need to be strengthened

Given that global mean temperature is already 0.85° C above pre-industrial levels, adaptation expenditure is essential for safeguarding livelihoods and human life. This is particularly urgent in countries where there is greater exposure and where infrastructure and health services need to be strengthened for coping with and recovering from climate hazards. According to the IPCC Fifth Assessment Report, existing estimates of adaptation costs range from $70 billion to $100 billion per year by 2050 within developing countries alone (compared with the $25 billion spent on adaptation projects in 2015 (figure V.2)). An updated UNEP review indicates that it is highly likely that these numbers are an underestimate. The difficulty of estimating adaptation costs is explained by the significant uncertainty in future climate scenarios and the multidimensional development areas that adaption must address if it is to be achieved. The true totality of financing needs is dependent on greenhouse gas emission levels: costs nearly double for a 4° C versus a 2° C pathway by mid-century, and higher rates of climate change across the modelled scenarios indicate exponential cost differentials (UNEP, 2016). Hence, it stands to reason that quantifying the financing gap implies identifying a moving target, in view of the uncertainties associated with climate projections (see chaps. III and IV for a discussion on the importance of including uncertainty in assessments and in the design of policy interventions). In addition, as noted in chapters I and II, adaptation requires a continuum of development policies under changing conditions which need to effect incrementally the transformations required for climate resilience.

In recognition of the fact that political processes have not kept pace with the severity and impacts revealed by climate science, developing countries and small island developing States have taken steps since 2006 to advance the adaptation agenda (alongside the mitigation agenda). As climate impacts worsened, developing countries and small island developing States negotiated effectively for the establishment of the Warsaw international mechanism for loss and damage associated with climate change impacts[18] at the Conference of the Parties to the Convention at its nineteenth session, held in Warsaw from 11 to 23 November 2013. Thus, the spectrum of climate finance includes money spent on climate mitigation activities, funds allocated towards adapting and promoting resilience to climate hazards, and a relatively new tranche of funding for payouts associated with climate catastrophes which hurt those least responsible for climate change such as small island developing States and the least developed countries, which have produced historically minimal emissions levels.

---

18   FCCC/CP/2013/10/Add.1, decision 2/CP.19.

Adaptation needs and the need for anticipatory climate adaptation action and finance are highest in developing countries. Unfortunately, the to mirror broader trends in global inequality, where those least well off have the highest level of need for anticipatory climate adaptation action and finance. The results of a recent assessment of municipal spending on climate adaptation within 10 megacities indicate that current financing trends will exacerbate inequalities. The assessment entailed calculation both of the municipal spending per capita and of that spending as a proportion of municipal gross domestic product allocated for adaptation. It was found that the spending on adaptation by developing countries as a proportion of municipal gross domestic product was less than the corresponding proportion for their developed-country counterparts: for each of the developing-country megacities studied, the proportion was approximately 0.15 per cent, except for Beijing, for which the figure was 0.33 per cent. In contrast, the corresponding figure for each of the developed-country megacities was 0.22 per cent. Further, developing-country spending per capita was significantly less than that of their developed-country counterparts (Beijing again being the exception). The study suggests that adaptation financing is driven by wealth rather than by vulnerability and that major population centres in developing and emerging economies are underserved (Georgeson and others, 2016).

Adaptation actions and financing are most needed in developing countries

Mitigation investments, and their returns, are (relatively) quantifiable

Mitigation investments are relatively easy to evaluate for effectiveness: the cost per ton of abated greenhouse gas emissions is a metric of investment effectiveness. The international carbon market established under the Kyoto Protocol to the United Nations Framework Convention on Climate Change[19] has created a method for translating greenhouse gas mitigation efforts into carbon offset credits, which can be traded and sold on various internationally regulated and voluntary markets. Under the Paris Agreement, a future role is explicitly nominated for market instruments in the 2020 climate regime, indicating a likely long-term upward trend in utilizing market mechanisms to integrate climate action into the global economy.

Beyond the establishment of carbon markets and its status as a global public good, mitigating climate change is increasingly becoming a feasible business proposition on its own. According to one estimate, 93 per cent of the $391 billion in total global climate finance in 2014 was directed towards mitigation projects, of which the vast proportion (81 per cent) went for investments in renewable energy (Climate Policy Initiative, 2015). Technical innovations aimed at increasing the efficiency and diversifying the supply of energy make sound business sense under any climate scenario. Admittedly, part of the reason why investments in renewable energy make up such a large share of climate finance is the lack of data on private investments beyond this sector (ibid.).

An estimated 93 per cent of the $391 billion in global climate finance in 2014 was directed towards mitigation projects, with the vast proportion for investments in renewable energy

The Paris Agreement makes the clear business case to the private sector that investments in a green economy will pay off (Krauss and Bradsher, 2015). In order to invest, private investors need "long, loud, and legal" policy to reduce their investment risk (Hamilton, 2009). Further, the Addis Ababa Action Agenda, which sets the framework for financing for development for the next 15 years, calls for the rationalization of fossil fuel subsidies, as one of many measures for mobilizing financing for sustainable development.

---

19   United Nations, *Treaty Series*, vol. 2303, No. 30822.

Barriers to adaptation finance

Explanations for the existence of the adaptation financing gap are wide-ranging, but most analyses tend to target one of four characteristics of adaptation project design.

Public, local good nature of adaptation projects

Adaptation investments often benefit a local group, without actually producing an economic profit. For example, the Adaptation Fund is financing a project on ecosystem-based adaptation to climate change in Seychelles, which enhances the region's ability to store adequate water in dry seasons. Climate change has resulted in more net annual precipitation than expected (historically speaking), but the rainfall is intermittent and Seychelles lacks storage capacity to retain the water. The ecosystem-based adaptation employed by the project essentially entails a concerted effort to restore wetlands, support natural coastal processes and maintain the watershed systems so that Seychelles is able to achieve its maximum water storage capacity even with intermittent inflows. The United Nations Development Programme (UNDP) is implementing the project with an incremental grant which will total $6,455,750; further, the projected benefits for the poor and vulnerable justify the use of public funds (UNDP, 2011).

The complexity of quantifying adaptation impacts

Economic gains can often be derived from an adaptation project, but quantifying and attributing those gains make for a complex undertaking

While economic gains are often to be derived from an adaptation project, quantifying and attributing those gains in terms of a payout to an individual organization can make for a highly complex undertaking. For example, the World Health Organization (WHO) reports that China has the highest rate of cerebro-cardiovascular disease and respiratory illness in the world and that labour-related losses and associated health-care costs are above $2,500 million annually. Heat waves cause an increase in the incidence of those types of illnesses. Vulnerable population groups such as seniors and infants—whose members are also the least equipped to advocate for themselves—are particularly at risk for serious injury or death in a heat wave, at a level that is 2-3 times above the normal (Ebi, 2015) (see chap. II for a more detailed discussion of these types of exposure and vulnerability).

Following record-breaking summer temperatures in China in 1988, 1990, 1994, 1998, 1999 and 2002-2008, WHO, the Institute for Environmental Health and Related Product Safety (Beijing), the Centers for Disease Control and Prevention (CDC) China and UNDP decided to implement an early warning system designed to predict heat waves and provide guidance on mounting a coordinated response through preparing and educating vulnerable populations. While the need for enhanced information and improved preparation in responding to heat waves remains beyond dispute, quantifying or attributing benefits from the project to a specific implementation organization or individual is all but impossible.

Lack of an operational definition of adaptation

That there is no internationally agreed process for identifying what constitutes an adaptation project renders it difficult to catalogue potential adaptation activities and estimate the cost of investment in those activities: investment in adaptation remains identified and priced on a case-by-case basis (Barbier, 2015). IPCC (2007) defines adaptation as "adjustment in natural or human systems in response to actual or expected climatic stimuli or their effects, which moderates harm or exploits beneficial opportunities". The all-encompassing nature of this definition accords with the fact that adaptation project outcomes are highly varied. As with financing development projects more generally, the goals are specific to local needs at the point of implementation. Any outcome (economic, environmental, social) that increases people's options and resources for adapting to crises can potentially qualify as a metric for project success. This being the case, wide room is left for interpretation, which increases the difficulty of comparing adaptation outcomes across a portfolio of projects.

The difficulty of separating adaptation investment from other forms of development investment

Separating adaptation finance from development assistance is a complex and often subjective exercise (Abadie, Galarraga and Rübbelke, 2012). In order to achieve the IPCC goal of implementing "no-regret policies", any development project should be able to integrate climate-adaptation components. On the other hand, if they are effectively integrated within all sectors of development, adaptation activities become all the more difficult to track. Efforts to mitigate climate change through reducing emissions from deforestation and forest degradation (REDD), which include adaptation components, provide an illustrative example. Such projects often include rehabilitating riparian zones, increasing forest diversity, incorporating fruit- and nut-bearing trees into a forested area for sustainable crop cycles, and other types of enhanced forest management which both increase the forest's ability to serve a region sustainably as a carbon sink and to act as a natural buffer against heat waves and floods. Given the difficulty of separating adaptation and mitigation activities, the need for policy coherence and the mainstreaming of adaptation with other development priorities and interventions becomes more salient (see chap. IV).

> Adaptation and mitigation activities require coherence for effective policy implementation

Similarly, investments in infrastructure may include an energy-efficiency component which could be considered an adaptation investment; and improvements to water storage and management systems will, arguably, almost always yield a benefit for climate change adaptation as well (Christiansen, Olhoff and Traerup, 2011). The amount of the investment in adaptation in all of these situations is based on a subjective calculation and, as a secondary objective, adaptation may even be excluded from the project developer's initial calculations.

In the lead-up to the twenty-first session of the Conference of the Parties to the Convention, the six large multilateral development banks and the International Development Finance Club adopted Common Principles for Climate Change Adaptation Finance Tracking, in a coordinated effort to establish harmonized definitions of adaptation finance for the purpose of achieving better accounting, transparency and accountability.[20] In support of this, OECD is undertaking efforts to fine-tune its Rio marker definitions to reflect the criteria established by the Common Principles, indicating some degree of convergence and standardization which will certainly benefit both donors and developing countries in their adaptation efforts.

Implications for adaptation

The barriers to increasing the financial resources available for adaptation are daunting, but they are not insurmountable nor do they affect all sectors of adaptation activities equally.

---

20   See http://pubdocs.worldbank.org/en/222771436376720470/010-gcc-mdb-idfc-adaptation-common-principles.pdf.

For example, the assessment by the Climate Policy Initiative of adaptation financing indicates that of the $25 billion allocated to adaptation in 2014, $14 billion in spending went towards water and wastewater management. The next largest sector, agriculture, forestry and land use, received just $3 billion (figure V.3). This discrepancy in funding is worth investigating—that is to say, why is water management more appealing to donors/investors than other adaptation activities? The initial indication is that water-related management often includes a technical component, one that can be commercially viable for entrepreneurs and corporate interests. Furthermore, activities within the water sector are easily identifiable as "climate change adaptation" activities, whereas projects that enhance climate change resilience in land use and the energy sector are likely counted as mitigation activities.

Figure V.3
Total adaptation finance by sector, 2014

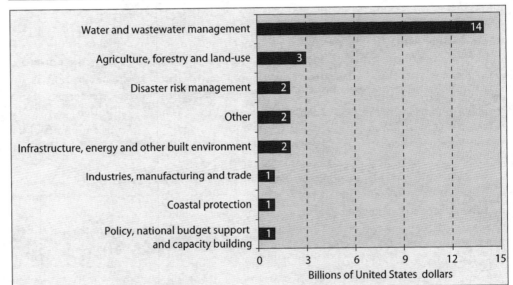

Overcoming barriers: policy scenarios for scaling up adaptation finance

Adaptation financing requires more resources from the public sector

Climate-resilient investments, such as in coastal protection efforts and other forms of disaster risk management, are often characterized by steep upfront costs, long investment timelines and low private returns to investment, making them prime candidates for public funds. There are some adaptation measures—the introduction and dissemination, for example, of adaptation technologies such as those involving drought-resistant seeds and solar-powered cooling systems for the home that expand access to electricity by reducing dependency on electrical grids while also reducing emissions—that align themselves well with business interests. However, in practice, kick-starting such adaptation measures requires a boost from the public sector. This being the case, the focus of the first policy scenario for increasing adaptation financing should simply be: more resources from the public sector.

Yet, no matter how active the public sector might be in the field of adaptation, participation of all levels of this sector is required to meet the scale of the adaptation challenge and should range from private financial institutions to small-scale entrepreneurs. Three major types of policy interventions can help in redesigning the landscape of adaptation financing prospects so as to render it more hospitable to private interests.

International and donor-level initiatives

The international agreement achieved at the twenty-first session of the Conference of the Parties to the Convention indicates that a coherent and coordinated international climate regime will exist far beyond 2020. Hence, the potential for establishing international policy leadership for the improvement of adaptation-related financial flows is high. Indeed, a clear example of regulatory action designed to increase funding for adaptation is provided by the Green Climate Fund, which is mandated to allocate 50 per cent of its funds towards adaptation.

Government regulation, in addition to effecting the direct financing of adaptation efforts, can also play a deciding role in the leveraging of private finance for adaptation measures. For example, the European Union Water Framework Directive[21] imposes legally binding requirements with respect to adaptation-relevant investments on private sector actors engaged in water-related development efforts.

Government regulation can also play a deciding role in the leveraging of private finance for adaptation measures

Regulation can also create markets from the ground up, as was the case with the flexible market mechanisms for greenhouse gas emissions under the Kyoto Protocol. As noted above, the Paris Agreement promises an enhanced role for utilization of market mechanisms for payment of environmental services; and the next generation of market tools for sustainable development could make adaptation deliverables a focus (Persson, 2011).

International and developed-country support for enabling institutions

International and national government intervention plays a pivotal role in transforming adaptation investment barriers into private sector opportunities (Dzebo and Pauw, 2015). For example, investments in infrastructure and early warning systems must precede the delivery of some adaptation measures such as improved crop distribution, enhanced delivery of medical services during a heat wave and rapid response to extreme weather events. It would be impossible for the private sector to implement crop insurance systems without there being weather monitoring stations in operation; however, the act of setting up such stations historically falls within the purview of the public sector.

International and national development banks are capable of reducing adaptation activities-related risk and leveraging large amounts of private sector financing. In recent years, development banks have facilitated increased levels of participation of the private sector in financing their adaptation portfolios (Climate Policy Initiative, 2015).

Targeted domestic policy incentives

Developing countries can catalyse private investment for specific adaptation interventions, e.g., by reducing import tariffs on adaptation-friendly technologies and equipment, such as irrigation systems. In addition to providing incentives, Governments can regulate private sector participation in sustainable environmental practices that support adaptation.

---

21   Directive 2000/60/EC of the European Parliament and of the Council establishing a framework for the Community action in the field of water policy, adopted on 23 October 2000.

Regulation need not be punitive over the long term, particularly if it includes feedback mechanisms that ultimately protect a sustainable resource base. Payment-for-ecosystem services schemes which generate revenue and then redistribute that revenue to vulnerable populations constitute one example of regulatory measures that provide incentives to protect natural resources. National authorities are favourably positioned to implement "benefit transfer" and "Nexus approach" solutions, terms that speak to a policy's ability to distribute gains throughout a community and to simultaneously consider multiple priority areas (such as water, food security, energy and health).[22]

Data and statistics for climate resilience

Improved capacities for producing and using complex sources of information to monitor progress towards climate-resilient development is imperative

The need to generate large, stable sources of financing for climate-resilient development is an issue that without doubt ranks high in the international agenda. A second focus of international attention is the imperative need to improve capacities for producing and using the large and complex sources of information required to monitor progress towards achieving climate-resilient development.

Pursuant to the adoption of the 2030 Agenda for Sustainable Development, the international community has turned its attention towards identifying the indicators that will support the follow-up and review of the 17 Sustainable Development Goals and 169 targets set therein. At its forty-sixth session, held from 3 to 6 March 2015, the Statistical Commission endorsed the formation of the Inter-agency and Expert Group on Sustainable Development Goal Indicators, which consists of 28 representatives of national statistical offices and includes, as observers, representatives of regional commissions and regional and international agencies.[23] The Inter-Agency and Expert Group was tasked to develop an indicator framework for the goals and targets under the 2030 Agenda for Sustainable Development at the global level. At its forty-seventh session, held from 8 to 11 March 2016, the Commission agreed on a global indicator framework for monitoring progress towards achieving the Sustainable Development Goals, which includes 230 global indicators, as proposed by the Inter-Agency and Expert Group.[24] It is a framework intended for follow-up and review of progress at the global level towards achieving the 17 Sustainable Development Goals. The Inter-agency and Expert Group will continue its technical work on reviewing and refining the indicators, as needed, and on further developing the methodologies for estimation, also as needed.

Meeting the new demands for data under the sustainable development agenda is a highly challenging task, which requires greater harmonization and integration among a wide range of data programmes across the economic, social and environmental domains, as well as improved analytical capacities for understanding the meaning of the intersections that occur across a multiplicity of disciplines. The present section discusses, within this larger framework, the challenge of producing the statistics and indicators required by

---

22   For more details on the Water-Energy-Food Security Nexus approach, see chap. III.

23   See the report of the Statistical Commission on its forty-sixth session (*Official Records of the Economic and Social Council, 2015, Supplement No. 4* (E/2015/24)), chap. I, sect. C, decision 46/101.

24   See the report of the Statistical Commission on its forty-seventh session (*Official Records of the Economic and Social Council, 2016, Supplement No. 4* (E/2016/24)), chap. I, sect. B, decision 47/101. See also the report of the Inter-Agency and Expert Group on Sustainable Development Goal indicators (E/CN.3/2016/2/Rev.1), in particular annex IV containing the final list of proposed Sustainable Development Goal indicators.

countries to identify population groups vulnerable to climate hazards, including through the use of the integrated assessments needed to inform policymakers (see chap. III).

International cooperation on the development of data and statistics needed to implement the 2030 Agenda builds on the experience of successful cooperation over the last 15 years. Implementation of the Millennium Development Goals agenda brought international attention and resources to bear on improving the methodologies and information systems that supported Millennium Development Goal monitoring and policy implementation. The Millennium Development Goals Report 2015, while confirming that there have been significant improvements in country coverage of core human development indicators, also recognizes that large gaps remain in respect of ensuring the quality and timely availability of data, including data disaggregated by geographical region, ethnicity, disability and other socioeconomic attributes, which are critical to the understanding of inequalities and vulnerability.

Erecting the statistical architecture that will help identify population groups vulnerable to climate hazards is a challenge in its own right, but it is even more of a challenge considering the gaps remaining in basic statistics. A World Bank study cited in *The Millennium Development Goals Report 2015* found that almost half of 155 countries examined lacked adequate data for monitoring poverty. And in sub-Saharan Africa, where poverty is most severe, 61 per cent of countries lacked data for monitoring poverty trends. Vital statistics disaggregated by geographical region, ethnicity, disability and other characteristics are also lacking. Overall, in spite of progress made in the last 15 years, systematic statistics are lacking on the size, geographical distribution and characteristics of vulnerable populations in developing regions. Such statistics, produced on a regular and coordinated basis, are essential for monitoring populations at risk and informing integrated climate impact assessments.

Missing data on vulnerable population groups

Public perceptions of climate change are largely conditioned by extreme events and the resulting disasters, whether or not they can be individually linked to climate change. In the case of weather events, for example, linkage is difficult to establish but there is currently considerable progress being made in attribution research (Cornwall, 2016; Solow, 2015). The international definition of disaster for statistical purposes has been established by the International Federation of Red Cross and Red Crescent Societies, in cooperation with the Centre for Research on the Epidemiology of Disasters (CRED) based in Louvain, Belgium. A "common accord" classification of disasters for operational purposes was published by CRED and the Munich Reinsurance Company (Munich RE) in 2009 (Below, Wirtz and Guha-Sapir, 2009). By compiling and analysing extensive data from its EM-DAT/ International Disasters Database covering the period 2005-2014, CRED was able to prepare tables on disasters for the *World Disasters Report 2015* (International Federation of Red Cross and Red Crescent Societies, 2015) presenting data by number, continent, phenomenon, numbers of people reported killed and affected, estimated damage and level of human development of the countries of occurrence.

The rural populations of the poorer developing countries in low-elevation coastal areas and deltas, including small island developing States, and people living in drylands and in mountainous and other remote areas, seem generally to be the populations most vulnerable to climate change. As noted in chapter I, those populations predominantly and

The Millennium Development Goals helped improve country coverage of human development indicators, but large gaps remain

more specifically include small-scale agricultural, pastoral, fishing and forest households and workers, who depend mainly on their own production for basic food security, water supply and housing and whose livelihoods are centred around climate-sensitive resources. These populations have been studied by the Food and Agriculture Organization of the United Nations (FAO) (2010; 2015a; 2016a) and the International Food Policy Research Institute (IFPRI) (Reij, Tappan and Smale, 2009; Spielman and Pandya-Lorch, 2009), but the data compiled have been limited. More generally, even though "three out of four poor people in developing countries live in rural areas…over the last two decades the quantity and quality of agricultural statistics have undergone a serious decline" and "(m) any countries, especially in the developing world, lack the capacity to produce and report even the minimum set of agricultural statistics required to monitor national trends" (FAO, World Bank and United Nations Statistical Commission, 2012, p. XI).

In addition, "(r)apid urbanization and the growth of megacities…have led to the emergence of highly vulnerable urban communities, particularly through informal settlements and inadequate land management", with vulnerable populations also including "refugees, internally displaced people, and those living in marginal areas" (IPCC, 2012, p. 8). These important factors relate to the mega-trends discussed in chapter I of this *Survey*, where the point was clearly made that those trends interact closely with climate change.

While much progress has been made in the production of the basic statistics needed to capture the impact of extreme climate hazards, as reported in chapter I, the statistics available on the basic characteristics of vulnerable population groups remain rough estimates. There are no systematic data available on the size of the population groups most vulnerable to climate hazards, including on their demographic characteristics and their livelihoods. The acquisition of a better understanding of the impact of climate hazards and policies effective in reducing people's vulnerability to them, for example, through the integrated climate impact assessments discussed in chapter III and other methodologies, urgently requires well-established information systems, based on systematic information derived from standardized data-collection processes (CRED, 2015).

> There are no systematic data on the size of the population groups most vulnerable to climate hazards, including their demographic characteristics and livelihoods

Improving statistics and indicators for addressing climate change vulnerability

In every area of data analysis on populations vulnerable to climate hazards, researchers have cited critical gaps in data sources and methods as impediments to compilation of reliable data series consistent over time and comparable across domains of research. While there are a large number of research projects and ongoing analysis focused on the wide range of topics related to the impact of climate change, the data sources generated by those projects, albeit useful for meeting the specific research objectives of those projects, do not, taken all together, offer complete systematic information on vulnerable populations. This patchwork of information on vulnerable populations, including indicators, derived from the results of those projects has gaps and possesses very limited geographical detail, frequency and continuity.

> International organizations can play a key role in development of guidelines and recommendations on how to improve data availability through coordinated technical cooperation

As the process of producing reliable and continuous statistics and indicators on the impact of climate hazards is at an early stage of its development, it requires considerable additional research, practical testing and development of capacities through advanced training on basic data sources and methods of compilation of statistics related to several fields including, among many others, hydrology, fisheries, forests and ecology, along with reliable disaggregated sociodemographic information. International organizations with responsibilities in those fields can play a key role through development of guidelines and recommendations and through partnerships, provision of training materials on methods and coordinated technical cooperation. For example, the Statistics Division of the Department of Economic and Social Affairs of the United Nations, in response to increased demands for climate change statistics and indicators, prepared, in collaboration with the Economic Commission for Europe (ECE), the report of the Secretary-General on climate change statistics, for submission to the Statistical Commission at its forty-seventh session (United Nations, Economic and Social Council, Statistical Commission, 2015).[25] In decision 47/112, adopted at its forty-seventh session on 11 March 2016 (see E/2016/24, chap. I, sect. B), the Commission requested the Statistics Division to review the set of climate change-related statistics and indicators being developed by ECE and to consider it as a basis for developing a global set of climate change statistics and indicators, applicable to countries at various stages of development (para. (h)).[26]

Harmonization and integration of data sources, concepts and methods

Basic data in countries, developed according to national circumstances and priorities, provide the foundation for indicator compilation, in particular for rural and urban populations susceptible to climate change impacts. As noted, population groups particularly vulnerable to climate hazards, as identified in this *Survey* (i.e., people in low-elevation coastal zones, floodplains, deltas, dryland zones, and mountainous and remote areas), are largely rural and rely to a great extent on subsistence production for food security, energy, water and sanitation, and shelter. Further, climate change impacts stemming from rising sea levels and extreme temperature events are compounded by pressures stemming from population growth, rapid urbanization, water shortages and pollution.

Basic planning to enable anticipation of and adaptation to climate change impacts requires basic indicators on populations in vulnerable zones, which meet international criteria for standardized sources and methods, frequency and continuity and are easy to understand. Much of the information available thus far is derived from the work of those in academia and specialized researchers and has been prepared through the use of varied and often inconsistent concepts, methods and classifications. This work covers only periods of a few years and the years chosen differ among researchers. The research does provide a basic foundation for continuing work on concepts and methods, and for benchmark approximations. However, the data and information underpinning the research must, for official monitoring and policy purposes, become part of official national and international programmes, compiled and issued on a regular basis by or in association with official specialized services. Consequently, harmonization and integration are required among a wide range of data programmes, including official statistics of populations and their main characteristics and distribution by ecozones and by urban/rural, and extensive data on water and oceans and weather. Such statistics—with indicators to be specified within the technical context of the Sustainable Development Goals indicators programme =and produced on a regular, internally consistent and coordinated basis—are essential for

Harmonization and integration among a wide range of data programmes, including official statistics of population and its main characteristics, are needed

---

25 Available at http://unstats.un.org/unsd/statcom/47th-session/documents/2016-15-Climate-change-statistics-E.pdf.

26 Available at http://unstats.un.org/unsd/statcom/47th-session/documents/Report-on-the-47th-session-of-the-statistical-commission-E.pdf.

routine monitoring of populations at risk and for supporting assessments of policy options for addressing exposure, impact and adaptation at national, subnational and local levels.

The need to harmonize and integrate the variety of data sources through common concepts and methodologies has been well recognized. Recommendations have been endorsed under the Sendai Framework for Disaster Risk Reduction 2015-2030[27] on the need to establish international standards and harmonize definitions and classifications relating to vulnerable ecozones and regions and their vulnerabilities in and among countries. Also important is the need to ensure the capacity to "layer" detailed data on population and population characteristics, including occupation, urban/rural area of residence and poverty levels in small administrative areas so that population can be placed in the appropriate geographical ecozones and regions. The development of these data requires greater efforts to establish national capacity to compile time series on vulnerable populations from national and international sources.

Based on current information, it is difficult to assess populations at risk. In his study of coastal populations, for example, Woodroffe (2010) argues that "the population data are not at sufficient resolution for detailed hazard analysis" and that "(s)uch vulnerability analyses should be focused on detailed local topography and integration with other variables such as flood level, land use, and other relevant factors". Specifically with respect to the "poorest and hungry", a study issued by IFPRI (Ahmed, Hill and Wiesmann, 2007) concluded that "without context-specific and timely information it is *difficult* to design programs that fit their needs". On a limited scale, FAO (2015a) reported on two case studies, in Ecuador and Malawi, where vulnerability of mountain peoples to food insecurity was assessed from household surveys specifically designed to verify the results obtained in a modelling exercise. This kind of information could be obtained at a much greater scale if geo-referenced households were available for all countries.

Official national statistics including geospatial information are critical to the production of integrated data series

Interfacing data sources, especially official national statistics containing global geospatial information, is needed critically for the production of integrated data series, which must rely on substantially different collection methods. An illustration of the difficulties involved is provided in the case of compilation of water statistics in the United States of America. Currently, comprehensive and detailed national statistics on water are compiled every five years, but cover information for only one year, as they must be derived from hundreds of independent entities, with their own mandates and responsibilities, which use a multiplicity of concepts, methods and microdata sources (Fishman, 2016). In the Seoul Declaration on Global Geospatial Information Management issued at the first High-level Forum on Global Geospatial Information Management, held in Seoul from 24 to 26 October 2011, Forum participants recognized "the need for full interoperability of multidimensional geospatial information and integration with other data sources at national, regional, and global levels, in order to provide an effective information base for the resolution of global and local issues".

Complex statistical sources and methods, notably population censuses and surveys, are indeed widely used in all countries to measure population, and its social and economic characteristics and growth, and for regional and international comparisons and analyses. However, in general, they cannot be integrated easily with the wide variety of sources and methods used for linking geospatial measurement and environmental conditions. This is

---

27   Adopted by the Third World Conference on Disaster Risk Reduction, held in Sendai City, Miyagi Prefecture, Japan, from 14 to 18 March 2015, and endorsed by the General Assembly in its resolution 69/283 of 3 June 2015, and contained in annex II of that resolution.

due, among many other factors, to incompatible definitions and classifications for, e.g., subnational administrative boundaries and ecozones, and for geospatial identification of large cities and other urban and rural areas, and the varying and irregular time periods covered. Intensive collaboration among data producers across a range of disciplines, including water management, ecology, agronomy, forestry, meteorology and demography, is essential for establishing officially recognized and compatible guidelines and recommendations.

Geospatial information for building climate resilience

Geospatial information is a powerful tool for exhibiting the interconnections among land, oceans, atmosphere and human activities; it supports the development of plausible climate change scenarios and their impact on specific geographical locations. To the extent that geospatial information originates mainly from satellite observations, making it available to developing countries—especially those in special situations (i.e., least developed countries, landlocked developing countries and small island developing States), which are the most vulnerable to the impact of climate hazards—requires strong mechanisms of international cooperation and capacity development.

Making geospatial information available to developing countries requires strong mechanisms of international cooperation and capacity development

Through the use of geospatial information, for example, it is possible to assess the adverse impact of climate change due to sea-level rise along the coasts of small island developing States. Geospatial information includes profiles of the land, natural hazards, exposure of livelihoods and the location of vulnerable populations (United Nations, Economic and Social Council, Statistical Commission. 2015). Remote monitoring of the Earth by satellite can provide crucial data on deforestation and crop patterns which may indicate potential food shortages, and early warning on climate hazards (United Nations, Economic Commission for Latin America and the Caribbean, and European Union, 2011).

The Committee of Experts on Global Geospatial Information Management[28] is the intergovernmental mechanism that has been established to set the direction for the production and use of geospatial information within national and global policy frameworks. International cooperation on satellite imagery, in particular, has already supported capacity development efforts in different countries. For example, in Thailand, regional cooperation for sharing satellite data and survey measures of poverty levels, together with local placement rules for protected green areas, had a positive impact on reforestation, consumption and poverty reduction. The intervention also increased local revenues from ecotourism (Greenstone and Jack, 2015). Along similar lines, in a study by Scaria and Vijayan (2012) of India, the importance was underscored of international cooperation on spatial information technology for the country's rural development, including delivery of reliable baseline information on natural resources at the regional and micro levels, together with support for an integrated analysis of the natural resources inventory and management as well as a strategic plan for sustainable rural development.

While geospatial information is used in some developing countries, additional international cooperation is needed to expand timely access to information; to build the computation and storage capacity in those countries; and to strengthen technical capacity for using this technology effectively in supporting quantitative and qualitative assessments which inform policy decisions on climate-resilient development.

There are a number of public-private partnership initiatives to build from, including those being undertaken at the African Climate Policy Centre and the International

---

28 See ggim.un.org.

Research Institute for Climate and Society at Columbia University, New York City, which are linking climate satellite information with demographics in order to build vulnerability maps that layer physical and social sources of vulnerability. Other successful partnerships reveal the potential for strengthening collaboration among international organizations, large data providers and national Governments, as illustrated in box V.I with respect to the improved monitoring of forests in tropical countries. Information and expertise, are still disseminated, however, in multiple centres with limited coordination and harmonization of concepts and data-collection processes.

Strengthened collaboration across disciplines and across borders

Institutional experience and capacity to monitor climate change and impacts in exposed populations are dispersed across Governments and international organizations

Institutional experience, capacity and responsibility for the statistics needed to monitor and analyse climate change, exposed populations and impact are widely dispersed across Governments and international organizations and their collaborating institutions, as well as among and within governments; and frequently, there is little communication among the different specialties. In the developing regions, only a few Governments have adequate capacities for the needed data collection and analysis; and often, they continue to lack strong mechanisms for essential national and international collaboration in many instances.

Box V.1
Monitoring of forests in tropical countries

The experience of monitoring forests in tropical countries offers an illustration of effective multilateral cooperation in support of national capacity development efforts and resilience-building. The monitoring of forest cover and forest functions provides information crucial to the sustainable protection and management of forests, which is particularly important for tropical countries and populations whose livelihoods depend on forests. National forest monitoring systems estimate forest coverage, forest cover change and carbon stock change.

Romijn and others (2015) assessed the status of and changes in national forest monitoring and reporting capacities in 99 tropical countries using FAO Global Forest Resources Assessment data for 2015, complemented by data for 2010 and 2005 (FAO, 2016a). Forest area change monitoring and remote sensing capacities improved considerably between 2005 and 2015. For 54 of the 99 countries, the total tropical forest area that was monitored with good forest area change monitoring and remote sensing capacities increased from 69 per cent (1,435 million hectares) in 2005 to 83 per cent (1,699 million hectares) in 2015. This positive development has been the result of effective use of internationally free and open-source high-resolution satellite (remote sensing) data such as Landsat and of other available techniques for assessing historical forest cover change and improving countries' national forest monitoring.

Moreover, the total tropical forest area that was monitored with good "forest inventory capacities" increased for 40 countries, from 38 per cent (785 million hectares) in 2005 to 66 per cent (1,350 million hectares) in 2015. That "carbon pool reporting capacities" did not display as much improvement indicates the need for greater support for production of accurate emission factors and improved greenhouse gas reporting. The study also revealed that there was a positive adjustment in the net change in forest area in cases where countries with lower capacities had had the tendency in the past to overestimate areas of forest loss. The results underlined the effectiveness of capacity-building programmes such as those led by FAO and the multilateral initiative REDD+, which rewards developing countries financially for their verified efforts to reduce emissions and enhance removals of greenhouse gases through a variety of forest management options.[a]

Source: UN/DESA, based on Romijn and others (2015).
a REDD+ is a set of guidelines established for developing countries on how to report on forest resources and forest management strategies and their results in terms of reducing emissions and enhancing removal of greenhouse gases. See also footnote 16 above.

Few among the least developed countries, landlocked developing countries, small island developing States and other countries in special situations, such as conflicts, have such capacities.

These challenges are being taken up by the Statistical Commission and the Statistics Division, FAO, UNEP, the United Nations Office for Disaster Risk Reduction, the World Bank, the World Water Assessment Programme and the International Federation of Red Cross and Red Crescent Societies, and under the United Nations Convention to Combat Desertification in Those Countries Experiencing Serious Drought and/or Desertification, Particularly in Africa.[29] Specific programmes supported by international organizations, including the Partnership in Statistics for Development in the 21st Century (PARIS21), bilateral technical assistance and data development programmes and non-governmental organizations such as Open Data Watch,[30] are also making an important contribution to the strengthening of the statistical capacity of countries in need. Box V.II provides examples of significant global and regional experiences within the framework of emerging new mechanisms for data sharing. However, policies designed to build resilience across the wide range of vulnerable population groups requires unprecedented levels of new forms of data development, integration and analysis to support the demanding goal of achieving sustainable development in a context of continuous population growth, rapid urbanization and climate change.

Systematic official statistics, for all countries, are needed at least in the areas listed below (the names of the international institutions that bear responsibility for the development of those statistics in each area are given in parentheses):

a. Population and demography, including income, occupation and poverty, education and health (Statistics Division and Population Division, both of the Department of Economic and Social Affairs of the United Nations; the International Labour Organization (ILO); the United Nations Children's Fund (UNICEF); the United Nations Educational, Scientific and Cultural Organization (UNESCO); the World Bank; and WHO));

b. Economic activity in agriculture, fishing and forestry (Statistics Division, FAO and ILO);

c. Cartography and geographic information systems (Statistics Division, Committee of Experts on Global Geospatial Information Management, FAO and UNEP);

d. Meteorology (World Meteorological Organization);

e. Geology and land use, hydrology and ecology (Statistics Division and FAO);

f. Disasters (United Nations Office for Disaster Risk Reduction, International Federation of Red Cross and Red Crescent Societies and national emergency management offices).

Foundations for partnerships going forward

This chapter has discussed two critical areas where international cooperation for climate resilience needs to be strengthened. International cooperation is needed to generate stable and large sources of financing for climate-resilient development. At the same time, it is

---

29   United Nations, *Treaty Series*, vol. 1954, No. 33480.

30   See opendatawatch.org.

Box V.2
International cooperation efforts towards data sharing

Various public and private organizations are developing new partnerships to facilitate data sharing, with different degrees of open access. The Megacities Carbon Project, for example, is developing and testing methods for monitoring greenhouse gas emissions from megacities and their impact on people. The project, which operates under the principle of open and transparent data sharing, encompasses collaborative research of several partners. It is anticipated that the Los Angeles component of the data portal will be ready for public access in 2016. The Los Angeles component of the project is jointly funded by the US National Institute of Standards and Technology (NIST), the National Aeronautics and Space Administration (NASA), the National Oceanographic and Atmospheric Administration (NOAA) and the Keck Institute for Space Studies (KISS) . The California Air Resources Board and the University of California Discovery programme provide in-kind contributions.

Along similar lines, the Open Data for Africa platform portal, created by the African Development Bank under its statistical capacity-building programme, provides free online data for monitoring development indicators at national and subnational levels. The portal provides data derived from national, international and other sources. Users can disseminate data and share data content directly with others through social media. All African countries and nine regional institutions contribute to this platform, which also offers data users the capability to access data in machine-readable format under Statistical Data and Metadata eXchange (SDMX) standards.[a] The African Development Bank and the International Monetary Fund (IMF) have partnered to standardize and streamline the data submission process through a leveraging of the platform across different agencies (e.g., national statistical offices, central banks and ministries of finance) in all African countries.

The Africa Platform for Knowledge and Data Sharing on Earth Observation disseminates free maps, geographic information system (GIS) data sets and satellite images to assist in the monitoring and management of natural resources and agriculture.

Sources: African Development Bank Group (2011); and Megacities Project website (https://megacities.jpl.nasa.gov/portal/collection-network/).

[a] SDMX is an initiative sponsored by seven international organizations aimed at developing standards for the exchange of statistical information. These orgnaizations are the Bank for International Settlements (BIS), the European Central Bank, the Statistical Office of the European Union (EUROSTAT), IMF, OECD, the United Nations and the World Bank.

---

imperative that the capacities be strengthened for developing and using the large and complex sources of information and data needed to guide policymaking for climate resilience.

Increased funding from public domestic and international efforts are required to fill the gap in areas in which the private sector is unlikely to invest

Given that many adaptation efforts, such as the creation of levies and the installation of weather monitoring systems, support the public good, there is a strong case to be made for support from the public sector. Increased funds from public domestic and international efforts are required to fill the gap in areas in which the private sector is unlikely to invest adequately, in particular in projects aimed at the most marginalized areas and population groups. Adaptation efforts are successful only when they integrate the needs of the disenfranchised into a given policy's central goals and are responsive to the existence of inequalities that determine exposure and vulnerability (see chap. I). While in some cases (such as that of philanthropy), the private sector will aim for redistributive outcomes, in most, an adaptation agenda will require public funding.

Notwithstanding, the private sector does have a wider role to play; and in order to support private sector participation, public institutions can create enabling environments for the transformation of some of the challenges associated with adaptation financing into economic possibilities for the private sector. And what does the creation of such enabling environments entail? As noted in this chapter, the vigorous participation of national and international public agencies is a prerequisite for success. In addition, creating incentives for private sector participation may help catalyse and redirect private sector support.

This chapter's exploration of the adaptation financing landscape indicates that there is no single, universal adaptation measure which is applicable to every context and every financing structure. This insight can be of particular use to policymakers in helping them direct limited adaptation funds to the areas of greatest need, while allowing other types of adaptation (e.g., improved seed dissemination and improved irrigation technologies) to reach scale in relation to the policy levers discussed above. Clearly, careful assessments of the different policy options most suitable to the areas of highest need are a necessity.

There is no single, universal adaptation measure which is applicable to every context and every financing structure

To respond to this challenge, the Third International Conference on Financing for Development adopted the Addis Ababa Action Agenda. Heads of State and Government and High Representatives, who gathered for the Conference in Addis Ababa from 13 to 16 July 2015, committed to the realigning of financial flows with public goals, the drawing upon all sources of finance, technology and innovation, the promotion of trade and debt sustainability, the harnessing of data and the addressing of systemic issues. The Addis Ababa Action Agenda, which establishes a strong foundation for support of the implementation of the 2030 Agenda for Sustainable Development, provides:

- A comprehensive set of policy actions aimed at financing sustainable development, transforming the global economy and achieving the Sustainable Development Goals
- A framework for financing sustainable development which aligns all financing flows and policies with economic, social and environmental priorities and ensures that financing is stable and sustainable

Mobilization of public and private sector action to build resilience and adaptive capacity will also entail meeting the challenge of identifying those vulnerable to climate hazards, understanding the risk they incur, and monitoring the effect of interventions in reducing that vulnerability. The level of complexity associated with the production of the consistent statistics needed to achieve this is much higher than that associated with efforts to strengthen the human development statistics required to reach the Millennium Development Goals. Production of statistics on the impact of climate hazards requires the development of consistent concepts and classifications as a component of official national and international programmes for the establishment of officially recognized and compatible guidelines. Understanding the interlinkages between vulnerability and climate hazards requires intensive collaboration, harmonization and integration among a wide range of data programmes and across a range of disciplines, including official statistics of population, its main characteristics and its distribution by ecozones.

Understanding the interlinkages between vulnerability and climate hazards requires intensive collaboration, harmonization and integration among a wide range of data programmes and across a range of disciplines

A wide range of official data developers beyond the national statistical offices, including national and subnational government agents across sectors (including agriculture, water, sanitation, energy, mining and environment) will need to work together within a framework of intensive collaboration and adequate coordination. At this point in time, not only are institutional experience, capacity and responsibility—with respect to statistics for monitoring and analysing climate change and hazards, exposed populations, impacts and policy responses—widely diffused across Governments and international organizations, but there is often very little communication among the different specialities within governments.

These challenges have been recognized in the 2030 Agenda for Sustainable Development and are being taken up by international organizations, led by the Statistical Commission. Efforts in this direction will require unprecedented levels of cooperation at the global and national levels. Strengthened international cooperation needs to be the foundation for a new form of data development and for support of the building of capacity to use those data effectively, including within the context of integrated climate impact assessments.

Bibliography

Abadie, L. M., I. Galarraga and D. Rübbelke (2012). An analysis of the causes of the mitigation bias in international climate finance. *Mitigation and Adaptation Strategies for Global Change*, vol. 18, No. 7), pp. 943-955.

Abdi, Omar A., Edinam K. Glover and Olavi Luukkanen (2013). Causes and impacts of land degradation and desertification: case study of the Sudan. *International Journal of Agriculture and Forestry*, vol. 3, No. 2, pp. 40-51.

Adepetu, A. A., and A. Berthe (2007). Vulnerability of rural Sahelian households to drought: options for adaptation. Final report submitted to Assessments of Impacts and Adaptations to Climate Change (AIACC), Project No. AF 92. Washington, D.C.: International START Secretariat.

Adiku, Samuel G.K., and others (2015). Climate change impacts on West African agriculture: an integrated regional assessment (CIWARA). In *Handbook of Climate Change and Agroecosystems: The Agricultural Model Intercomparison and Improvement Project (AgMIP) Integrated Crop and Economic Assessments*, part 2, Cynthia Rosenzweig, and Daniel Hillel, eds. ICP Series on Climate Change Impacts, Adaptation, and Mitigation, vol. 3. London: Imperial College Press. Sect. I, chap. 1, Pp. 25-74. doi: 10.1142/9781783265640_00.

African Development Bank (AfDB), Asian Development Bank (ADB), European Bank for Reconstruction and Development (EBRD), European Investment Bank (EIB), Inter-American Development Bank (IDB), International Finance Corporation (IFC) and World Bank (WB) (2015). 2014 joint report on multilateral development banks' climate finance. June.

African Development Bank Group (2011). Open Data Platform for Africa: Data Submission and Dissemination Tool. User Manual V 1.0. Abidjan.

Agricultural Model Intercomparison and Improvement Project (AgMIP) (2015). Protocols for AgMIP Regional Integrated Assessments, Version 6. 23 June. Available from http://www.agmip.org/.

Ahmed, Akhter U., Ruth Vargas Hill and Doris M. Wiesmann (2007). 2020 focus brief on the world's poor and hungry people: the poorest and hungry – looking below the line. Washington, D.C.: International Food Policy Research Institute. October.

Ahmed, Syud A., Noah S. Diffenbaugh and Thomas W. Hertel (2009). Climate volatility deepens poverty vulnerability in developing countries. *Environmental Research Letters*, vol. 4, No. 3, pp. 1-8.

Akter, Sonia, and Bishawjit Mallick (2013). The poverty-vulnerability-resilience nexus: evidence from Bangladesh. *Ecological Economics*, vol. 96 (December), pp. 114-124.

Andersen, Lykke E. (2015). Opportunities in a changing climate: policies for reducing vulnerability, poverty and inequality. Background paper prepared for *World Economic and Social Survey 2016*. December.

_____, and Marcelo Cardona (2013). Building resilience against adverse shocks: what are the determinants of vulnerability and resilience? Development Research Working Paper No. 02/2013. La Paz: Institute for Advanced Development Studies. June.

Andersen, Lykke E., Lotte Lund and Dorte Verner (2010). Migration and climate change. In *Reducing Poverty, Protecting Livelihoods, and Building Assets in a Changing Climate: Social Implications of Climate Change in Latin America and the Caribbean*, Dorte Verner, ed. Washington, D.C.: World Bank. Chap. 7, pp 195-220.

Andersen, Lykke E., Addy Suxo and Dorte Verner (2009). Social impacts of climate change in Peru: a district level analysis of the effects of recent and future climate change on human development and inequality. World Bank Policy Research Working Paper No. 5091. Washington, D.C. October.

Andersen, Lykke E., and Dorte Verner (2010). Social impacts of climate change in Chile: a municipal level analysis of the effects of recent and future climate change on human development and inequality. World Bank Policy Research Working Paper No. 5170. Washington, D.C. January.

Andersen, Lykke E., and others (2016). *Climate Change Impacts and Household Resilience: Prospects for 2050 in Brazil, Mexico, and Peru*. IFPRI Food Policy Report. Washington, D.C.: International Food Policy Research Institute. April.

Anthoff, David, Cameron Hepburn and Richard S.J. Tol. (2009). Equity weighting and the marginal damage costs of climate change. *Ecological Economics*, vol. 68, No. 3, pp. 836–849.

Anthoff, David, and Richard S.J. Tol. (2010). On international equity weights and national decision-making on climate change. *Journal of Environmental Economics and Management*, vol. 60, No. 1, pp. 14–20.

Antle, John M., and Roberto O. Valdivia (2016). Assessing climate change impact, adaptation, vulnerability, and food security of farm households: the AgMIP regional integrated assessment approach. Background paper prepared for *World Economic and Social Survey 2016*.

Antle, John M., and others (2015). AgMIP's trans-disciplinary agricultural systems approach to regional integrated assessment of climate impacts, vulnerability, and adaptation. In *Handbook of Climate Change and Agroecosystems: The Agricultural Model Intercomparison and Improvement Project Integrated Crop and Economic Assessments*, part 1, Cynthia Rosenzweig and Daniel Hillel, eds. . ICP Series on Climate Change Impacts, Adaptation, and Mitigation, vol. 3. London: Imperial College Press.

Arimah, Ben C. (2011). Slums as expressions of social exclusion: explaining the prevalence of slums in African countries. Paper presented at the International Conference on Social Cohesion and Development, Paris, 20 and 21 January 2011.

Arup (2014). City Resilience Index. Research Report Vol. 1: Desk Study. London. April.

Baez, Javier, Alejandro de la Fuente and Indhira Santos (2010). Do natural disasters affect human capital? an assessment based on existing empirical evidence. IZA Discussion Paper No. 5164. Bonn: Institute for the Study of Labor. September.

Baird, Rachel (2008). *The Impact of Climate Change on Minorities and Indigenous Peoples*. Briefing. London: Minority Rights Group International. April. Available from http://www.ohchr.org/Documents/Issues/ClimateChange/Submissions/Minority_Rights_Group_International.pdf.

Barbier, Bruno, and others (2009). Human vulnerability to climate variability in the Sahel: farmers' adaptation strategies in northern Burkina Faso. *Environmental Management*, vol. 43, No. 5, pp. 790-803.

Barbier, Edward B. (2010). Poverty, development and environment. *Environment and Development Economics*, vol. 15, No. 6, pp. 635-660.

_____ (2015). Climate change impacts on rural poverty in low-elevation coastal zones. World Bank Policy Research Working Paper No. 7475. Washington, D.C. November.

Barrett, Christopher B., Alexander J. Travis and Partha Dasgupta (2011). Biodiversity conservation and poverty traps. *Proceedings of the National Academy of Sciences of the United States of America*, vol. 108, No. 34, pp. 13907-13912.

Barry, Ellen (2016). In India, a small band of women risk it all for a chance to work. *New York Times*, 30 January.

Below, Regina, Angelika Wirtz and Debarati Guha-Sapir (2009). Disaster category classification and peril terminology for operational purposes: common accord. Brussels: Centre for Research on the Epidemiology of Disasters (CRED); and Munich, Germany: Munich Reinsurance Company (Munich RE). Working Paper No. 264. October.

Ben Mohamed, Abdelkrim (2011). Climate change risks in Sahelian Africa. *Regional Environmental Change*, vol. 11, Supplement No. 1 (March), pp. 109-117.

Berkes, Fikret (2007). Understanding uncertainty and reducing vulnerability: lessons from resilience thinking. *Natural Hazards*, vol. 41, No. 2, pp. 283-295.

Bhave, Ajay Gajanan, and others (2016). Integrated assessment of no-regret climate change adaptation options for reservoir catchment and command areas. *Water Resources Management*, vol. 30, No. 3 (February), pp. 1001–1018.

Bourguignon, FranÇois. (2015). *The Globalization of Inequality*. Princeton, New Jersey: Princeton University Press.

Boyce, James K. (1994). Inequality as a cause of environmental degradation. *Ecological Economics*, vol. 11, No. 3 (December), pp. 169-178.

_____ (2003). Inequality and environmental protection. Political Economy Research Institute PERI Working Paper No. 52. Amherst, Massachusetts: University of Massachusetts, Political Economy Research Institute.

Brainard, Lael, Abigail Jones and Nigel Purvis, eds. (2009). *Climate Change and Global Poverty: A Billion Lives in the Balance?* Washington, D.C.: Brookings Institution Press.

Braun, Boris, and Tibor Aßheuer (2011). Floods in megacity environments: vulnerability and coping strategies of slum dwellers in Dhaka/Bangladesh. *Natural Hazards*, vol. 58, No. 2 (August), pp. 771-787.

Brookings Institution (2005). New Orleans after the storm: lessons from the past, a plan for the future. Special analysis. Washington, D.C. October.

Brooks, Nick (2006). Climate change, drought and pastoralism in the Sahel. Discussion note for the World Initiative on Sustainable Pastoralism.

Brouwer, Roy, and others (2007). Socioeconomic vulnerability and adaptation to environmental risk: a case study of climate change and flooding in Bangladesh. *Risk Analysis*, vol. 27, No. 2, pp. 313-326.

Burkett, V.R., and others (2014). Point of departure. In *Climate Change 2014: Impacts, Adaptation, and Vulnerability. Part A: Global and Sectoral Aspects.* Working Group II Contribution to the Fifth Assessment Report of the Intergovernmental Panel on Climate Change, C.B. Field and others, eds. Cambridge, United Kingdom: Cambridge University Press. Pp. 169-194.

Butt, Tanveer A., Bruce A. McCarl and Alpha O. Kergna (2006). Policies for reducing agricultural sector vulnerability to climate change in Mali. *Climate Policy*, vol. 5, No. 6, pp. 583-598.

Campanella, Richard (2011). An initial interpretation of 2010 racial and ethnic geographies of greater New Orleans. June.

Carter, Michael, and others (2007). Poverty traps and natural disasters in Ethiopia and Honduras. *World Development*, vol. 35, No. 5, pp. 835-856.

Carvajal-Velez, Liliana (2007). Impacts of climate change on human development. Human Development Report Office Occasional Paper. New York: United Nations Development Programme. March.

Carvalho, Laura, and Armon Rezai (2014). Personal income inequality and aggregate demand. Working Paper 2014-23. São Paulo, Brazil: University of São Paulo.

Centre for Research on the Epidemiology of Disasters (CRED) (2015). The human cost of weather related disasters 1995-2015. Brussels and Geneva. Available from http://www.unisdr.org/files/46796_cop21weatherdisastersreport2015. pdf.

Cervigni, Raffaello, and others, eds. (2015). *Enhancing the Climate Resilience of Africa's Infrastructure: The Power and Water Sectors.* Washington D.C.: World Bank.

Chainey, Ross (2015). Which is the world's most polluted city? World Economic Forum Agenda. Based on the World Health Organization "Outdoor air pollution in cities" database (2003-2010). 25 June.

Chakraborty, Jayajit, and others (2014). Social and spatial inequalities in exposure to risk: a case study in Miami, Florida. *Natural Hazards Review*, vol. 15, No. 3 (August).

Chambwera, M., and others (2014). Economics of adaptation. In *Climate Change 2014: Impacts, Adaptation, and Vulnerability. Part A: Global and Sectoral Aspects.* Working Group II Contribution to the Fifth Assessment Report of the Intergovernmental Panel on Climate Change, C.B. Field and others, eds. Cambridge, United Kingdom: Cambridge University Press. Pp. 945-977.

Chatterjee, Urmila, Rinku Murgai and Martin Rama (2015). Job opportunities along the rural-urban gradation and female labor force participation in India. World Bank Policy Research Working Paper No. 7412. Washington, D.C. January.

_____ (2016). What explains the decline in female labour force participation in India? Ideas for India for more evidence-based policy. Website managed by International Growth Centre, New Delhi. 13 January.

Chen, C., and others (2015). University of Notre Dame Global Adaptation Index: country index technical report. November. Available from http://index.nd-gain.org:8080/documents/nd-gain_technical_document_2015.pdf. Accessed 2 March 2016.

Christenson, Elizabeth, and others (2014). Climate-related hazards: a method for global assessment of urban and rural population exposure to cyclones, droughts and floods. *International Journal of Environmental Research and Public Health*, vol. 11, No. 2, pp. 2169-2192.

Christiansen, Lars., Anna Olhoff and Sara Traerup (2011). *Technologies for Adaptation: Perspectives and Practical Experiences*. Roskilde, Denmark: United Nations Environment Programme (UNEP) Risø DTU National Laboratory for Sustainable Energy.

Church, J.A., and others (2013). Sea level change. In *Climate Change 2013: The Physical Science Basis*. Working Group I Contribution to the Fifth Assessment Report of the Intergovernmental Panel on Climate Change, Thomas F. Stocker and others, eds. Cambridge, United Kingdom: Cambridge University Press. Pp. 1137–1216.

Cicowiez, Martín, and Marco V. Sánchez (2011). Efectividad y viabilidad de la política pública frente a los choques externos: un análisis mediante simulaciones. In *Vulnerabilidad económica externa, protección social y pobreza en América Latina,* Marco V. Sánchez and Pablo Sauma, eds. Santiago de Chile: Economic Commission for Latin America and the Caribbean; New York: Department of Economic and Social Affairs of the United Nations Secretariat; and Quito: Facultad Latinoamericana de Ciencias Sociales (FLACSO). Pp. 79-158.

City of Chicago (2016). Chicago Climate Action Plan. Available from http://www.chicagoclimateaction.org/pages/adaptation/11.php. Accessed 21 April 2016.

Clarke, Daniel, and Stefan Dercon (2015). Insurance, credit, and safety nets for the poor in a world of risk. In *Financing for Overcoming Economic Insecurity*, Nazrul Islam and Rob Vos, eds. United Nations Series on Development. London: Bloomsbury Academic.

Climate Policy Initiative (2014). The global landscape of climate finance 2014. Authors: Barbara Buchner and others. November Available from climatepolicyinitiative.org/publication/global-landscape-of-climate-finance-2014/.

_____ (2015). Global landscape of climate finance 2015. Authors: Barbara K. Buchner and others. November. Available from http://climatepolicyinitiative.org/wp-content/uploads/2015/11/Global-Landscape-of-Climate-Finance-2015.pdf.

Coleman, James M., Oscar K. Huh and DeWitt Braud, Jr. (2008). Wetland loss in world deltas. *Journal of Coastal Research,* vol. 24, No. 1A, pp. 1-14.

Coles, Ashley R., and Christopher A. Scott (2009). Vulnerability and adaptation to climate change and variability in semi-arid rural southeastern Arizona, USA. *Natural Resources Forum*, vol. 33, No. 4 (November), pp. 297-309.

Colton, Craig (2006). Vulnerability and place: flat land and uneven risk in New Orleans. *American Anthropologist*, vol. 108, No. 4, pp. 731-734.

Cornwall, Warren (2016). Efforts to link climate change to severe weather gain ground. *Science,* vol. 351 No. 6279 (18 March), pp. 1249-1250.

Cotula, Lorenzo (2006). Water rights, poverty and inequality: the case of dryland Africa. Human Development Report Office Occasional Paper No. 2006/2. New York: United Nations Development Programme.

Dabla-Norris, Era, and others (2015). *Causes and Consequences of Income Inequality: A Global Perspective.* IMF Staff Discussion Note 15/13. Washington, D.C.: International Monetary Fund. June.

Dani, Anis A., and Arjan de Haan, eds. (2008). *Inclusive States: Social Policy and Structural Inequalities.* Washington, D.C.: World Bank.

Dasgupta, Susmita, and others (2010). Vulnerability of Bangladesh to cyclones in a changing climate: potential damages and adaptive cost. World Bank Policy Research Working Paper No. 5280. Washington, D.C.: World Bank. April.

_____ (2014). Climate change, soil salinity, and the economics of high-yield rice production in coastal Bangladesh. World Bank Policy Research Working Paper No. 7140. Washington, D.C.: World Bank. December.

Davoudi, Simin (2012). Resilience: a bridging concept or a dead end? *Planning Theory and Practice*, vol. 13, No. 2 (June), pp. 299-307.

_____, Elizabeth Brooks and Abid Mehmood (2013). Evolutionary resilience and strategies for climate adaptation. *Planning Practice and Research*, vol. 28, No. 3 (June).

de Bono, Andrea, and Bruno Chatenoux (2014). A global exposure model for GAR 2015. Input paper prepared for the Global Assessment Report on Disaster Risk Reduction 2015. UNEP/GRID-Geneva. July.

de Bruin, Kelly C., Rob B. Dellink and Richard S.J. Tol (2009). AD-DICE: an implementation of adaptation in the DICE model. *Climatic Change*, vol. 95, Nos. 1-2 (July), pp. 63-81.

de Janvry, Alain, and others (2006). Can conditional cash transfer programs serve as safety nets in keeping children at school and from working when exposed to shocks? *Journal of Development Economics*, vol. 79, No. 2, pp. 349-373.

del Ninno, Carlo, and others (2001). *The 1998 Floods in Bangladesh: Disaster Impacts, Household Coping Strategies, and Response.* International Food Policy Research Institute Research Report No. 122. Washington, D.C.: International Food Policy Research Institute.

Dennig, Francis, and others (2015). Inequality, climate impacts on the future poor, and carbon prices. *Proceedings of the National Academy of Sciences of the United States of America*, vol. 112, No. 52, pp. 15827–15832. Available from http://www.pnas.org/content/112/52/15827.

Dercon, Stefan (2004). Growth and shocks: evidence from rural Ethiopia. *Journal of Development Economics*, vol. 74, No. 2 (August), pp. 309-329.

Dercon, Stefan., John Hoddinott and Tassew Woldehanna (2005). Shocks and consumption in 15 Ethiopian villages, 1999-2004. *Journal of African Economies*, vol. 14, No. 4 (February), pp. 559-585.

Deressa, Temesgen Tadesse, and others (2009). Determinants of farmers' choice of adaptation methods to climate change in the Nile Basin of Ethiopia. *Global Environmental Change*, vol. 19, No. 2 (May), pp. 248-255. Special issue: *Traditional Peoples and Climate Change.*

Deryugina, Tatyana, Laura Kawano and Steven Levitt (2014). The economic impact of Hurricane Katrina on its victims: evidence from individual tax returns . Unpublished paper. September. Available at http://deryugina.com/2014-09-15-hurricane_katrina_draft.pdf.

D'haen, Sarah Ann Lise, Jonas Østergaard Nielsen and Eric F. Lambin (2014). Beyond local climate: rainfall variability as a determinant of household nonfarm activities in contemporary rural Burkina Faso. *Climate and Development*, vol. 6, No. 2, pp. 144-165.

Dietz, A.J., R. Ruben and A. Verhagen, eds. (2004). *The Impact of Climate Change on Drylands: With a Focus on West Africa.* Dordrecht, Netherlands: Kluwer Academic Publishers.

Di Lernia, Savino (2006). Building monuments, creating identity: cattle cult as a social response to rapid environmental changes in the Holocene Sahara. *Quaternary International*, vol. 151, No. 1, pp. 50-62.

Dorling, Danny (2010a). Is more equal more green? Monday night lecture delivered on 17 May 2010 at the Royal Geographical Society, London.

_____ (2010b). Social inequality and environmental justice. *Environmental Scientist*, vol. 19, No. 3, pp. 9-13.

Douglas, Ian, and others (2008). Unjust waters: climate change, flooding and the urban poor in Africa. *Environment and Urbanization*, vol. 20, No. 1, pp. 187-205.

Dzebo, A., and P. Pauw (2015). Private finance for adaptation in LDCs? spelling out the options. SEI discussion brief. Stockholm: Stockholm Environment Institute.

Ebi, Kristie L. (2008). Adaptation costs for climate change-related cases of diarrhoeal disease, malnutrition, and malaria in 2030. *Global Health*, vol. 4, No. 9. doi:10.1186/1744-8603-4-9.

_____ (2015). Terminal evaluation of UNDP/WHO GEF Project "Piloting Climate Change Adaptation to Protect Human Health". UNDP Evaluation Resource Centre. February. Available from https://erc.undp.org/evaluation/evaluations/detail/7756.

Ecofys, Climate Analytics, NewClimate Institute and Potsdam Institute for Climate Impact Research (PIK) (2014). Tracking INDCs. Climate Action Tracker. Available from http://climateactiontracker.org/indcs.html. Accessed 16 February 2016.

Egeru, Anthony, Eseza Kateregga and Gilber Jackson Mwanjalolo Majaliwa (2014). Coping with firewood scarcity in Soroti district of eastern Uganda. *Open Journal of Forestry*, vol. 4, No. 1 (January), pp. 70-74.

Ensor, Jonathan, and Rachel Berger, eds. (2009). *Understanding Climate Change Adaptation: Lessons from Community-Based Approaches*. Bourton-on-Dunsmore, United Kingdom: Practical Action.

Few, Roger, Katrina Brown and Emma L. Tompkins (2007). Public participation and climate change adaptation: avoiding the illusion of inclusion. *Climate Policy*, vol. 7, No. 1 (January).

Field, C. B., and others (2014). Technical summary. In *Climate Change 2014: Impacts, Adaptation, and Vulnerability. Part A: Global and Sectoral Aspects*. Contribution of Working Group II to the Fifth Assessment Report of the Intergovernmental Panel on Climate Change, C.B. Field and others, eds. Cambridge, United Kingdom: Cambridge University Press.

Finch, Christina, Christopher T. Emrich and Susan L. Cutter (2010). Disaster disparities and differential recovery in New Orleans. *Population and Environment*, vol. 31, No. 4, pp. 197-202.

Fishman, Charles (2016). Water Is Broken : data can fix it. Opinion pages. *New York Times*, 17 March.

Food and Agriculture Organization of the United Nations (2010). *Agricultural Based Livelihood Systems in Drylands in the Context of Climate Change: Inventory of Adaptation Practices and Technologies of Ethiopia*. Environment and Natural Resources Management Working Paper No. 38. Authors : Kidane Georgis, Alemneh Dejene and Meshack Maio. Rome.

_____ (2012). *The State of Food Insecurity in the World 2012: Economic Growth is Necessary but Not Sufficient to Accelerate Reduction of Hunger and Malnutrition*. Rome.

_____ (2013). *The State of Food and Agriculture: Food Systems for Better Nutrition*. Rome.

_____ (2015a). *Climate Change and Food Systems: Global Assessments and Implications for Food Security and Trade*, Aziz Elbehri, ed. Rome.

_____ (2015b). *Mapping the Vulnerability of Mountain Peoples to Food Insecurity*, R. Romeo and others, eds. Rome.

_____ (2016a). Global Forest Resources Assessments. Available from http://www.fao.org/forest-resources-assessment/current-assessment/en/. Accessed 7 March 2016.

_____ (2016b). Google and FAO partner to make remote sensing data more efficient and accessible. News article. Available from http://www.fao.org/news/story/en/item/350761/icode/. Accessed 6 January 2016.

_____, Fisheries and Aquaculture Department (n.d.). Fishing people.

Food and Agriculture Organization of the United Nations, Forestry Policy and Planning Division and Regional Office for Asia and the Pacific (1977). People and forests in Asia and the Pacific: situation and prospects. Asia-Pacific Forestry Sector Outlook Study Working Paper No. APFSOS/WP/27. Authors: R.J. Fisher and others. Rome. December.

Food and Agriculture Organization of the United Nations, Mountain Partnership Secretariat, United Nations Convention to Combat Desertification secretariat, Swiss Agency for Development and Cooperation and Centre for Development and Environment of the University of Bern (2011). *Highlands and Drylands: Mountains, A Source of Resilience in Arid Regions*. Rome.

Food and Agriculture Organization of the United Nations, World Bank and United Nations Statistical Commission (2012). *Action Plan of the Global Strategy to Improve Agricultural and Rural Statistics for Food Security, Sustainable Agriculture and Rural Development*. Rome.

Food and Agriculture Organization of the United Nations, World Food Programme and International Fund for Agricultural Development (2012). *The State of Food Insecurity in the World: Economic Growth is Necessary but Not Sufficient to Accelerate Reduction of Hunger and Malnutrition*. Rome: FAO.

Foresight: Migration and Global Environmental Change (2011). Migration and global environmental change: future challenges and opportunities - final project report. London: Government Office for Science.

Forouzanfar, Mohammad H., and others (2015). Global, regional, and national comparative risk assessment of 79 behavioural, environmental and occupational, and metabolic risks or clusters of risks in 188 countries, 1990–2013: a systematic analysis for the Global Burden of Disease Study 2013. *Lancet*, vol. 386, No. 10010 (5 December), pp. 2287-2323.

Frumkin, Howard, and Anthony J. McMichael (2008). Climate change and public health. *American Journal of Preventive Medicine*, vol. 35, No. 5 (November), pp. 403-410.

Gault, Barbara, and others (2005). The women of New Orleans and the Gulf Coast: multiple disadvantages and key assets for recovery. Part I: poverty, race, gender and class. IWPR briefing paper No. D464. Washington, D.C.: Institute for Women's Policy Research. October.

Gentle, Popular, and Tek Narayan Maraseni (2012). Climate change, poverty and livelihoods: adaptation practices by rural mountain communities in Nepal. *Environmental Science Policy*, vol. 21 (August), pp. 24-34.

Gentle, Popular, and others (2014). Differential impacts of climate change on communities in the middle hills region of Nepal. *Natural Hazards*, vol. 74, No. 2 (November), pp. 815-836.

Georgeson, L., and others (2016). Adaptation responses to climate change differ between global megacities. *Nature Climate Change* , pp. 1-6. February. doi:10.1038/nclimate2944.

Gilens, Martin, and Benjamin I. Page (2014). Testing theories of American politics: elites, interest groups, and average citizens. *Perspectives on Politics*, vol. 12, No. 3, pp. 564-581.

Gillis, Justin (2016). Climate model predicts West Antarctic ice sheet could melt rapidly. *New York Times*, 30 March.

Gonzales, Christian, and others (2015). *Catalyst for Change: Empowering Women and Tackling Income Inequality*. IMF Staff Discussion Note No. 15/20. Washington, D.C.: International Monetary Fund. 22 October.

Gorakhpur Environmental Action Group (GEAG) (2014). Developing climate resilient ward plan: a guideline. Gorakhpur, India. September.

Green Climate Fund (2015). Green Climate Fund approves first 8 projects. Incheon City, Republic of Korea.

_____ (2016). Funding. Available from http://www.greenclimate.fund/ventures/funding. Accessed 28 March 2016.

Greenstone, M., and B. Kelsey Jack (2015). Envirodevonomics: a research agenda for an emerging field. *Journal of Economic Literature*, vol. 53, No. 1 (March), pp. 5-42.

Groen, Jeffrey A., and Anne E. Polivka (2008). The effect of Hurricane Katrina on the labor market outcomes of evacuees. *American Economic Review*, vol. 98, No. 2, pp. 43-48.

Gu, Danan, and others (2015). Risks of exposure and vulnerability to natural disasters at the city level: a global overview. Population Division Technical Paper No. 2015/2. New York: Department of Economic and Social Affairs of the United Nations Secretariat.

Guha-Sapir, Debarati, and Philippe Hoyois (2012). Measuring the human and economic impact of disasters. Report produced for the Government Office for Science, Foresight project « Reducing risks of future disasters : priorities for decision makers ». London. 27 November.

Hallegatte, Stephane, and others (2014). Climate change and poverty: an analytical framework. World Bank Policy Research Working Paper No. 7126. Washington, D.C.: World Bank.

_____ (2016). *Shock Waves: Managing the Impacts of Climate Change on Poverty*. Climate Change and Development Series. Washington, D.C.: World Bank.

Hamilton, Kirsty (2009). Unlocking finance for clean energy: the need for 'investment grade' policy. Energy, Environment and Development Programme Paper No. 09/04. London: Chatham House. December.

Hammill, Anne, Oli Brown and Alec Crawford (2005). Forests, natural disasters and human security. *Arborvitae*, No. 27 (March). Available from http://www.iisd.org/pdf/2005/security_ arborvitae27.pdf. Accessed 29 February 2016.

Hanson, Susan, and others (2010). A global ranking of port cities with high exposure to climate extremes. *Climatic Change*, vol. 104, pp. 89-111.

Hardoy, Jorgelina, and Gustavo Pandiella (2009). Urban poverty and vulnerability to climate change in Latin America. *Environment and Urbanization*, vol. 21, No. 1, pp. 203-224.

Hashizume, Masahiro, and others (2008). Factors determining vulnerability to diarrhoea during after severe floods in Bangladesh. *Journal of Water and Health*, vol. 6, No. 3, pp. 323-332.

Hein, Lars, Marc J. Metzger and Rik Leemans (2009). The local impacts of climate change in the Ferlo, Western Sahel. *Climatic Change*, vol. 93, pp. 465-483.

Heinrich Böll Stiftung (HBF) and Overseas Development Institute (2016). Least Developed Countries Fund. Climate Funds Update. Available from http://www.climatefundsupdate.org/listing/least-developed-countries-fund. Accessed 26 April.

_____ (n.d.). Climate Funds Update. Available from http://www.climatefundsupdate.org/.

Heinrigs, Philipp (2010). Security implications of climate change in the Sahel region: policy considerations. Paris: Organization for Economic Cooperation and Development, Sahel and West Africa Club Secretariat.

Hertel, Thomas W., Marshall B. Burke and David B. Lobell (2010). The poverty implications of climate-induced crop yield changes by 2030. GTAP Working Paper No. 59. West Lafayette, Indiana: Global Trade Analysis Project, coordinated by the Center for Global Trade Analysis, Department of Agricultural Economics, Purdue University,

Hertel, Thomas W., and Stephanie D. Rosch (2010). Climate change, agriculture and poverty. World Bank Policy Research Working Paper No. 5468. Washington D.C.: World Bank.

Hill, Ruth, and Carolina Mejia-Mantilla (2015). Welfare and shocks in Uganda. Background paper prepared for the World Bank Uganda Poverty Assessment. Washington, D.C.: World Bank.

Holthuijzen, Wieteke, and Jacqueline Maximillian (2011). Dry, hot and brutal: climate change and desertification in the Sahel of Mali. *Journal of Sustainable Development in Africa*, vol. 13, No. 7, pp. 245-268.

Homann-Kee, Tui S., and others (2016). Co-designing scenarios towards reduced vulnerability to climate change in semi-arid southern Africa. Draft presentation for the Agricultural Model Intercomparison and Improvement Project (AgtMIP) Phase 2 Integration Workshop, Dakar, 22-27 February 2016.

_____ (forthcoming). Re-designing smallholder farming futures for reduced vulnerability to climate change in semi-arid southern Africa. *European Journal of Agronomy*.

Hongbo, Wu (2015). Closing statement. Delivered at the Economic and Social Council Development Cooperation Forum Uganda High-level Symposium on "Development cooperation for a new era: making the renewed global partnership for sustainable development a reality", Kampala, 4-6 November 2015.

Hossain, Md Sarwar, and others (2015). Recent trends of human wellbeing in the Bangladesh delta. *Environmental Development,* vol. 17 (January), pp. 21-32. Available from www.elsevier.com/locate/envdev.

Howe, Caroline, and others (2013). Elucidating the pathways between climate change, ecosystem services and poverty alleviation. *Current Opinion in Environmental Sustainability*, vol. 5, No. 1, pp. 102-107.

Howells, Mark, and others (2013). Integrated analysis of climate change, land-use, energy and water strategies. *Nature Climate Change,* vol. 3, No. 7, pp. 621-626. doi:1038/nclimate1789.

Hughes, Barry B., and others (2012). Exploring future impacts of environmental constraints on human development. *Sustainability*, vol. 4, No. 5, pp. 958-994.

Hulme, Mike, and others (2001). African climate change: 1900-2100. *Climate Research*, vol. 17, pp.145-168.

Hutton, David (2008). *Older People in Emergencies: Considerations for Action and Policy Development*. Geneva: World Health Organization.

Imberman, Scott A., Adriana D. Kugler and Bruce J. Sacerdote (2012). Katrina's children: evidence on the structure of peer effects from hurricane evacuees. *American Economic Review*, vol. 102, No. 5 (August), pp. 2048-2082.

Intergovernmental Panel on Climate Change (2007). *Climate Change 2007: Synthesis Report*. Contribution of Working Groups I, II and III to the Fourth Assessment Report of the Intergovernmental Panel on Climate Change, R.K. Pachauri and A. Reisinger, eds. Geneva.

_____ (2007). *Climate Change 2007: Impacts, Adaptation and Vulnerability*. Contribution of Working Group II to the Fourth Assessment Report of the Intergovernmental Panel on Climate Change, M.I. Parry and others, eds. Cambridge, United Kingdom: Cambridge University Press.

_____ (2012). *Managing the Risks of Extreme Events and Disasters to Advance Climate Change Adaptation*. Special Report of Working Groups I and II of the Intergovernmental Panel on Climate Change, C.B. Field and others, eds. Cambridge, United Kingdom: Cambridge University Press.

_____ (2013). Summary for Policymakers, Technical Summary and Frequently Asked Questions. In *Climate Change 2013: The Physical Science Basis*. Part of the Working Group I Contribution to the Fifth Assessment Report of the Intergovernmental Panel on Climate Change, T.F. Stocker and others, eds. Cambridge, United Kingdom: Cambridge University Press.

_____ (2014a). *Climate Change 2014: Impacts, Adaptation, and Vulnerability. Part A: Global and Sectoral Aspects*. Working Group II Contribution to the Fifth Assessment Report of the Intergovernmental Panel on Climate Change, C.B. Field and others, eds. Cambridge, United Kingdom: Cambridge University Press.

_____ (2014b). *Climate Change 2014: Impacts, Adaptation, and Vulnerability. Part B: Regional Aspects*. Working Group II Contribution to the Fifth Assessment Report of the Intergovernmental Panel on Climate Change, V.R. Barros and others, eds. Cambridge, United Kingdom: Cambridge University Press.

_____ (2014c). *Climate Change 2014: Synthesis Report*. Contribution of Working Groups I, II and III to the Fifth Assessment Report of the Intergovernmental Panel on Climate Change, Rajendra K. Pachauri and Leo Meyer, eds. Geneva.

_____ (2014d). Summary for Policymakers. In *Climate Change 2014: Impacts, Adaptation, and Vulnerability. Part A: Global and Sectoral Aspects*. Working Group II Contribution to the Fifth Assessment Report of the Intergovernmental Panel on Climate Change, C.B. Field and others, eds. Cambridge, United Kingdom: Cambridge University Press.

_____ (2014e). Summary for Policymakers. In *Climate Change 2014: Synthesis Report*. Contribution of Working Groups I, II and III to the Fifth Assessment Report of the Intergovernmental Panel on Climate Change, R.K. Pachauri and L.A. Meyer, eds. Cambridge, United Kingdom: Cambridge University Press.

International Federation of Red Cross and Red Crescent Societies (2015). *World Disasters Report 2015: Focus on Local Actors - The Key to Humanitarian Effectiveness*. Geneva.

International Renewable Energy Agency (IRENA) (2015). Renewable energy in the water, energy and food nexus. Abu Dhabi.

IRIN (2012). Coping versus adapting. 2 April. Available from http://www.irinnews.org/report/95224/climate-change-coping-versus-adapting. Accessed 6 November 2015.

Islam, A.K.M. Saiful, and others (2014). Impact of climate change on heavy rainfall in Bangladesh. Final report R01/2014. Dhaka: Bangladesh University of Engineering and Technology (BUET), Institute of Water and Flood Management (IWFM). October.

Islam, S. Nazrul (2015). Inequality and environmental sustainability. DESA Working Paper No. 145. New York: Department of Economic and Social Affairs of the United Nations Secretariat. August. ST/ESA/2015/DWP/145.

Ivanic, Maros, Will Martin and Hassan Zaman (2012). Estimating the short-run poverty impacts of the 2010-2011 surge in food prices. *World Development*, vol. 40, No. 11, pp. 2302-2317.

Jackson, Jeremy B.C., and others (2001). Historical overfishing and the recent collapse of coastal ecosystems. *Science,* vol. 293, No. 5530 (27 July), pp. 629-637.

Jankowska, Anna, Arne Nagengast and José Ramón Perea (2012). The product space and the middle-income trap: comparing Asian and Latin American experiences. OECD Development Centre Working Paper No. 311. Paris: Organization for Economic Cooperation and Development. April.

Jalan, Jyotsna, and Martin Ravallion (2001). Household income dynamics in rural China. World Bank Policy Research Working Paper No. 2706. Washington, D.C.: World Bank. November.

Jaumotte, Florence, and Carolina Osorio Buitron (2015). Power from the people. *Finance and Development*, vol. 52, No. 1, pp. 29-31.

Jena, Manipadma. (2015). India holds up farmers' plight from extreme weather for COP21 delegates. Inter Press Service News Agency, 2 December.

Jiménez Cisneros, B.E., and others (2014). Freshwater resources. In *Climate Change 2014: Impacts, Adaptation, and Vulnerability. Part A: Global and Sectoral Aspects*. Contribution of Working Group II to the Fifth Assessment Report of the Intergovernmental Panel on Climate Change, C.B. Field and others, eds. Cambridge, United Kingdom: Cambridge University Press. Pp. 229-269.

Johnston, Robert (2010). "Poverty or income distribution: which do we want to measure?. In *Debates on the Measurement of Global Poverty,* Sudhir Anand, Paul Segal and Joseph E. Stiglitz, eds. Initiative for Policy Dialogue Series. Oxford: Oxford University Press.

_____ (2016). What data analytics are needed to identify and monitor populations vulnerable to climate change in developing countries? Background paper prepared for *World Economic and Social Survey 2016*. 27 April.

Jones, R.N., and others (2014). Foundations for decision making. In *Climate Change 2014: Impacts, Adaptation, and Vulnerability. Part A: Global and Sectoral Aspects*. Contribution of Working Group II to the Fifth Assessment Report of the Intergovernmental Panel on Climate Change, C.B. Field and others, eds. Cambridge, United Kingdom: Cambridge University Press. Pp. 195–228.

Kates, R.W., William R. Travis and Thomas J. Wilbanks (2012). Transformational adaptation when incremental adaptations to climate change are insufficient. *Proceedings of the National Academy of Sciences of the United States of America*, vol. 109, No. 19 (8 May).

Khandlhela, Masingita, and Julian May (2006). Poverty, vulnerability and the impact of flooding in the Limpopo Province, South Africa. *Natural Hazards*, vol. 39, No. 2 (October), pp. 275-287.

Koohafkan, P., and B.A. Stewart (2008). *Water and Cereals in Drylands*. London: FAO and Earthscan.

Kovats, Sari, and Rais Akhtar (2008). Climate, climate change and human health in Asian cities. *Environment and Urbanization*, vol. 20, No. 1 (April), pp. 165-175.

Kovats, R. Sari, and Shakoor Hajat (2008). Heat stress and public health: a critical review. *Annual review of Public Health*, vol. 29, No. 1 (January), pp. 41-55. doi:10.1146/annurev.publhealth.29.020907.090843.

Kraay, Aart, and David McKenzie (2014). Do poverty traps exist? assessing the evidence. *Journal of Economic Perspectives*, vol. 28, No. 3, pp. 127-148.

Krauss, Clifford, and Keith Bradsher (2015). Climate deal is signal to industry: the era of carbon reduction is here. *New York Times*, 13 December.

Kriegler, Elmar, and others (2012). The need for and use of socio-economic scenarios for climate change analysis: a new approach based on shared socio-economic pathways. *Global Environmental Change*, vol. 22, No. 4 (October), pp. 807-822.

Kronik, Jakob, and Dorte Verner (2010). *Indigenous Peoples and Climate Change in Latin America and the Caribbean*. Washington, D.C.: World Bank.

Kuhn, Katrin, and others (2005). *Using Climate to Predict Infectious Disease Epidemics*. Geneva: World Health Organization.

Lal, P.N., and others (2012). National systems for managing the risks from climate extremes and disasters. In *Managing the Risks of Extreme Events and Disasters to Advance Climate Change Adaptation*. A Special Report of Working Groups I and II of the Intergovernmental Panel on Climate Change, C.B. Field and others, eds. Cambridge, United Kingdom: Cambridge University Press. Pp. 339-392.

Lebel, Louis, and Bach Tan Sinh (2009). Risk reduction or redistribution? flood management in the Mekong region. *Asian Journal of Environment and Disaster Management*, vol. 1, No. 1, pp. 25-41.

Leichenko, Robin, and Julie A. Silva (2014). Climate change and poverty: vulnerability, impacts and alleviation strategies. *WIREs Climate Change*, vol. 5, No. 4 (July/August), pp. 539-556.

Le Masson, Virginie, and others (2016). Gender and resilience: from theory to practice. Working paper. London: Overseas Development Institute. January.

Li, Xiaodong, and others (2016). Evaluating the impacts of high-temperature outdoor working environments on construction labor productivity in China: a case study of rebar workers. *Building and Environment*, vol. 95, No. 1 (January), pp. 42-52.

Little, Peter D., and others (2006). Moving in place: drought and poverty dynamics in South Wollo, Ethiopia. *Journal of Development Studies*, vol. 42, No. 2, pp. 200-225.

Lloyd, S.J., R.S. Kovats and Z. Chalabi (2011). Climate change, crop yields, and undernutrition: development of a model to quantify the impact of climate scenarios on child undernutrition. *Environmental Health Perspectives*, vol. 119, No. 12 (December), pp. 1817-1823.

Logan, John R. (2006). The impact of Katrina: race and class in storm-damaged neighborhoods. Providence, Rhode Island: Brown University, Spatial Structures in the Social Sciences.

Lowrey, A. (2013). The inequality of climate change. *New York Times*, 12 November.

Luber, George, and Michael McGeehin (2008). Climate change and extreme heat events. *American Journal of Preventive Medicine*, vol. 35, No. 5 (November), pp. 429-435. doi:http://dx.doi.org/10.1016/j.amepre.2008.08.021.

Luo, Tianyi, and others (2015). World's 15 countries with the most people exposed to river floods. World Resources Institute blog. 5 March. Available from http://www.wri.org/blog/2015/03/world%E2%80%99s-15-countries-most-people-exposed-river-floods.

Macchi, Mirjam, Amanda Manandhar Gurung and Brigitte Hoermann (2015). Community perceptions and responses to climate variability and change in the Himalayas. *Climate and Development*, vol. 7, No. 5, pp. 414-425.

Maccini, Sharon, and Dean Yang (2009). Under the weather: health, schooling and economic consequences of early-life rainfall. *American Economic Review*, vol. 99, No 3, pp. 1006-1026.

Magnan, Alexandre (2014). Avoiding maladaptation to climate change: towards guiding principles. *S.A.P.I.E.N.S.* (Surveys and Perspectives Integrating Environment and Society), vol. 7, No. 1 (March).

Margulis, Sergio, Carolina Burle Schmidt Dubeux and Jacques Marcovitch, coordinators (2011). *The Economics of Climate Change in Brazil: Costs and Opportunities*. São Paulo, Brazil: School of Economics, Business Administration and Accountancy, University of São Paulo.

Markandya, Anil, and others (2001). Costing methodologies. In *Climate Change 2001: Mitigation*. Contribution of Working Group III to the Third Assessment Report of the Intergovernmental Panel on Climate Change, Bert Metz and others, eds. Cambridge, United Kingdom: Cambridge University Press. Available from http://www.ipcc.ch/ipccreports/tar/wg3/pdf/7/pdf.

Marshall, Fiona, and Elisabeth Hildebrand (2002). Cattle before crops: the beginnings of food production in Africa. *Journal of World Prehistory*, vol. 16, No. 2, pp. 99-143.

Masikati, Patricia, and others (2015). Crop-livestock intensification in the face of climate change: exploring opportunities to reduce risk and increase resilience in southern Africa by using an integrated multi-modeling approach. In *Handbook of Climate Change and Agroecosystems: The Agricultural Model Intercomparison and Improvement Project Integrated Crop and Economic Assessments*, part 2, Cynthia Rosenzweig and Daniel. Hillel, eds. ICP Series on Climate Change Impacts, Adaptation, and Mitigation, vol. 3. London: Imperial College Press.

Masozera, Michel, Melissa Bailey and Charles Kerchner (2006). Distribution of impacts of natural disasters across income groups: a case study of New Orleans. *Ecological Economics*, vol. 63, Nos. 2-3 (1 August), pp. 299-306.

Matin, Nilufar, and others (2014). Group inequality and environmental sustainability: insights from Bangladesh and Kenyan forest commons. *Sustainability*, vol. 6, No. 3, pp.1462-1488.

McDowell, Julia Z., and Jeremy J. Hess (2012). Accessing adaptation: multiple stressors on livelihoods in the Bolivian highlands under a changing climate. *Global Environmental Change*, vol. 22, No. 2 (May) pp. 342-352.

McMichael, A.J., and others, eds. (1996). *Climate Change and Human Health*. Geneva: World Health Organization.

Mekonnen, Mesfin M., and Arjen Y. Hoekstra (2016). Four billion people facing severe water scarcity. *Science Advances*, vol. 2, No. 2, pp. 1-6.

Mertz, Ole, and others (2011). Adaptation strategies and climate vulnerability in the Sudano-Sahelian region of West Africa. *Atmospheric Science Letters*, vol. 12, No. 1 (January/March) pp. 104-108.

Met Office Hadley Centre (2010). Sahelian climate: past, current, projections. Paris: Organization for Economic Cooperation and Development Sahel and West Africa Club Secretariat. February.

Mideksa, Torben K. (2010). Economic and distributional impacts of climate change: the case of Ethiopia. *Global Environmental Change*, vol. 20, No. 2 (May), pp. 278-286.

Milanovic, Branko (2011). *The Haves and the Have-Nots: A Brief and Idiosyncratic History of Global Inequality*. New York: Basic Books.

Miller, F., and others (2010). Resilience and vulnerability: complementary or conflicting concepts? Ecology and Society, vol. 15, No. 3), p. 11. Available from http://www.ecologyandsociety.org/vol15/iss3/art11/.

Mimura, N., and others (2014) Adaptation planning and implementation. In *Climate Change 2014: Impacts, Adaptation, and Vulnerability. Part A: Global and Sectoral Aspects*. Contribution of Working Group II to the Fifth Assessment Report of the Intergovernmental Panel on Climate Change, C.B. Field and others, eds. Cambridge, United Kingdom: Cambridge University Press. Pp. 869–898.

Moreno, Alvaro, and Susanne Becken (2009), A climate change vulnerability assessment methodology for coastal tourism. *Journal of Sustainable Tourism*, vol. 17, No. 4 (June).

Morin, Véronique M., Mokbul Morshed Ahmad and Pennung Warnitchai (2016). Vulnerability to typhoon hazards in the coastal informal settlements of Metro Manila, the Philippines. *Disasters*. 8 January. doi:10.1111/disa.12174.

Moser, Caroline (2007). Asset accumulation policy and poverty reduction. In *Reducing Global Poverty: The Case for Asset Accumulation,* Caroline O.N. Moser, ed. Washington, D.C.: Brookings Institution Press.

Mosley, Paul (2015). Assessing the success of microinsurance programmes in meeting the insurance needs of the poor. In *Financing for Overcoming Economic Insecurity*, Nazrul Islam and Rob Vos, eds. United Nations Series on Development. London: Bloomsbury Academic.

Moss, R.H., and others (2012). Ready or not: towards a resilience framework for making climate-change adaptation decisions. Report prepared for the World Bank by the Joint Global Change Research Institute.

Müller, Christoph, and others (2011). Climate change risks for African agriculture. *Proceedings of the National Academy of Sciences of the United States of America*, vol. 108, No. 11, pp. 4313-4315.

Mutter, John C. (2015). *Disaster Profiteers: How Natural Disasters Make the Rich Richer and the Poor Even Poorer.* New York: St. Martin's Press.

National Academies of Sciences, Engineering, and Medicine (2016). *Attribution of Extreme Weather Events in the Context of Climate Change.* Washington, D.C.: National Academies Press.

Navrud, Ståle, Tran Huu Tuan and Bui Duc Tinh (2012). Estimating the welfare loss to households from natural disasters in developing countries: a contingent valuation study of flooding in Vietnam. *Global Health Action,* vol. 5, pp. 1-11.

Nawrotzki, R. J., and others (2015). Undocumented migration in response to climate change. *International Journal of Population Studies*, vol. 1, No. 1, pp. 60-74.

Neumann, Barbara, and others (2015). Future coast population growth and exposure to sea-level rise and coastal flooding: a global assessment. *PLoS ONE*, vol. 10, No. 3, pp. 1-34.

Neumann, James. (2009). Adaptation to climate change: revisiting infrastructure norms. Issue brief No. 09-15. Washington, D.C.: Resources for the Future. December.

Neumayer, Eric, and Thomas Plümper (2007). The gendered nature of natural disasters: the impacts of catastrophic events on the gender gap in life expectancy, 1981-2002. *Annals of the Association of American Geographers*, vol. 97, No. 3, pp. 551-566.

Nicholls, Robert J., and Richard S.J. Tol (2006). Impacts and responses to sea level rise: a global analysis of the SRES scenarios over the twenty-first century. *Philosophical Transactions of the Royal Society A*, vol. 364, No. 1841 (April), pp. 1073-1095.

Nkedianye, Davie, and others (2011). Mobility and livestock mortality in communally used pastoral areas: the impact of the 2005-2006 drought on livestock mortality in Maasailand. *Pastoralism: Research, Policy and Practice*, vol. 1, pp. 1-17.

Noack, Frederik, and others (2015). Responses to weather and climate: a cross-section analysis of rural incomes. World Bank Policy Research Working Paper No. 7478. Washington, D.C.: World Bank.

Noble, I. R., and others (2014). Adaptation needs and options. In *Climate Change 2014: Impacts, Adaptation, and Vulnerability. Part A: Global and Sectoral Aspects*. Contribution of Working Group II to the Fifth Assessment Report of the Intergovernmental Panel on Climate Change, C. B. Field and others, eds. Cambridge, United Kingdom: Cambridge University Press. Pp. 833-868.

Nordbeck, Ralf, and Reinhard Steurer (2015). Integrated multi-sectoral strategies as dead ends of policy coordination: lessons to be learned from sustainable development. *InFER Discussion Paper*, No. 5-2015. Vienna: Institute of Forest, Environmental, and Natural Resource Policy.

Nordhaus, William D. (2007). A review of the *Stern Review on the Economics of Climate Change, Journal of Economic Literature*, vol. XLV, No. 3, pp. 686-702.

Nurse, L.A., and others (2014). Small islands. In *Climate Change 2014: Impacts, Adaptation, and Vulnerability. Part B: Regional Aspects*. Contribution of Working Group II to the Fifth Assessment Report of the Intergovernmental Panel on Climate Change, V.R. Barros and others, eds. Cambridge, United Kingdom: Cambridge University Press. Pp. 1613–1654.

O'Brien, K., and others (2007). Why different interpretations of vulnerability matter in climate change discourses. *Climate Policy*, vol. 7, No. 1, pp. 73-88.

_____ (2012). Toward a sustainable and resilient future. In *Managing the Risks of Extreme Events and Disasters to Advance Climate Change Adaptation*. A Special Report of Working Groups I and II of the Intergovernmental Panel on Climate Change, C.B. Field and others, eds. Cambridge, United Kingdom: Cambridge University Press. Pp. 437-486.

Olhoff, Anne, and J.M. Christensen (2015). Opportunities for bridging the gap. In *The Emissions Gap Report 2015. A UNEP Synthesis Report*. Nairobi: United Nations Environment Programme. Part II, chap. 4.

Olsson, L., and others (2014). Livelihoods and poverty. In *Climate Change 2014: Impacts, Adaptation, and Vulnerability. Part A: Global and Sectoral Aspects*. Contribution of Working Group II to the Fifth Assessment Report of the Intergovernmental Panel on Climate Change, C.B. Field and others, eds. Cambridge, United Kingdom: Cambridge, University Press. Pp. 793-832.

Open Data Watch (2016). Strategy and Guidance. Available from www.opendatawatch.com.

Oppenheimer, M., and others (2014). Emergent risks and key vulnerabilities. In *Climate Change 2014: Impacts, Adaptation, and Vulnerability. Part A: Global and Sectoral Aspects*. Contribution of Working Group II to the Fifth Assessment Report of the Intergovernmental Panel on Climate Change, C.B. Field and others, eds. Cambridge, United Kingdom: Cambridge University Press. Pp. 1039-1099.

_____, and Marcio Cruz (2014). GIDD Sectoral Wage Bill Database by workers' skill level. GTAP Resource No. 4503. West Lafayette, Indiana: Purdue University, Department of Agricultural Economics, Center for Global Trade Analysis. Available from https://www.gtap.agecon.purdue.edu/resources/res_display.asp?RecordID=4503.

Organization for Economic Cooperation and Development (2015a). Climate finance in 2013-14 and the USD 100 billion goal. Report by the OECD in collaboration with Climate Policy Initiative. Available from http://www.oecd.org/environment/cc/OECD-CPI-Climate-Finance-Report.htm.

Organization for Economic Cooperation and Development (2015b). *OECD Companion to the Inventory of Support Measures for Fossil Fuels 2015*. Paris. 21 September. OECD Publishing, Available from http://www.oecd.org/environment/oecd-companion-to-the-inventory-of-support-measures-for-fossil-fuels-2015-9789264239616-en.htm.

Osorio Rodarte, Israel (2016). Sustainable pathways, climate change and the evolution of inequalities. Background paper prepared for *World and Economic and Social Survey 2016*.

Ospina, Angelica Valeria, and Richard Heeks (2010). Linking ICTs and climate change adaptation: a conceptual framework for e-resilience and e-adaptation. Publication of the Centre for Development Informatics, Institute for Development Policy and Management, SED, University of Manchester, Manchester, United Kingdom.

Overeem, Irina, and James P.M. Syvitski, eds. (2009). Dynamics and vulnerability of delta systems. *LOICZ Reports and Studies*, No. 35. Geesthacht, Germany: GKSS Research Center.

Oxfam (2015). Extreme carbon inequality. Oxfam media briefing. 2 December.

Paavola, Jouni (2008). Livelihoods, vulnerability and adaptation to climate change in the Morogoro region, Tanzania. *Environmental Science and Policy*, vol. 11, No. 7, pp. 642-654.

Page, Benjamin I., Larry M. Bartels and Jason Seawright (2013). Democracy and the policy preferences of wealthy Americans. *Perspectives on Politics*, vol. 11, No. 1, pp. 51-73.

Painter, James (2007). Deglaciation in the Andean region. Human Development Report Office Occasional Paper No. 2007/55. New York: United Nations Development Programme.

Patankar, Archana (2015). The exposure, vulnerability, and ability to respond of poor households to recurrent floods in Mumbai. World Bank Policy Research Working Paper No. 7481. Washington, D.C.: World Bank.

Patz, J.A., M.L. Grabow and V.S. Limaye (2014). When it rains, it pours: future climate extremes and health. *Annals of Global Health*, vol. 80, No. 4, pp. 332-344.

Pereira de Lucena, Andre Frossard, Roberto Schaeffer and Alexandre Salem Szklo (2010). Least-cost adaptation options for global climate change impacts on the Brazilian electric power system. *Global Environmental Change*, vol. 20, No. 2, pp. 342-350.

Perez, Carlos, and others (2015). How resilient are farming households and communities to a changing climate in Africa? a gender-based perspective. *Global Environmental Change*, vol. 34 (September), pp. 95-107.

Persson, Åsa. (2011). Institutionalising climate adaptation finance under the UNFCCC and beyond: could an adaptation « market » emerge? Stockholm Environment Institute Working Paper No. 2011-03. Stockholm: Stockholm Environment Institute.

Petherick, Anna (2014), Adaptation with participation, *Nature Climate Change*, vol. 4, No. 8 (August), pp. 660-661.

Petley, D. N. (2010). On the impact of climate change and population growth on the occurrence of fatal landslides in South, East and SE Asia. *Quarterly Journal of Engineering Geology and Hydrogeology,* vol. 43, No. 4 (November), pp. 487-496.

Piketty, Thomas (2014). *Capital in the Twenty-First Century.* Translated by Arthur Goldhammer. Cambridge, Massachusetts: Belknap Press.

Pitman, Michael G., and André Läuchli (2002). Global impact of salinity and agricultural ecosystems. In *Salinity: Environment – Plants – Molecules*, André Läuchli and Ulrich Lüttge, eds. Dordrecht, Netherlands: Kluwer Academic Publishers.

Porter, J.R., and others (2014). Food security and food production systems. In *Climate Change 2014: Impacts, Adaptation, and Vulnerability. Part A: Global and Sectoral Aspects.* Contribution of Working Group II to the Fifth Assessment Report of the Intergovernmental Panel on Climate Change, C.B. Field and others, eds. Cambridge, United Kingdom: Cambridge University Press. Pp. 485–533.

Portier, C.J., and others (2010). A human health perspective on climate change: a report outlining the research needs on the human health effects of climate change. Research Triangle Park, North Carolina: Environmental Health Perspectives/National Institute of Environmental Health Sciences. April.

Purvis, Matthew J., Paul D. Bates and Christopher M. Hayes (2008). A probabilistic methodology to estimate future coastal flood risk due to sea level rise. *Coastal Engineering*, vol. 55, No. 12 (December), pp. 1062-1073.

Rabbani, Golam, and Saleemul Huq (2016). Climate change and inequality in Bangladesh. Background paper prepared for *World Economic and Social Survey 2016.*

Rabbani, Golam, Atiq Rahman and Khandaker Mainuddin (2009). Women's vulnerability to water-related hazards: comparing three areas affected by climate change in Bangladesh. *Waterlines*, vol. 28, No. 3, pp. 235-249.

_____(2013). Salinity-induced loss and damage to farming households in coastal Bangladesh. *International Journal of Global Warming*, vol. 5, No. 4, pp. 400-415.

Rahman, K. M. Mizanur (2009). Erosion and flooding in northern Bangladesh. In *Understanding Climate Change Adaptation: Lessons from Community-Based Approaches*, Jon Ensor and Rachel Berger, eds. Bourton-on-Dunsmore, United Kingdom: Practical Action Publishing. Chap. 2, pp. 39-54.

Rana, S.M. Masud, and others (2011). Changes in cyclone pattern with climate change perspective in the coastal regions of Bangladesh. *Environmental Research, Engineering and Management*, vol. 56, No. 2, pp. 20-27.

Ranger, N., and others (2011). A preliminary assessment of the potential impact of climate change on flood risk in Mumbai. *Climatic Change*, vol. 104, No. 1 (January), pp. 139-167.

Reij, Chris, Gray Tappan and Melinda Smale (2009). Agroenvironmental transformation in the Sahel: another kind of « green revolution ». IFPRI Discussion Paper No. 00914. Washington, D.C.: International Food Policy Research Institute. November.

Reisinger, A., and others (2014). Australasia. In *Climate Change 2014: Impacts, Adaptation, and Vulnerability. Part B: Regional Aspects*. Working Group II Contribution to the Fifth Assessment Report of the Intergovernmental Panel on Climate Change, V.R. Barros, and others, eds. Cambridge, United Kingdom: Cambridge University Press. Pp. 1371–1438.

Renaud, Fabrice G., Karen Sudmeier-Rieux and Marisol Estrella, eds. (2013). *The Role of Ecosystems in Disaster Risk Reduction*. Tokyo: United Nations University Press.

REN21 Renewable Energy Policy Network for the 21st Century (2005). Renewables 2005: global status report. Lead author: Eric Martinot. Washington, D.C.: Worldwatch Institute.

_____ (2016). *Renewables 2016: Global Status Report*. Paris.

Rhinard, Mark, and Bengt Sundelius (2010). The limits of self-reliance: international cooperation as a source of resilience. In *Designing Resilience: Preparing for Extreme Events*, Louise K. Comfort, Arjen Boin and Chris C. Demchak, eds. Pittsburgh, Pennsylvania: University of Pittsburgh Press.

Rist, Ray C. (2016). Introduction.I In *Poverty, Inequality, and Evaluation: Changing Perspectives*, Ray C. Rist, Frederic P. Martin and Ana Maria Fernandez, eds. Washington, D.C.: World Bank Group.

Romijn, Erika, and others (2015). Assessing change in national forest monitoring capacities of 99 tropical countries. *Forest Ecology and Management,* vol. 352 (7 September), pp. 109-123.

Rosen, Harvey S. (1985). *Public Finance*. Homewood, Illinois: Richard D. Irwin:.

Rosenzweig, Cynthia, and Daniel Hillel, eds. (2015). *Handbook of Climate Change and Agroecosystems: The Agricultural Model Intercomparison and Improvement Project (AgMIP) Integrated Crop and Economic Assessments*, part 2. ICP Series on Climate Change Impacts, Adaptation, and Mitigation, vol. 3. London: Imperial College Press.

Sabates-Wheeler, Rachel (2006). Asset inequality and agricultural growth: how are patterns of asset inequality established and reproduced? Background paper prepared for *World Development Report 2006*. Washington, D.C.: World Bank.

Sánchez, Marco V. (2016). Analytical dimensions of inequality in integrated climate impact assessments. Background paper prepared for World and Economic and Social Survey 2016.

Sánchez, Marco V., and Martín Cicowiez (2014). Trade-offs and payoffs of investing in human development. *World Development*, vol. 62, Issue C (October), pp. 14–29.

Sánchez, Marco V., and Rob Vos, eds. (2013). Financing Human Development in Africa, Asia and the Middle East. United Nations Series on Development. London and New York: Bloomsbury Academic.

Sánchez, Marco V., and Eduardo Zepeda (2016). Achieving sustainable development: investment and macroeconomic challenges. In *Technology and Innovation for Sustainable Development*, Rob Vos and Diana Alarcón, eds. New York: Bloomsbury Academic. Chap. 5.

Sánchez, Marco V., and others, eds. (2010). *Public Policies for Human Development: Achieving the Millennium Development Goals in Latin America*. London: Palgrave Macmillan.

Satterthwaite, David, and others (2007). *Adapting to Climate Change in Urban Areas: The Possibilities and Constraints in Low- and Middle-Income Nations*. Human Settlements Discussion Paper. London: Human Settlements Group and Climate Change Group at the International Institute for Environment and Development.

Scaria, Richard, and P. K. Vijayan (2012). Sustainable rural development with the application of Spatial Information Technology and Mahatma Gandhi national rural employment guaranteed scheme. *International Journal of Geomantics and Geosciences,* vol. 2, No. 4 (April), p. 1048.

Scholl, Adam (2012). Map room: hidden waters. *World Policy Journal*, vol. 29, No. 4, pp. 9-11.

Schultz, Jürgen. (2005). *The Ecozones of the World: The Ecological Divisions of the Geosphere*, 2nd ed. Berlin: Springer.

Sen, Amartya. (1999). *Development as Freedom*. New York: Oxford University Press.

Seo, S. Niggol, and Robert Mendelsohn (2008): Animal husbandry in Africa: climate change impacts and adaptations. *African Journal of Agricultural and Resource Economics*, vol. 2, No. 1 (March), pp. 65-82.

Seo, S. Niggol, and others (2009). Adapting to climate change mosaically: an analysis of African livestock management by agroecological zones. *B.E. Journal of Economic Analysis and Policy*, vol. 9, No. 2 (March), pp. 1-35. doi:10.2202/1935-1682.1955.

Sepúlveda, S.A., and D.N. Petley (2015). Regional trends and controlling factors of fatal landslides in Latin America and the Caribbean. *Natural Hazards Earth Systems Science*, vol. 15, pp. 1821-1833.

Shameem, Masud Iqbal Md., Salim Momtaz and Ray Rauscher (2014). Vulnerability of rural livelihoods to multiple stressors: a case study from the southwest coastal region of Bangladesh. *Ocean and Coastal Management*, vol. 102, part A (December), pp. 79-87.

Shaw, Keith (2012). "Reframing" resilience: challenges for planning theory and practice. *Planning Theory and Practice*, vol. 13, No. 2 (June), pp. 308-312.

Sherwood, Amy (2013). Community adaptation to climate change: exploring drought and poverty traps in Gituamba location, Kenya. *Journal of Natural Resources Policy Research*, vol. 5 Nos. 2-3, pp. 147-161.

Shrinath, Nihal, Vicki Mack and Allison Plyer (2014). Who lives in New Orleans and metro parishes now? The Data Center. 6 October. Available from http://www.datacenterresearch.org/data-resources/who-lives-in-new orleans-now/.

Silva, Humberto R., Patrick E. Phelan and Jay S. Golden (2010). Modeling effects of urban heat island mitigation strategies on heat-related morbidity: a case study for Phoenix, Arizona, USA. *International Journal of Biometeorology*, vol. 54, No. 1 (January), pp. 13-22.

Silva, Julie A. (2016). The effects of changes in rainfall patterns, water availability, and desertification on multidimensional inequality. Background paper prepared for *World Economic and Social Survey 2016*.

Sindhu, Abdul Shakoor, Jonathan Ensor and Rachel Berger (2009). Desert and floodplain adaptation in Pakistan. In *Understanding Climate Change Adaptation: Lessons from Community-Based Approaches*, Jon Ensor and Rachel Berger, eds. Bourton-on-Dunsmore, United Kingdom: Practical Action Publishing.

Sissoko, Keffing, and others (2011). Agriculture, livelihoods and climate change in the West African Sahel. *Regional Environmental Change*, vol. 11, Supplement 1 (March), pp. 119-125.

Skoufias, Emmanuel, Mariano Rabassa and Sergio Olivieri (2011). The poverty impacts of climate change: a review of the evidence. World Bank Policy Research Working Paper No. 5622. Washington, D.C.: World Bank.

Skoufias, Emmanuel, ed. (2012). *The Poverty and Welfare Impacts of Climate Change: Quantifying the Effects, Identifying the Adaptation Strategies*. Washington, D.C.: World Bank.

Smith, K.R., and others (2014). Human health: impacts, adaptation, and co-benefits. In *Climate Change 2014: Impacts, Adaptation, and Vulnerability. Part A: Global and Sectoral Aspects*. Contribution of Working Group II to the Fifth Assessment Report of the Intergovernmental Panel on Climate Change, C.B. Field and others, eds. Cambridge, United Kingdom: Cambridge University Press. Pp. 709–754.

Snorek, Julie, Fabrice G. Renaud and Julia Kloos (2014). Divergent adaptation to climate variability: a case study of pastoral and agricultural societies in Niger. *Global Environmental Change*, vol. 29 (November), pp. 371-386.

Solow, Andrew R. (2015). Extreme weather, made by us? individual climate events cannot be attributed to anthropogenic climate change. *Science*, vol. 349, No. 6255 (25 September), pp. 1444-1445.

Somanathan, E., and Rohini Somanathan (2009). Climate change: challenges facing India's poor. *Economic and Political Weekly*, vol. 44, No. 31 (1-7 August), pp. 51-58.

Somanathan, E., and others (2014). The impact of temperature on productivity and labor supply: evidence from Indian manufacturing. Indian Statistical Institute Discussion Paper 14-10. New Delhi: Indian Statistical Institute, Delhi, Economics and Planning Unit. November.

Spielman, David J., and Rajul Pandya-Lorch (2009). *Millions Fed: Proven Successes in Agricultural Development* (2009). Washington, D.C.: International Food Policy Research Institute.

Statistics Division of the Department of Economic and Social Affairs of the United Nations Secretariat (2016a). Millennium Development Goals indicators: the official United Nations site for the MDG indicators. Country level data: population below national poverty line - urban, rural (percentage). Available from http://mdgs.un.org/unsd/mdg/Data.aspx. Accessed 2 February.

_____ (2016b). Side event entitled "Geospatial information and Earth observations: supporting official statistics in monitoring the SDGs". Held at the forty-seventh session of the Statistical Commission, 7 March 2016. Coverage of the meeting is provided at http://unstats.un.org/unsd/statcom/47th-session/side-events/20160307-1M-geospatial-information-and-earth-observations/. Accessed 3 March 2016.

Stern, Nicolas (2006). *The Stern Review on the Economics of Climate Change*. London: HM Treasury.

Stiglitz, Joseph E. (2012). *The Price of Inequality: How Today's Divided Society Endangers Our Future*. New York: W. W. Norton and Company.

_____ (2015). Rewriting the Rules of the American Economy: An Agenda for Growth and Shared Prosperity. New York: Roosevelt Institute.

Straus, Scott (2011). Mali and its Sahelian neighbors. World Development Report 2011 background case study. Washington, D.C.: World Bank.

Sutton, William R., Jitendra P. Srivastava and James E. Neumann (2013). *Looking Beyond the Horizon: How Climate Change Impacts and Adaptation Responses Will Reshape Agriculture in Eastern Europe and Central Asia*. Directions in Development. Washington, D.C.: World Bank.

Taylor, Anna, Katie Harris and Charles Ehrhart (2010). Adaptation key terms. *Tiempo*, No. 77 (October), pp. 10-13. Available from http://tiempo.sei-international.org/portal/archive/pdf/tiempo77low.pdf. Accessed 6 November 2015.

Tessler, Z.D., and others (2015). Profiling risk and sustainability in coastal deltas of the world. *Science*, vol. 349, No. 6248 (August), pp. 638-643.

Top 10 largest deltas in the world (2012). Top ten of the world. Blog. 7 June. Available from www.toptenofworld.blogspot.com. Accessed 15 December 2015.

Ullah, Akm Ahsan (2004). Bright city lights and slums of Dhaka City: determinants of rural-urban migration in Bangladesh. *Migration Letters*, vol. 1, No. 1, pp. 26-41.

United Nations (1993). *Report of the United Nations Conference on Environment and Development, Rio de Janeiro, 3-14 June 1992, vol. I, Resolutions Adopted by the Conference.* Sales No. E.93.I.8 and corrigendum. Resolution 1, annex I (Rio Declaration on Environment and Development). Resolution 1, annex II (Agenda 21).

_____ (2008). *Principles and Recommendations for Population and Housing Censuses, Revision 2.* Statistical Papers, Series M, No. 67/2. Sales No. E.07.XVII.8. Available from unstats.un.org.

_____ (2011a). Seoul Declaration on Global Geospatial Information Management. Adopted on 26 October 2011 at the first High-level Forum on Global Geospatial Information Management (GGIM), held in Seoul from 23 to 27 October 2011.

_____ (2011b). *World Economic and Social Survey 2011: The Great Green Technological Transformation.* Sales No. E.11.II.C.1.

_____ (2013). *World Economic and Social Survey 2013: Sustainable Development Challenges.* Sales No. E.13.II.C.1.

_____ (2015a). *Demographic Yearbook 2014.* Sixty-fifth issue. Sales No. B.16. XIII.1. Available from http://unstats.un.org./unsd/demographic/products/dyb/dyb2.htm.

_____ (2015b). World Urbanization Prospects: The 2014 Revision. ST/ESA/SER.A/366.

_____ (2016). *World Economic and Social Survey 2014/2015: Learning from National Policies Supporting MDG Implementation.* Sales No. E.15.II.C.1.

_____ (forthcoming). *Report on the World Social Situation 2016: Leaving No One Behind – The Imperative of Inclusive Development.*

_____, Department of Economic and Social Affairs, Division for Public Administration and Development Management (2015). Report of the expert group meeting on "Policy integration in government in pursuit of the Sustainable Development Goals", held at United Nations Headquarters on 28 and 29 January 2015. E/CN.16/2015/CRP.2. Available from www.un.org/esa/socdev/csocd/2016/egmreport-policyintegrationjan2015.pdf.

United Nations, Department of Economic and Social Affairs, Population Division (2014). World Urbanization Prospects: The 2014 Revision. Downloadable files available from https://esa.un.org/unpd/wup/. Accessed 1 March 2015.

_____ (2015a). World Populations Prospects: The 2015 Revision. Downloadable files available from https://esa.un.org/unpd/wpp/. Accessed 1 March 2015.

United Nations, Economic and Social Council (2016). Report of the Statistical Commission on the forty-seventh session (8-11 March 2016). *Official Records of the Economic and Social Council, 2016, Supplement No. 4.* E/2016/24. Available from http://unstats.un.org/unsd/statcom/47th-session/documents/Report-on-the-47th-session-of-the-statistical-commission-E.pdf.

_____, Statistical Commission (2015). Report of the Secretary-General on climate change statistics. E/CN.3/2016/15. 18 December. Available from http://unstats.un.org/unsd/statcom/47th-session/documents/2016-15-Climate-change-statistics-E.pdf.

United Nations, Economic and Social Council, United Nations Forum on Forests (2009a). Report of the Secretary-General on forests and climate change. E/CN.18/2009/4. 11 February.

_____ (2009b). Report of the Secretary-General entitled "Reversing the loss of forest cover, preventing forest degradation in all types of forests and combating desertification, including in low forest cover countries". E/CN.18/2009/5. 26 January.

United Nations, Economic Commission for Africa (2010). Climate change and human development. Issues paper No. 3, prepared for the Seventh African Development Forum on "Acting on climate change for sustainable development in Africa". Addis Ababa, 10-15 October 2010.

United Nations, Economic Commission for Latin America and the Caribbean, and European Union (2011). ICT and environment. eLAC2015 Newsletter, No. 14 (March).

United Nations Children's Fund (2009). *Understanding Urban Inequalities in Bangladesh: A Prerequisite for Achieving Vision 21.* Dhaka: UNICEF Bangladesh. November.

United Nations Development Programme (2006). *Human Development Report 2006: Beyond Scarcity - Power, Poverty and the Global Water Crisis.* Basingstoke, United Kingdom: Palgrave Macmillan.

_____ (2008). *Human Development Report 2007/2008: Fighting Climate Change - Human Solidarity in a Divided World.* Basingstoke, United Kingdom: Palgrave Macmillan.

_____ (2011). Ecosystem adaptation in the Seychelles. Available from http://adaptation-undp.org/projects/af-seychelles. Accessed 2/19/16.

_____, and United Nations Convention to Combat Desertification Secretariat (2011). The forgotten billion: MDG achievement in the drylands. New York and Bonn.

United Nations Environment Management Group (2011). Global drylands: a UN system-wide response. October.

United Nations Environment Programme (2015). *The Emissions Gap Report 2015.* A UNEP Synthesis Report. Nairobi. November.

_____ (2016). *Adaptation Finance Gap Report.* Nairobi.

United Nations Framework Convention on Climate Change secretariat (2013). Third synthesis report on technology needs identified by Parties not included in Annex I to the Convention. Note by the secretariat. Submitted to the Subsidiary Body for Scientific and Technological Advice at its thirty-ninth session, Warsaw, 11-16 November 2013, under item 7 (c) of the provisional agenda, entitled "Development and transfer of technologies and implementation of the Technology Mechanism: third synthesis report on technology needs identified by Parties not included in Annex I to the Convention". 21 October.

_____ (2014). UNFCCC Standing Committee on Finance: 2014 biennial assessment and overview of climate finance flows report. Bonn.

_____ (2015). Report of the Standing Committee on Finance to the Conference of the Parties. 20 November. FCCC/CP/2015/8.

_____ (2016). Report of the Conference of the Parties to the United Nations Framework Convention on Climate Change on its twenty-first session, Paris, 30 November-13 December 2015. Part two: action taken by the Conference of the Parties at its twenty-first session. 29 January. FCCC/CP/2015/10/Add.1. Decision 1/CP.21 entitled "Adoption of the Paris Agreement".

United Nations Human Settlements Programme (UN-Habitat) (2003). *Slums of the World: The Face of Urban Poverty in the New Millennium?* Working paper. Nairobi.

United Nations World Water Assessment Programme (WWAP) (2015a). *The United Nations World Water Development Report 2015: Water for a Sustainable World*. Paris: United Nations Educational, Scientific and Cultural Organization.

_____ (2015b). *UNESCO's Contribution to the United Nations World Water Development Report: Facing the Challenges - Case Studies and Indicators*. Paris: United Nations Educational, Scientific and Cultural Organization.

United States Census Bureau (2016). Website of the Opportunity Project: let's build something amazing together. Opportunity.census.gov. Accessed 10 March 2016.

Valdivia, Roberto O., and others (2015). Representative agricultural pathways and scenarios for regional integrated assessment of climate change impacts, vulnerability and adaptation. In *Handbook of Climate Change and Agroecosystems: The Agricultural Model Intercomparison and Improvement Project Integrated Crop and Economic Assessments,* part 1, Cynthia Rosenzweig and Daniel Hillel, eds. ICP Series on Climate Change Impacts, Adaptation, and Mitigation, vol. 3. London: Imperial College Press.

van der Mensbrugghe, Dominique (2015). Shared socio-economic pathways and global income distribution. Paper prepared for the Eighteenth Annual Conference on Global Economic Analysis, Melbourne, Australia, 17-19 June 2015.

van Ruijven, Bas J., Brian C. O'Neill and Jean Chateau (2015). Methods for including income distribution in global CGE models for long-term climate change research. *Energy Economics,* vol. 51 (September), pp. 530-543.

Verhagen, A., and others (2003). Climate change and food security in the drylands of West Africa. In *Global Environmental Change and Land Use*, A.J. Dolman, A. Verhagen and C.A. Rovers, eds. Dordrecht, Netherlands: Kluwer Academic Publishers.

Verner, Dorte, ed. (2010). *Reducing Poverty, Protecting Livelihoods, and Building Assets in a Changing Climate: Social Implications of Climate Change for Latin America and the Caribbean*. Washington, D.C.: World Bank.

Veronesi, Marcella, and Salvatore Di Falco (2012). How can African agriculture adapt to climate change? a counterfactual analysis from Ethiopia. *University of Verona Department of Economics Working Paper,* No. 14. Verona, Italy. March.

Vincent, K., and others (2014). Cross-chapter box on gender and climate change. In *Climate Change 2014: Impacts, Adaptation, and Vulnerability. Part A: Global and Sectoral Aspects.* Contribution of Working Group II to the Fifth Assessment Report of the Intergovernmental Panel on Climate Change, C.B. Field and others. Cambridge, United Kingdom: Cambridge University Press. Pp. 105-107.

Volkery, Axel, and Teresa Ribeiro (2009). Scenario planning in public policy: understanding use, impacts and the role of institutional context factors. *Technological Forecasting and Social Change*, vol. 76, No. 9 (November), pp. 1198-1207.

Vos, Rob, and Marco V. Sánchez (2010). A non-parametric microsimulation approach to assess changes in inequality and poverty. *International Journal of Microsimulation*, vol. 3, No. 1, pp. 8-23.

Ward, Philip J., and others (2010). Partial costs of global climate change adaptation for the supply of raw industrial and municipal water: a methodology and application. *Environmental Research Letters*, vol. 5, No. 4. doi:10.1088/1748-9326/5/4/044011.

Watkiss, Paul (2015). A review of the economics of adaptation and climate-resilient development. Centre for Climate Change Economics and Policy Working Paper No. 231. Leeds, United Kingdom: University of Leeds, Centre for Climate Change Economics and Policy. September.

Weitzman, Martin L. (2007). A review of *The Stern Review on the Economics of Climate Change. Journal of Economic Literature,* vol. XLV, No. 3 (September), pp. 703-724.

Welsch, M., and others (2014). Adding value with CLEWS: modelling the energy system and its interdependencies for Mauritius. *Applied Energy*, vol. 113 (January), pp. 1434–1445.

Weragoda, Rohana, Jonathan Ensor and Rachel Berger (2009). Increasing paddy salinity in coastal Sri Lanka. In *Understanding Climate Change Adaptation: Lessons from Community-Based Approaches,* Jonathan Ensor and Rachel Berger, eds. Bourton-on-Dunsmore, United Kingdom: Practical Action Publishing.

White, Jeffrey W., and others (2011) Methodologies for simulating impacts of climate change on crop production. *Field Crops Research*, vol. 124, No. 3 (December), pp. 357–368.

White, Robin P., and Janet Nackoney (2003). Drylands, people and ecosystem goods and services: a web-based geospatial analysis. Washington, D.C.: World Resources Institute. February. Available from www.wri.org.

Williams, Erica, and others (2006). The women of New Orleans and the Gulf Coast: multiple disadvantages and key assets for recovery. Part II: Gender, race, and class in the labor market. IWPR briefing paper No. D465. Washington, D.C.: Institute for Women's Policy Research. August.

Wilson Steven G., and Thomas R. Fischetti (2010). Coastline population trends in the United States: 1960 to 2008 - population estimates and projections. Current Population Report No. P25-1139. U.S. Census Bureau. May.

Winsemius, Hessel, and others (2015). Disaster risk, climate change, and poverty: assessing the global exposure of poor people to floods and droughts. World Bank Policy Research Working Paper No. 7480. Washington, D.C.: World Bank.

Wodon, Quentin, and others, eds. (2014). *Climate Change and Migration: Evidence from the Middle East and North Africa.* Washington, D.C.: World Bank.

Wong, P.P., and others (2014). Coastal systems and low-lying areas. In *Climate Change 2014: Impacts, Adaptation, and Vulnerability. Part A: Global and Sectoral Aspects.* Contribution of Working Group II to the Fifth Assessment Report of the Intergovernmental Panel on Climate Change, C.B. Field and others, eds., Cambridge, United Kingdom:Cambridge University Press. Pp. 361–409.

Woodroffe, Colin D. (2010). Assessing the vulnerability of Asian megadeltas to climate change using GIS. In *Coastal and Marine Geospatial Technologies*, David R. Green, ed. Dordrecht, Netherlands: Springer. Part VI, chap. 36.

World Bank (2003). *World Development Report 2003: Sustainable Development in a Dynamic World -Transforming Institutions, Growth, and Quality of Life.* Washington, D.C.: World Bank; and New York: Oxford University Press. Available from https://openknowledge.worldbank.org/handle/10986/.

_____ and others (2003). Poverty and climate change: reducing the vulnerability of the poor through adaptation.

_____ (2005). *World Development Report 2006: Equity and Development.* New York: Oxford University Press; and Washington, D.C.: World Bank.

_____ (2008). *Global Monitoring Report 2008: MDGs and the Environment – Agenda for Inclusive and Sustainable Development.* Washington, D.C.

_____ (2013). *Turn Down the Heat: Climate Extremes, Regional Impacts, and the Case for Resilience.* Washington, D.C.

_____ (2015). Development banks agree common approach to measure climate finance. Press release. 9 July.

World Commission on Environment and Development (1987). *Our Common Future.* Oxford: Oxford University Press.

World Economic Forum (2016). The Global Risks Report 2016, 11th ed. Available from http://wef.ch/risks2016. Accessed 7 March 2016.

World Health Organization (1990). Potential health impacts of climate change: report of a WHO Task Group. Geneva.

_____ (2009). Improving public health responses to extreme weather/ heat-waves. Summary for policy-makers: – EuroHEAT – technical summary. Copenhagen: WHO Regional Office for Europe.

_____ (2014). *WHO Guidelines for Indoor Air Quality: Household Fuel Combustion.* Geneva.

_____ (2016). Public health, environmental and social determinants of health (PHE): burden of disease from ambient and household air pollution. Available from www.who.int.

World Meterological Organization (2014). *Atlas of Mortality and Economic Losses from Weather, Climate and Water Extremes* (1970–2012). Geneva.

Yamamura, Eiji (2013). Impact of natural disasters on income inequality: analysis using panel data during the period 1965 to 2004. MPRA Working Paper No. 45623. Munich, Germany: Munich Personal RePEc Archive. 20 March.

Zhang, Ke, and others (2015). Poverty alleviation strategies in eastern China lead to critical ecological dynamics. *Science of the Total Environment*, vols. 506-507 (15 February), pp. 164-181.

Zivin, Joshua Graff, and Matthew J. Neidell (2014). Temperature and allocation of time: implications for climate change. *Journal of Labor Economics*, vol. 32, No. 1, pp. 1-26.

Zoleta-Nantes, Doracie B. (2002). Differential impacts of flood hazards among the street children, the urban poor and residents of wealthy neighborhoods in Metro Manila, Philippines. *Migration and Adaptation Strategies for Global Change*, vol. 7, No. 3 (September), pp. 239-266.

DATE DUE

GAYLORD   PRINTED IN U.S.A.

United Nations publication
ISBN 978-92-1-109174-8
eISBN: 978-92-1-058231-5